Which Door has the Cadillac

Which Door has the Cadillac

✦

Adventures of a Real-Life Mathematician

Andrew Vazsonyi, Ph.D.

Writers Club Press
New York Lincoln Shanghai

Which Door has the Cadillac
Adventures of a Real-Life Mathematician

Writers Club Press
an imprint of iUniverse, Inc.

For information address:
iUniverse, Inc.
2021 Pine Lake Road, Suite 100
Lincoln, NE 68512
www.iuniverse.com

ISBN: 0-595-26062-4

Printed in the United States of America

Dedicated to the memory of Herbert A. Simon, my lifelong friend, icon and professional inspiration.

Contents

Acknowledgments

First and foremost, I am deeply indebted to my daughter and co-author, Bobbi Chaney, M.A. Without her, the book would have been quite different. As soon as I'd finish a chapter, I'd e-mail it to her, and she would set me straight. Her constant reviews filtered out my "textbook" flavor, and her additions kept the book lively and people oriented.

Hal Jacobs, my friend and managing editor of the Decision Sciences Institute, reviewed and rewrote the text in professional style. His splendid talent as a writer shines through every page of the book.

Barbara Schreiber did the final edit and brought the book to a perfect, print-ready copy.

1

WHICH DOOR HAS THE CADILLAC?

o o o o o o o o o o o o o o o o o o o o o o o o o o o o o o

I have found you an argument; but I am not obliged to find you an understanding.

—Samuel Johnson (1709–1784)

No theory is good except on the condition that one can use it to go beyond.

—Adapted from André Gide (1869–1951)

It is one of those beautiful, windless days on the Pacific. Nothing but blue skies and big waves from California all the way to Japan. As I stroll along the beach near Goat Rock with my son-in-law's father, Dick, I hit golf balls off an extra long golf tee. The beach is perfect for my "tee-ball" game because it offers me an infinitely large sand trap. Also, when I play without my regular golf partners, I don't have to listen to them gripe about my using a tee on every shot.

Actually, my tee-ball game is off today because I'm trying to do too many things at once: teeing off shots, talking with Dick, keeping one eye peeled for sleeper waves. The Goat Rock area is notorious for swallowing up people in rogue waves; I estimate the probability of being washed away in a sleeper wave at 1/100,000 because two to three people drown here every year. This quickly leads me to think it might a good example of catastrophe theory I can use in my writing. Just then another thought flickers through my mind: Why does the ocean swallow so many of my golf balls?

Then Dick asks if I can solve the puzzle of the Cadillac and two goats.

The situation is based on the old "Let's Make A Deal" game show in which the host and contestant stand in front of three closed doors. Behind one door is a shiny new Cadillac. Behind the other two doors are goats. The game is quite simple. Choose the correct door and win the automobile. Choose the wrong door and take home a goat. Only the game show host knows which door leads to the automobile.

And that's where it gets interesting. Let's say the contestant picks door #1. Before showing what's behind that door, however, the host opens door #3 and reveals a goat. Now he asks if the contestant would like to change his mind. Based on this new information, should the contestant switch from door #1 to door #2?

As soon as Dick poses the problem, I realize once again why I dislike puzzles so much.

First, it takes me too long to understand them.

Second, I can never solve them.

Third, because I'm a mathematician most people assume I can solve them.

Still, there is something about this problem that tickles my interest. I think about it as I tee up a ball, launch it into the blue sky and watch it plop down softly in the sand just before being swallowed by a wave.

My gut feeling is: "It makes no difference! The chances are the same that the car is behind any of the doors, namely, one in three." But immediately the image of Tomas Bayes—the English theologian and mathematician from the eighteenth century who was the first to use probability inference—flashes through my mind. So I quickly over-rule my gut and say, "I don't know." (*According to my hero, Nobel laureate Richard P. Feynman, that's the answer to most questions.*)

I start to look at the problem, as always, through the lens of math. In the beginning, I have no way of knowing which door the car is behind. But after the host opens one door and shows me a goat, that tells me I should revise my view of the future.

Our decisions are always influenced by new information. Why do physicians use tests to determine what we're allergic to? So they can receive new information and make better choices for our treatment. Is there a difference between a doctor choosing between allergy treatments and me choosing between closed doors to win a Caddy?

To switch or not to switch. That is the question. It was the kind of problem that would stay with me long after my last tee shot on the beach.

As Dick and I drive back to my home in Santa Rosa, I realize that I can use a decision tree to work out the problem. Each branch of the tree will show a choice that either I can make or have made for me by chance, as well as the direction it will take. In this case, some branches of the tree lead to Cadillacs, while other branches lead to goats. To find the correct answer, I have to climb all over the tree like a monkey.

Let's say I pick door #1 and, by good luck, I'm right. This is the first branch of my tree.

Of course, the host won't open door #1 right away. Instead, he'll drag out the game and show me the goat behind door #2 or #3.

So let's say the following occurs. He opens door #2 and invites me to change my answer. I switch to Door #3 and go home with a goat. Perhaps in some remote parts of the world, a goat might be preferable to a Cadillac. But not in California.

Suddenly, Dick calls out, "Red light!"

This new information prompts a quick decision—I hit the brakes on my automobile, which is, coincidentally, a Cadillac. After the antilock braking system and seatbelts do their job, Dick takes over the driving. I know better than trying to operate heavy machinery while under the influence of math.

Next I visualize the second branch of the tree.

Suppose I guess door #2, and the host replies by opening door #3. That goat again. If I then switch to door #1, the Caddy is mine.

"Szerencse (Luck)!" I say to myself, lapsing into my native Hungarian.

Now suppose I start the game by choosing door #3, the third branch of the tree. The host will reveal the goat behind door #2, and I switch to car door #1. Another win!

I can't believe it. By switching my pick each time, I win two out of three trials. Two of the three branches of the decision tree lead to the Cadillac. So the probability is 2/3 if I switch. It seems hard for me to believe, so I keep mum about it to Dick.

Later that evening I check my calculations on a piece of paper. By golly, I'm right! Of course, it makes no sense, but Newton's law makes no sense either. Who could have believed such nonsense that the moon causes the tides to rise and fall from such a great distance? But I feel really good, like I've just slain the dragon—or won the Cadillac.

The next day I call Dick and tell him my findings. He's really impressed. Especially after he went home and read that the probability of winning the Cadillac was just as I said.

"But how did you figure it out?" he asks.

I start to tell him about my decision tree approach, but he interrupts.

"Cut the technical bullshit," he says. "Just tell me why."

◆   ◆   ◆

Two years later when I told the Cadillac problem to Paul Erdös, a long-time friend and math hero, I was totally unprepared for his reaction. Erdös, who passed away in 1996, was one of the most famous mathematicians of the 20th century—he published more than a thousand research papers in many areas of pure mathematics. Number theorists, who deal with the mathematical properties of whole numbers, consider him to have been one of the world's foremost experts in probability theory.

During one of his many visits with me, we were talking about using probability theory in decision making. At some point I brought up the game show puzzle. I told Erdös that the contestant stood a better chance of winning the Cadillac if he switched his answer when the game show host showed him a door with a goat.

When he heard this, he reacted as if he had just been stung by a bee.

"No, that is impossible," he said. "It should make no difference if you switch."

At this point I could have kicked myself for bringing up the subject. I'm not the only mathematician who becomes agitated over puzzles. But there was no way to bow out gracefully, so I told Erdös about Bayes' theorem. Then I showed him the decision tree solution I had used in my undergraduate courses at the University of Rochester.

I reminded him that probability is not a fixed, static thing—it changes as time goes by.

To my amazement, Erdös remained unconvinced. He didn't want to hear about decision trees. He wanted a straightforward explanation.

I gave up. I didn't have a common-sense explanation that would satisfy him. If you understand decision trees, you can work it. Otherwise, it's pretty confusing.

And that's pretty much what I told Erdös, adding, "Now put on your earphones, listen to your music and stop bothering me."

Let me explain. During an earlier visit to our home, Erdös had unpacked his radio to tune into classical music, which he lovingly called "noise". Unfortunately, there are hills between our house and the broadcasting station in San Francisco. As a result, Erdös picked up mostly static on his radio, that is, real noise. He solved this problem by playing the radio in our living room, which was connected by cable, from 5:00 am to midnight. Although my wife and I loved the music, we also enjoyed periodic interludes of silence. Finally, nearly desperate, I dashed down to Radio Shack and bought an Optimus transmitter set. I wired the transmitter to his radio, and Erdös wore the wireless headset during this and subsequent visits.

So, after Erdös rejected my solution to the Cadillac problem, I felt a little low. I gazed out our family room window, which overlooks a golf course, and watched a golfer desperately trying to get out of a sand trap. He made one, two, three, four, five swings with no success. Finally, he became so furious that he threw his club on the green and kicked the ball. Perfect approach! The ball dropped into the cup. After seeing that, I decided to expand my tee-ball game to include kick-putts, happily anticipating the grief this would cause my golf partners, especially my brother-in-law, Judson. This cheered me up quite a bit.

An hour later, Erdös came looking for me.

"What's the matter with you?" he said. "Why aren't you telling me the reason that I should switch?"

He was so upset that I tried another explanation—a visual, simulation approach that I had developed on my computer.

The Monte Carlo method was well known to Erdös because it was first introduced by his good friend and collaborator, Stanislaw Ulam (1909–1984), a mathematician who played a major role in the development of the hydrogen bomb at Los Alamos.

On the computer screen I displayed pictures of a sequence of scenarios. First we see the contestant, who chooses door #1. Then we see the host open door #2 and reveal the goat. That's followed by the contestant sticking with his original guess, and the host throwing open that door to reveal the other goat.

In the second version, the same events occur. But this time the contestant wins the Cadillac, and the host cries because he must pay for the car out of his own salary.

Screen after screen followed. Meanwhile, the computer kept running totals of smiling and crying hosts. I ran the program without the pictures 100,000 times and found that *if the contestant does not switch, the host will smile in about 2/3 of the time. But if the contestant switches, the host will cry about 2/3 of the time.*

Erdös objected that he still did not understand the reason why, but was convinced, somewhat reluctantly, that I was right.

A few days after his visit, he telephoned to say that his friend and frequent collaborator Ron Graham, a research mathematician at AT&T, had explained the reasoning and now everything was perfectly clear. Then he proceeded to share the explanation with me.

It made no sense at all. Apparently, Graham and Erdös had developed a private language that I wasn't privy to.

◆   ◆   ◆

Later, I gained more insight into the puzzle by reading Marilyn vos Savant's column, "Nation's Mathematicians Guilty of 'Innumeracy,'" in the *Skeptical Inquirer* (Vol. 15, Summer 1991, pp. 342–345). The problem was submitted to vos Savant, whose specialty is answering brain teasers in her syndicated magazine column.

Vos Savant answered the question of "to switch or not to switch" by saying, "Yes, you should switch," and giving her explanation.

According to her, the chance is 1/3 that the car is actually at #1, and in that case you lose when you switch. The chance is 2/3 that the car is either at #2 (in which case the host first opens #3) or at #3 (in which case he first opens #2). In these cases, when the host reveals a goat, he shows you how to switch and win.

In a later column she published signed letters from four PhDs—some quite nasty—that chastised her for misleading the public. So she gave an alternate explanation. Later still, she followed up with letters from five more PhDs, who unanimously agreed that she was an idiot. All the explanations, including von Savant's, had hidden errors that could be uncovered only by math savants or people well-versed in probability theory.

The fact is, this problem has appeared numerous times, not only in the popular press but in technical and statistical articles and textbooks as well. Whenever it reappears, heated debates follow. Most people defend the "obvious" answer: There is no logical reason for the contestant to switch doors. Not only plain citizens, but high-powered statisticians defend this common sense answer.

I get a big kick out of all this. In everyday life we change our views all the time based on new information. That seems like common sense to me.

Let me give an example. Late one evening, my son-in-law, Sky, was driving the Cadillac back from his father's house in Sacramento. I woke up from a deep sleep in the back seat to find us stopped by the side of the road. We were out of gas.

So here we were, stranded on some small country road in total darkness, with nothing around for miles. It wouldn't have been so bad, but my wife, Laura, was starting to say, "I told you so." Unfortunately, this time she was right.

Fortunately, Sky had his cell phone handy and called AAA emergency service. In less than an hour we were on our way home.

Here's the rub. When Sky purchased his cell phone and suggested that I get one, I thought it was ridiculous. Who would I call? But running out of gas on a dark country road gave me new information. The next morning I drove down to Radio Shack and bought myself a cell phone.

Still, the goat controversy stirred up another question that baffled me. How could somebody like Erdös not know anything about Bayes' theorem, which I consider to be a bridge between the world of pure math and the real world?

So I did some research. I checked my books and found little, almost nothing, about Bayes' theorem. If it was discussed, only an incomprehensible formula was included that no one could understand, much less apply to anything useful.

No wonder the PhDs were jumping on vos Savant. They didn't know anything about Bayes, and most of them couldn't care less.

Then I thought about my own circumstances. If somebody had given me the problem in the 1950s before I was involved in decision making, my reaction would have been like Erdös'. Back then I was interested in math purely for its own sake, or for applying to the exact sciences. I had no use for Bayes—not until I began using math for real-life decision making.

◆　　◆　　◆

Recently, Dick and his wife, Johna, got together with their clan at their cabin in Lake Tahoe. I called my daughter, Bobbi, and we had a long talk.

"What goes about Dick?" I asked.

She chuckled. "Oh, he's having a great time. He and the guys are going on and on about the Cadillac problem. But Johna says she hates those damn goats. She says she wishes he would just buy her a new Cadillac and be done with it!"

The next day I got a phone call from Dick.

"I have a good solution to the Cadillac problem," he said. "You assume that there is a box around the first two doors…" and on and on he rambled. "I don't get it," I said, meaning that I didn't have the patience to follow his reasoning.

What I've realized is this: I'm not interested in unique solutions invented by clever people. I want a method that works for lots of problems.

I'm not looking for hundreds of keys to solve these problems. I want one key that opens many doors.

My key is math for real-life decision making.

2

LIFE IN HUNGARY: THE MAKING OF A MATHEMATICIAN

I was touring around Yugoslavia in 1953, and remember peering down into the bronze footprint of the Serbian nationalist hero Gavrilo Princip. He assassinated Archduke Francis Ferdinand of Austria at Sarejevo on June 28, 1914. This single shot triggered the First World War, ending a century of order and stability and starting a century of change.

I was born in 1916, the dawn of the twentieth century. My parents often referred to the pre-war era as one of peace, prosperity and stability. Those were the days of the Hapsburgs, when life was good. This "Age of the Antebellum" was a product of the long rule of Franz Joseph, emperor of Austria-Hungary, who died in 1916, the year I was born. I was slated to live in the century of chaos.

When I look back at the world I was born into, I see war, violence and ethnic hatred. But I also see my childhood as sheltered from all that. I remember Sunday meals, afternoons of rowing on the Danube and long conversations with my father. Later, of course, the storm would engulf us, causing me to leave Hungary and claiming the lives of my brothers.

The year that I was born marked an important turning point for Hungary. After the death of Franz Joseph, King Károly assumed his place on the throne.

As a result of the assassination, Austria-Hungary and Serbia went to war against each other. Gradually the fighting grew into World War I, which involved thirty-two nations. In 1918, after about ten million people were killed, an armistice was signed that ended the fighting, but not the suffering.

I'll never forget the sight of disabled war veterans on the city streets. Or seeing soldiers whose legs had been blown away as they dragged themselves along the sidewalks in wooden boxes. Or seeing them beg on street corners because they received no help from the government. When I went with my brothers to the City Park, we would see many of the city's orphans playing there.

We were the fortunate ones. My family lived in a small apartment near the center of Budapest on the Pest, or the left side, of the Danube. For a time, we all slept in the same bedroom. My parents lay side by side in two bronze beds. My older brother, Karcsi, bedded down on the sofa, while I slept in a metal crib. After the birth of my younger brother, Pityu, Karcsi was relocated to the dining room.

In that little apartment, Karcsi used to bug me until I was in tears. The he and Pityu danced around me singing, "Cry baby, cry baby." Karcsi had terrible nightmares. He jumped out of bed and ran around hollering. Father was afraid that he would jump out of the window, and tied a rope around his ankle anchored to the bed stand.

A rather large kitchen was furnished with a cast-iron cooking stove, gas range and faucet with cold water only. Our bathroom came with a tub, sink and small iron stove where water could be heated for a hot bath. Our toilet was in a separate room. All the rooms opened onto a long dark entry hall, that gave me the creeps at night. There was also a tiny dark hole of a room in the back for the maid, a kind of domestic slave who never stayed around very long. Each room was furnished with a tile stove. During the winter, the maid would arrive early to light the fires. Getting out of bed on cold mornings was dreadful.

Our apartment was on the fifth floor. Many times I counted the one hundred and three steps as I climbed them. The elevator in our build-ing was run by the concierge, but it cost money to ride so we seldom used it. Whenever the concierge oiled the machinery, we would stand around and watch in fascination.

The apartment building itself was built around a large courtyard space, and on each floor there was a walkway that led to the front doors of each apartment. Down below, peddlers and beggars would appear in the central courtyard, loudly announcing their presence. When mother had a hole in one of her pots or a broken window, she would call down to the trader, who would arrive at our door with his tools. My brothers and I tossed pennies wrapped in newspaper to the beggars.

Of course, that wasn't all we tossed from our apartment. As we grew older, our mother began leaving us at home so that she could help out in my father's shoe store. Sometimes we would take light bulbs, which back then had sharp points on top, push the bulbs underwater in the sink, snip off the points and watch as the vacuum sucked them full of water. Then we tossed the water-filled bulbs out the fifth-floor window. They exploded with a wonderful blast on the street below. The beauty of this was that the concierge never caught us because he lived in the back of the building.

One day I got into a fight with my brother about who should toss the light bulb. During the fight I squeezed the bulb too hard, and it made a deep cut into my index finger—the scar is still visible today. I wasn't too upset, though. After my mother bandaged me up, I was excused from my piano lesson.

◆   ◆   ◆

My mother, Hermine, grew palm trees in front of the bay window in the dining/living room. Hungarian winters weren't ideal for growing palm trees, but my mother managed to keep them alive indoors. I remember her cleaning the leaves with a toothbrush. Many years later, when I moved to Los Angeles, she would visit and admire the towering palm trees that grew outdoors all by themselves.

Hermine was born in 1885 in Sárospatak, a village in the northeastern part of Hungary. Her father was a dry goods merchant, and she had nine brothers and sisters. Although her family was Jewish, she was educated by Catholic nuns who urged her to convert and join the convent. Instead she married my father in 1910—her sister later married my father's brother and left for the big city of Budapest.

When not raising three young boys or taking care of the house, my mother spent her time stitching fabulous needlework. She even set up a carpet-weaving loom to make imitation Oriental carpets, and eventually hired other women to assist her.

I was especially close to my father, Miksa Weiszfeld. He was born in 1880 in Nagyvázsony. At the age of eight, my grandfather, a boot maker, died and my father dropped out of school to become an apprentice in another shoe shop. He was a self-educated man who knew a great deal about running a successful business. This made a permanent impression on me that formal education was not a prerequisite for intelligence, knowledge or the better things in life.

At his elegant, mahogany-paneled shop in the fashionable shopping district of Budapest, my father became well-known for his custom-made shoes, although he never made a pair of shoes himself. When clients came, he carefully measured their feet and would instruct the lead workmen on making a wooden cast to match the measurements. Then one of the workmen made the shoe on the cast.

The mathematician Paul Erdös was cursed with shapeless feet. Nobody could make shoes for him—nobody except for my father. When Erdös left Hungary and after my father passed away, he became known as the man who always wore sandals.

At the time, Budapest was a city of one million people, but in some ways it was still a small town. People who mattered knew each other. I remember my father taking me for walks and him continuously lifting his derby hat to the greetings of his acquaintances. He was a large man, six feet tall and over two hundred pounds. Everybody knew that he and his brother made the best shoes in Hungary. In fact, my father was in direct competition with his brother Vilmos.

Father had a silly feud with his brother, but I had no idea why. He never referred to him as Vilmos but as the "Fat One." (Both of them were fat, but Vilmos was fatter.) Father probably forgot the reason for the feud. When they met on the street—something that happened quite frequently because their shops and their apartments were quite close—one of them would cross to the other side of the street so they did not have to face each other. The feud did not faze me because non-violent, transient, innocent feuds were quite common among relatives and friends in Hungary.

When I was about twelve, my father took me along with him to buy leather for his business. During these trips, we developed an excellent relationship. I was a precocious child with respect to business and had my early education from Father. For example, I remember him once explaining to me the meaning of inflation.

"You see," he said, "six months ago it cost me fifty kronen to make a pair of shoes. But today it will cost me one hundred kronen to replace it. So I must charge one hundred and thirty kronen with my markup. Some people say this is highway robbery. They say I am making a profit of eighty kronen and that I should sell the shoes for sixty-five kronen. But if I did that I would soon be out of business because I could not replace my stock of shoes."

Many years later, when we went through an inflationary period in the U.S., some people had problems understanding inflation. They were delighted to get a fifteen percent return on their money, not realizing that after an inflation rate of twelve percent they were really getting only three percent. Also, the growth of the mighty Dow Jones average is rarely shown adjusted for inflation. But I had no problem—all I had to do was to recall the business lessons I received from my father.

One day we were walking by a mansion, and he said, "A few years ago I could have bought this house on credit. Today I could pay it off for the price of a pack of cigarettes."

By the way, my father was a chain smoker. But rather than roll his own cigarettes as did most people in Budapest, he hired girls to do it for him. These young women would appear at our apartment in the morning with the tools of their trade. They would claim the largest table, lay out their little machines, tobacco and paper, and over the course of a few days roll thousands of cigarettes. Afterwards, my father's wooden roll top cabinet—reserved for cigarettes only—would be filled with little boxes of cigarettes.

Occasionally, we took trips together to the countryside. My father showed me his birthplace and his parents' graves, and introduced me to his relatives. To the chagrin of my brothers, I became his favorite. Father would go to bed early and would call on me to "come and talk." We would discuss current events, books, business and many other things.

Father assumed that I would take over his business. But after math took hold of me, he gave up that dream. To his credit, he remained supportive of my work, and I discussed my plans with him a great deal. It was a very special day when I received my PhD at Pázmány Péter University with him in the audience.

A few years before his death, our family moved to a more spacious apartment. After twenty years of sharing rooms with my brothers, I had my own room and a private desk where I could do my math in private.

◆   ◆   ◆

I suppose I was a sensitive child. I had terrible nightmares in which I was lost and trying desperately to find something, but I never knew what I was supposed to find.

Perhaps I was simply starting my career in mathematics and didn't know it.

Like other boys at the time, I collected stamps and played with tinker toys. My brothers and I played a game called "buttons," which had rules much like soccer. We would clear the room, remove the carpet and position the players—medium-sized buttons—on the wood floor. By squeezing them between our thumb and forefinger, we made them slide. The ball was a smaller button. Our objective was to get the ball to enter the goal, an open cardboard box.

One of my favorite toys was the "Feri," or little photographer. We would clip a small piece of film to a special photographic paper and hold it in the sun. When we got a small print—not quite black and white, but brown and white—we soaked it in salt water so it wouldn't fade.

Like other households, we did not have a radio yet, because the radio was a gadget for nerds. But we had a pair of wired-in earphones hanging on the wall, the "Hirmondo" (news medium), so we could listen to news and children tales.

I was a very serious child. By the age of eight I had fully developed my lifelong passion for reading and spent every spare minute reading novels. My nickname at the time was "Little Scholar." I read the *Count of Monte Cristo* by Alexandre Dumas so many times that it seemed real to me.

Years later, when I visited Chateau d'If, near Marseilles, I found myself reliving the episode from the novel when Edmond Dantes was imprisoned on the island. The people of Marseilles, addicted to fibs (in the spirit of great literature), had assigned two of the cells in the basement to the famous fictional characters: "Le numero 34: Edmond Dantes," and "Le numero 27: Abbe Faria." When I saw the spot, I froze and almost broke out in tears—much to the astonishment of the other sightseers.

I still have the original French version of the book, and when I feel particularly low I read parts of it again. Once, while reading *Captain*

Hatteras by Jules Verne, I dreamt that I was lost in the icebergs of Labrador.

I loved books so much that I even learned how to bind them. My father knew a professional bookbinder and hired him as a tutor. We drove two nails into a board and sewed each of the sixteen—or thirty-two-page signatures of the book to the nails. For the spine we used a special glue that we bought in solid blocks and cooked in water. We removed the nails and replaced them with heavy strings and glued on cardboard to form the hard covers. I took the books to a professional shop to print the gold-leaf titles. I bound about twenty books and was delighted with the results. Later I discovered that others believed that I had ruined the books because the margins were trimmed off and the bindings looked ugly.

The lycée I attended was in a lower middle class neighborhood. My friend George Vidor was considered the richest kid in class because his father was a successful wholesale paper merchant. Somehow I earned the reputation of being the second richest, though I never understood why. George's family had a much larger apartment than ours, as well as a horse-driven carriage that required a full-time coachman. Perhaps it was because both George and I flaunted our wristwatches. We also carried around fountain pens, but we weren't allowed to use them because we were required to write in calligraphy, something that could be achieved only with old-fashioned pens dipped in inkwells.

Back then it was the custom in middle class families for children to learn to play the piano, and I was tortured by lessons for a few years. Sad to say, this experience destroyed my love of music for almost the next thirty years. It was only much later in life, after marrying a pianist, that I discovered music as one of the great loves in my life.

◆   ◆   ◆

We spent one of our vacations on Lake Balaton with our Uncle David and his favorite daughter, my cousin Lotte. She had some very romantic ideas about Magyars that we carefully nurtured with many fancy tales. We told her that we rode to school on horses, and some other wild stories about fighting wolves. She got it into her head that she wanted an excursion on an ox-drawn carriage, "in true Hungarian style." Father, being a good sport, managed to arrange it, and I vividly remember all of us riding in all our glory on a rickety cart.

Uncle David, his son, Fritz, and Lotte often came to visit us in Budapest. Uncle David thought it would be a good idea for Fritz to start a lingerie business in Paris. This turned out to be a stroke of luck, because Fritz managed to transfer to Paris before the rise of Hitler and later was able to provide a safe refuge for most of his family. Fritz was extremely helpful to me when I was stranded in Paris, and today most of my relatives live there.

◆   ◆   ◆

The Danube River played an important role in my life. It is a wide, muddy river, not the beautiful "Blue Danube," a romantic illusion created by the Austrian musician Johan Strauss. This fast-moving river gave us recreation and adventure.

In the 1920s it was customary for middle-class families to escape from the summer heat of Budapest and spend a couple of months on the shores of the Danube. A horse-drawn carriage appeared on the street in front of our house accompanied by some husky guys. Some of our most important furnishings, like the beds, were put on the carriage, and our maid climbed in to keep an eye on things. We kids went with mother to West Railroad Station and took the train to Göd, abut fifteen miles from Budapest, upstream on the Danube, where our father had rented a summer cottage for us.

Our cottage was very primitive—no electricity, running water or indoor toilets—but perfect for our summer fun. Father stayed there at night and commuted to Budapest during the day to run the store.

Going to the train station in the afternoon to greet him was often the highlight of the day.

Every morning after breakfast, we put on our bathing suits and climbed into a wooden carriage. Mother pulled us to the shore of the Danube, and we spent most of the day playing in the sand. I also learned to swim. I was under the illusion that I knew how to swim, but was rudely awakened later in life when I went to pools and discovered that I knew only how to float downstream and could make no progress whatever in still water. But no matter. I did learn to love the water, and this prepared me to become an excellent swimmer. Eventually I would find myself plowing through giant waves in the Pacific, which my friends thought was totally out of character for such a math nerd.

Sundays in Göd were always great occasions. Large number of relatives and friends from the city would converge on our cottage, wanting to escape the heat and tedium of Budapest. Mother would prepare a banquet, which everyone ate with gusto. Then we would go to the shore of the Danube and have a great time swimming, sunning, frolicking and simply doing nothing.

As I grew older, the Danube became a place for high adventure. My friends and I would row out into the middle of the river in our small boat, then hitch a ride on a barge. Like the Mississippi, the Danube is an important international highway for huge ships and barges carrying large loads of grain and sand.

It was a risky business. When we saw a ship towing barges upstream, we would quickly row alongside it, then let the barges slide by until we could reach out and grab the final one. If everything worked, we received a nice ride upstream. But if we came too close to the lead boat, we could be run over. And if we didn't grab at just the right moment, we'd find ourselves in the middle of the swirling Danube headed downstream in the wrong direction.

I remember one time when things didn't work as planned. There were three of us: Otto and myself rowing hard together, with George at the helm. The high black walls of the barge passed by us quickly.

Because we were rowing backwards, I had no sense of direction. George suddenly yelled, "Now!"

Unfortunately, we were a split-second too early. The giant barge ran over our little wooden rowboat. Down we went. After we swam to the surface, we saw a gaping hole in the side of our boat, then watched in horror as it sank to the rim.

George began swimming to shore, but Otto and I realized that we had to save the borrowed rowboat. The cost of replacing it would have ruined us financially. So we slowly pulled the boat to shore. Eventually, we managed to get it fixed, but never spoke of the adventure to our parents.

◆   ◆   ◆

Sundays were always special days in our family. The store was open every other day of the week until 6:00 or 7:00 in the evening, but on Sundays it was closed all day.

Cooking for Sunday was always a big event. Mother spent all day Saturday preparing, and on Sunday morning she would finish cooking the fattened goose for noon dinner. The greatest delicacies of all were the goose liver and rind. There is an old Hungarian folk song that sings the praises of goose liver.

Father and we three kids stayed in bed late, jumping around and frolicking. Father always took a bath on Sunday morning, whether he needed it or not. Then the three little kids got all dolled up, and he took us around to visit his friends, proudly showing off his "quarter-of-a-dozen" boys.

In the summertime we went to the Weingruber, an open-air "bier hall" where father and his friends drank beer. We did not have a car, but took a taxi. The driver waited for us until we were ready to come home. Father never failed to send a glass of beer to the chauffeur, who we always called the "pilot" because it sounded more elegant than "chauffer."

Sometimes we took a taxi to the Hüvösvölgy summer home of my uncle Vilmos Bacsi. (Bacsi is the Hungarian word for "Uncle." Actually, children called any grownup Bacsi.) Father would not visit with him because of the feud. But Mother would take us to spend time with our aunt's side of the family, including my grandparents, who lived under the same roof.

◆　　◆　　◆

My brothers and I grew up knowing very little about the mysteries of the other sex. We overheard grownups whispering about Aunt Miszi, the French woman who lived next door. They said she lived in a "wild marriage," but we had no idea what was meant by this. Only later did we discover that she wasn't married to the man she lived with. Miszi had a dog and cat that we were very fond of visiting. Both of their deaths made a deep impression on me. Especially the cat Susu, who liked to sit in the fifth-floor window and contemplate the world. One day, however, she saw a bird and sprang after it, falling all the way to the ground. Although Susu managed to crawl back to the apartment, she later expired.

When I was eight, my friend Paul Forgács asked me, "Can you keep a secret?"

"Why, of course," I answered.

"Give me your word of honor," he insisted.

I did.

"Girls do not have penises," he said.

"That can't be. You're lying!"

Paul said that he had seen his sister naked. He also pointed out the anatomical details of a large oil painting by Szüle Peter on our wall that showed a naked woman. Our apartment was modest, but it was somewhat of a museum. Father had prominent painters and sculptors among his clients, so first-class paintings covered our walls and elegant statues were displayed on stands around the house.

"She is just hiding it between her legs," I insisted.

Paul said he would prove it and asked me to visit him in his apartment. But his sister wouldn't cooperate, and the issue was left open. Later he brought me a book that settled the argument. Reluctantly, I reconciled myself to this organic deficiency of girls.

◆   ◆   ◆

An important place to visit during my early years was Saint Marguerite's Island. It was a 1.5-mile-long island situated in the middle of the Danube, between Buda and Pest. In the 15th century it was uninhabited except by wildlife, especially rabbits, and was known as the "Island of Rabbits." Later, one of the kings sent a daughter named Marguerite to live there. After her death, this pious nun became a saint and the island was renamed for her.

Before World War I, the island was the private property of the Habsburgs; afterwards, it became a public park. There was a big difference between this and the other public parks; at Saint Marguerite there was a small entrance fee, which immediately excluded many of the poor. In the center of the park was a spa called the Palatinus, a large sandy area that sported three pools. One was large enough for swimming and was quite warm, another was like a good-sized hot tub and the third was a very cold fountain that was mostly for looks and extremely tough swimmers.

Before the invention of electricity, trolleys drawn by horses on rails were used for public transportation in cities. As an historic curiosity, much like the electric trolley cars in San Francisco, there was a horse-drawn trolley wagon on the island that accommodated about twenty-five people. As I write this, I count myself among the last living persons to ever ride a horse-drawn public trolley.

When I was about ten years old, my family would go to the Palatinus on Sundays to swim and have a family picnic. As a student, I went there with my friends for socializing and swimming. Later, a covered area with an Olympic-sized pool was added. The Hungarians are big on water polo and we used to go there for serious swimming.

Buda has many natural hot springs, and after the Turks defeated the Hungarians in 1526, they occupied the country for the next one hundred and fifty years, building many bathhouses and spas. At the Palatinus, the pools were continuously emptied and refilled from the natural hot springs—no chlorine was ever needed.

The island was the popular lover's lane and it's where I took my dates. My first true girlfriend was Aranka, whom I met in 1936 through our common interest in math. At the time, I was twenty years old and attending the university, while she was still enrolled in the lycée. Our relationship turned into a very serious love affair, and for all practical purposes we became engaged. After my graduation, we planned to get married after traveling to the U.S., where she had family. However, she died of influenza in New York while I was still in Paris awaiting my visa. This greatest tragedy of my entire life lies so buried in my mind that I don't want to meddle with it, and I don't want to talk about it.

◆   ◆   ◆

My father's ethical standards were very high; as a result, I was raised to be absolutely honest. Lying was an unforgivable sin and unimaginable offense. But this wasn't the typical Hungarian outlook.

Emile, an uncle on my mother's side, was clever with gadgets. When he developed an electric bypass so that he could get free electricity, his family was proud of him. Father said this was stealing.

Another black sheep from my mother's family was Dezsö. My father told me of the day that Dezso dropped by the house. When he saw my father wasn't home, he left with a few of my father's suits and pawned them. After a few brushes with the law, my grandfather bought Dezso a steamship ticket and sent him to "wild" America. Dezso managed to get a job, save money and return. But apparently he never reformed, because after a few more mishaps grandfather shipped him back to America. When World War I broke out, Dezso got stuck in Memphis, Tennessee.

One day I was missing some books, and we discovered that my cousin Laci stole them. Father forgave him, because he was a kind man. But when Laci stole some stuff from one of my aunts, he was sent to jail.

When I left Hungary, I was astounded by the different ethical standards in other countries. In the Zurich train station, I found paper and soap in the bathroom—something you'd never see in Hungary because people would have stolen it.

In 1939, George Pinter (Pintér) asked me to drop by his house in Zurich while he was in class at the university.

"Just step in and wait for me," he said.

"How do I get in?" I asked.

"The door is never locked," was his astonishing reply.

In the U.S., people stood in line at the post office, something I had never seen anyone do in Hungary. There were self-service stores. In Paris, I saw books openly displayed in a bookstore for anyone to steal—a Hungarian university student did just that and was caught, locked up and deported.

Also while in Paris, I was surprised to learn that passengers boarding a bus would take a number from the block and stand patiently in line as their number was called. When they tried this system in Budapest, people stole the block of numbers.

Until Laura, my wife, visited Hungary for the first time, she couldn't fully appreciate the joke, "A Hungarian is a person who enters after you in the revolving door and leaves ahead of you." When we boarded our plane in Budapest, we were the first ones in line at the gate, and the last to enter the plane.

Many years later a cousin (again on mother side) came into possession of a tape recorder and wanted me to send him a sworn affidavit, signed by a notary public, that I had sent the recorder to him. When I refused, he became so angry at me that I never heard from him again.

I could never figure out where my father picked up his high standards. But I followed them all my life, even if occasionally they didn't yield the shortest path to my goals.

◆   ◆   ◆

By the time I became a teenager, I developed an intolerance for the blind and belligerent patriotic attitude of the ruling elite. Countess Hedervary Héderváry expressed a typical feeling when she once congratulated my mother by saying, "You should be proud to have given three sons to the Fatherland."

In school we were saturated by the glory of Hungarian history and literature. We were constantly reminded of Hungary's proud history and encouraged to join an army that would fight for and reestablish our glorious past.

Of course, we never learned that we lost World War I, only that we were tricked out of victory. We understood that the Treaty of Versailles wasn't a treaty at all—it was actually a dictum of the Allied Powers. We weren't told that the so-called "lost" territories (Hungary lost nearly two thirds of its territory after the war) were mostly populated by minorities. Or that Woodrow Wilson wanted to divide this territory into independent, self-governing countries.

The official Hungarian attitude was that we must regain these lost territories, even if it meant a glorious war. We were supposed to hate the winners of WWI and arm ourselves to annex Slovakia, Czechoslovakia and Transylvania.

We started our classes with a prayer every morning that declared, "We believe in one God, one country and the resurrection of Hungary." As Magyars, we were the finest people on Earth, while people from other countries were pigs.

We were never told about the terrible atrocities committed by the German armies under the Kaiser. Incidents like the burning of cities and the massacre of civilians in Belgium were omitted from our history books. The press and cinema were censored, and international best sellers about the WWI were not available. My family and friends were absolute pacifists—we thought the government should concentrate on improving the lot of Hungarians, and not on resurrecting past glories. Of course, this was considered a most unpatriotic attitude and we never mentioned it publicly.

Later, this overzealous attitude resulted in Hungary allying itself with Hitler's Germany and losing World War II. Hundreds of thousands of Hungarians died, much of Budapest and the countryside were destroyed, and a communist government was installed that mismanaged the country's resources for many future generations.

◆　　◆　　◆

As a child, I wasn't really aware of being Jewish, or that there was a distinction between Jews and non-Jews. Of course, I knew there was something strange about Aunt Gizi, the wife of an uncle on my mother's side. But it wasn't until much later that I learned she was Christian and considered to be out of sync with the rest of the family.

The simple fact was, my father and mother never darkened a synagogue's door. We never observed sacred holidays, spoke Yiddish or lived in the Jewish section of Budapest. Because we were opposed to all forms of nationalism, we didn't agree with the Zionists who wanted Jews to return to Israel.

I guess we were atheists because I remember my father once telling me that there was no God.

"How do you know?" I asked.

"Because I overheard my dad say the same thing to his friend," he said.

As I got older, my awareness of being Jewish gradually sharpened. Twice a week our class in the lycée was split into three groups with a priest for the Catholics, a minister for the adherents of the reformed church and a rabbi for the Jewish students. Once a week the Jewish children were led to synagogue. At thirteen I was required to have my bar mitzvah in the synagogue—it was a near disaster because I didn't know my Hebrew name, and so I was called as the Son of Israel. My family and friends considered this mandatory religion to be complete nonsense, but we learned to hide our feelings in the lycée and in all official dealings with the government.

When Admiral Horthy came to power, there was a sudden outburst of anti-Semitism. Atrocities against Jews were committed, but they were mild in comparison to what Hitler encouraged. The mood of the times was perfectly expressed in a popular Hungarian joke: "An anti-Semite is a person who dislikes Jews more than is normal."

A merchant like my father wasn't affected at all. Some of the most prominent intellectuals, physicians, attorneys and business men were Jewish, and some were quite wealthy and prominent. However, the unwritten law of the day said that Jews couldn't be hired as policemen, teachers, professors or government employees.

◆   ◆   ◆

One Sunday morning my father announced that he was going to introduce me and my brothers to his cousin Vilmos Vazsonyi. I was six years old at the time and knew Vazsonyi was a distant relative and someone my father played cards with at the Democratic Club. I didn't realize that Vazsonyi was the most prominent Jew in Hungary, the "Hungarian Disraeli."

Vilmos Vazsonyi was the son of Janos Weiszfeld, a teacher. They were much better off than my father's family, and Vilmos went to the university at Budapest and became an attorney, in hopes of becoming a politician. At the time, however, having a German-sounding name like

Weiszfeld was considered a disadvantage. The national custom was to take on a Hungarian name, often related to the person's place of birth. His birthplace was Sümeg; unfortunately, there was already an important politician called Sümegi (meaning from Sümeg). So Vilmos decided to use the name of my father's birthplace and took the name Vazsonyi (from Vazsony). It didn't matter to him that there was in fact no village called Vazsony, only Nagyvazsony and Kisvazsony.

When we went to meet him at his villa, I was enthralled by his parrot, Lori, who could talk. I had never seen anything like it. Lori said: "Wolf, menj a pokolba" ("Wolf, go to hell"). Mr. Wolf was the worst, anti-Semitic, political opponent of Vilmos Vazsonyi. The other thing that amazed me was that he kept a gun with a pearl handle on his nightstand because the Horthy gang wanted to assassinate him. He was very friendly to me and lifted me up to see a typewritten document neatly framed and hanging on the wall. "Look at my diploma," he said. I can remember a typewritten page signed with the huge letters: Karoly. This document was his appointment by the king to the cabinet and the Privy Council.

Vilmos Vazsonyi became the highest ranking Hungarian Jew ever to be addressed as "His Grace." This was only possible because King Karoly, who was crowned in 1916, had no ill feelings towards the Jews.

The only hitch over Vazsonyi's appointment was that he refused to take the oath on the Christian Bible. He said he did not believe in it, and actually did not believe in any bible at all. Like my immediate family, he was a non-practicing Jew as a matter of principle. So King Karoly exempted him from the oath.

A few years after our visit, when Karoly IV abdicated his rule and Admiral Horthy began his anti-Semitic regime, Vazsonyi joined the opposition party, which was in strict violation of the government's repressive laws.

One day I was walking back from elementary school and turned to the left on the Terez Ring. A group of people were gathered at the closed gate in front of Vazsonyi's legal offices. I learned that earlier in the day, as Vazsonyi was leaving his office, an assassin jumped out of the bushes and fired his gun twice. When both shots failed, Vazsonyi lunged forward and hit the assassin on the head with his heavy walking stick. The would-be assassin was arrested, but released the next day because "he committed his patriotic act in a state of temporary mental confusion."

Vazsonyi died in Baden, Germany, in 1926, while "taking the waters." Six years later, while I was still in the lycée, Hungarians with Germanic-sounding names were pressured by the authorities to take on more traditional Hungarian names. My family decided that the three boys should take the name Vazsonyi. There was no point in my father changing his name because he had a successful business as a Weiszfeld. We submitted a petition to change our names, but nothing happened until March of 1937, when, quite out of the blue sky, we received decrees from the Hungarian government changing our names irrevocably to Vazsonyi. This put me in an embarrassing position, because I had already submitted my first math paper under the Weiszfeld name.

◆　　　◆　　　◆

By 1936 my father's business turned sour. He lost interest in his work and slowly in life. His relationships with my brothers turned bad, too. He had hoped my elder brother would take over the business, but Karcsi wanted to be a poet, a profession at which he had no hope of making a living. My younger brother, considered the smartest of the three, turned into an inventor and acquired a good job. But he hated Father and me, and our relationship became impossible. In 1938, during my last year in Hungary, my father's business finally collapsed. He left the country for a vacation to Semmering, Austria, and my brother was supposed to wind up the business. But he could not do it, and strangely I, without any business experience, had to step in. I negotiated with the lawyers and creditors as the business went into bankruptcy and final liquidation. Many years later this experience helped me to gain confidence in business dealings of my own.

One summer morning, while I was working at home, my father called me into his room, saying he wasn't feeling well. I was the only one at home, so I called our doctor but he was not available. I called a second, and finally a third agreed to come. I recall my father looking at me, sitting on the bed; he could not talk, but waved in a desperate way. The doctor started to examine him, but father fell back on the bed, went into final agony and died of a massive heart attack. I can still remember how our maid, a country girl, tied up his jaws with a napkin. I also associate the smell of hot tar with his death because at the time workers were patching asphalt on the street in front of our apartment.

Losing my father left a large gap in my life. Every step I had ever made was discussed with him in detail, and together we planned my future. This was the end of my real family life in Hungary. In a sad way, however, it may have been a blessing for my father to pass away before seeing the terrors of World War II and the Nazis and the murder of two of his sons.

Six months after his death I left Hungary for good.

3

MATHEMATICAL HUMPBACKS

o o o o o o o o o o o o o o o o o o o o o o o o o o o o

Jupiter bestowed on man far more passion than reason. More-over, he confined reason to a cramped corner of the head and left all the rest of the body to the passions.

—Desiderius Erasmus (c. 1466–1536)

During my fellowship at the Sorbonne, my friends in Paris would often greet me by saying, "Tien, voici le bossu Hongrois." ("Here comes the Hungarian humpback.") At first I thought my friends were comparing me to Quasimodo because I would often sit for hours in the Notre Dame Cathedral. Unlike the hunchback of Notre Dame, however, I would contemplate the stone gargoyles while thinking of math theorems. (Even today I have on my desk a little gargoyle working his desktop computer.) Later on I learned that the French use the word "hump" in the same way the English say "knack." To their Gallic eye, I had a hump for math.

Where did my hump come from?

Hungary was, and still is to some extent, math crazy—even now American students visit Budapest to experience the excitement of math—or, in other words, rub humps. In the early part of the 20th century, this culture produced an extraordinary number of math geniuses. Not only was there my friend Paul Erdös, but also Michael Polányi,

George Polya, Gabor Szegö, Leo Szilard, Edward Teller, Theodore von Kármán, John von Neumann, Abraham Wald and Eugene Wigner.

I have two explanations for this baby boom of mathematicians.

The first is the Bossu (Hump) Theory. In the early days of the 1900s, members of an alien race from a faraway planet, the Bossu, landed on Margit Island, which sits in the center of the Danube between Buda and Pest. The Bossu had an extraordinary knack for mathematics that may or may not have been related to the humps on their backs. Supposedly, this physical abnormality was a kind of portable office that enabled the Bossu to do their work at any time or place—say, for instance, at Notre Dame Cathedral.

As the Bossu exited their ship, a band of gypsies greeted them with singing and dancing and violin playing. So overwhelmed by the beauty of the music and the physical charms of the women, the Bossu promptly voted to end their exploration of deep space and put down their humps in Hungary.

For the next two decades, the Bossu roamed the Hungarian countryside, cavorting with gypsies, romancing young Hungarian women and exploring mathematical theorems. They might have stayed longer, but the threat of another world war darkened the horizon. Being sensible creatures, they left as abruptly as they came. Today we behold their legacy: an exceptional bunch of talented and somewhat eccentric mathematicians with an incredible hump for math.

My other explanation is grounded in my own experiences. Perhaps by holding up a mirror to myself, I can reflect what some of my fellow math Bossu went through.

When I was about fourteen years old, my hump began growing at an alarming rate. At the time, I was attending the lycèe, which was like a combination of middle school, high school and the first two years of college.

Hungarians put a high priority on learning, and the lycèe held high standards of classical education. In September 1926, I was ten years old when my mother first dropped me off at the Kemény Zsigmond Fö-

Reáliskola, a gray, three-story school building with high echoing ceilings. In a typical year, each grade had two classes with about thirty students. But in 1916, when I was born, the men were off fighting World War I and there were few births. So we had only one class with sixteen students.

Kemény Zsigmond was an experimental school. Some "harebrained ignoramus" (in the words of some classical education proponents) convinced Count Klieberberg, the Secretary of Education, that Latin shouldn't be a required course for everyone. For example, engineers could be exempt because they were practical types who didn't need "culture." So, to the great chagrin of the "cultured people," the "Real Iskola" (Real School) was started and Latin was dropped. This was lucky for me, because Latin was replaced with descriptive geometry, a subject I loved. The upside for me was that I avoided years of studying a boring, useless subject. The downside was that I could never understand the Latin words written on my Ph.D. diploma.

(Unfortunately, a few years later the conservative educators won out and forced the Secretary to return to the classical approach. The conservatives correctly pointed out that until 1850 the official language of Hungary was Latin and that the debates in the House of Representative had been conducted in Latin. Given this information, they incorrectly concluded that Latin was "good for the soul." Since there was no way to return to the good old days when Latin was useful, students were expected to learn it for its own sake. Currently there is a similar sentiment about algebra in U.S. high schools, but I will talk about that later.)

I was in my fifth year when a friend of mine from the technical university showed me his photograph in a national magazine called Középiskolai Matematikai Lapok, or KöMaL.

This monthly magazine featured math problems aimed at upper-grade math students from lycées all over Hungary. The publisher, a lycèe instructor named Farago, encouraged students to submit proofs of theorems. If Farago accepted your solution, he published your name beside the proof. As a bonus, those students who solved the most problems during the school year would have their photos published at the end of that year.

When my friend showed me his smiling mug shot in that magazine, I knew I wouldn't rest until my face graced those pages.

Around that same time, I had another experience that made a deep impression on me. My father, who was bursting with pride over my ability to solve intricate math problems, heard about a young math genius in Budapest. So he arranged a visit with Paul Erdös, whose parents were both math teachers. There was a story going around that when Erdös was four years old, his uncle posed a trick question: "What is one hundred less two hundred and fifty?" His answer came without hesitation: "One hundred and fifty below zero." The young math prodigy already understood the concept of negative numbers.

I was sitting in the office at the back of my father's shoe shop when I first met Paul Erdös. He was all of seventeen years old. By his own words, however, he was already old (throughout his entire life he referred to his old age, or his old bones). He certainly looked old as he walked in, his body twisted and hunched over, his eyes squinting at the world around him.

Just as a normal person would say "How are you?", his first words to me were: "Give me a four-digit number."

"Two thousand, five hundred and thirty-two," I replied.

"The square of it is six million, four hundred and eleven thousand and twenty-four," he said. "Sorry, I am getting old and cannot tell you the cube."

I was bewildered. I had never met anybody like him, nor would I ever again.

Erdös flew on to the next subject. "How many proofs of the Pythagorean Theorem do you know?"

"One."

"I know thirty-seven," he said.

"Did you know that the points of a straight line do not form a denumerable set?"

He proceeded to show me Cantor's proof for using the diagonal.

When he had finished drilling me, he said, "I must run." And, indeed, he never walked, but cantered with a weird, lopsided gait that made people on the street turn to watch him.

From our first meeting, it was clear to me that I had a lot to learn from him. And so, Paul Erdös became my life-long mathematics hero—we stayed in touch until his death in 1996. He was the most dedicated person I have ever met.

As teenagers, we spent much time together—ice skating and hiking in the hills of Buda, where I used to spin wild tales. We had our own code. If he had doubts about the authenticity of a story I was telling, he would ask, "Did this happen in China?" If I answered, "Yes," then he knew I was making it up. I learned to overlook the stares and comments that his strange walk would provoke. Often girls would ask me, "Who's the gorilla?"

Years later when I considered leaving mathematics to seek an engineering degree from the Technical University at Budapest, Erdös put the issue to rest by saying, "If you do, when you enter the gates of the Technical University, I will come out of hiding and shoot you." (Erdös had no tolerance for practical math and felt it would be a betrayal of my talent to dabble in it.)

Many more years later, when Erdös became world famous, some wits developed a way to rank mathematicians. According to this ranking system, the highest level mathematician had an Erdös number of one because he wrote a joint paper with Erdös. Those who never wrote a paper with the great mathematician himself, but wrote a paper jointly with a mathematician who had an Erdös number of one, would receive an Erdös number of two. Someone who co-wrote a paper with a colleague who had an Erdös number of two would be ranked three and so on. Supposedly, every creative mathematician had an Erdös number of five or less. Albert Einstein's Erdös number was two. My Erdös number is one. Skipping ahead a bit, this is how it happened.

In 1936, while still living in Budapest, I was doing research on a classical graph theorem, the Königsberg theorem of Euler, and managed to extend the theorem to infinite graphs. I had only the necessary but not the sufficient condition. Those days I was seeing Erdös almost daily and made the fatal error of telling him about my discovery. I say fatal because after I told him, he called me back in twenty minutes and told me the proof of sufficient condition.

"Damn," I thought, "now I have to write a joint paper with him."

Little did I know the fame that co-authoring a paper with Erdös would later bring me. Now whenever I meet a mathematician, I introduce myself, "I am Andrew Vazsonyi and my Erdös number is one." (One smart guy who also wrote a paper with Erdös once replied, "My Vazsonyi number is two.") When the biographies on Erdös were published, my friend Herb Simon (the Nobel Prize winner and one of my decision-making heroes) wrote that he was bothered all his life that his Erdös number was infinite. He suggested—tongue in the cheek—that we write a joint paper so that his number would be two.

♦   ♦   ♦

During that year at the lycèe, my math hump grew in the most virulent manner. I lost interest in all other subjects (except girls—like a good, old-fashioned Bossu Hungarian male I was also a hopeless romantic). Every month I waited breathlessly to see if my name would appear in the magazine below my solution. Each time it did, I wondered if I would be able to solve the next problem and the next, so that my photo would finally appear in the spring.

Eventually, all this effort paid off. During my last four years at the lycèe, my photograph was published each year, making me the Hungarian national champion from all the lycèes. It was a triumph that my whole family shared. The old nightmares of being lost and frightened went away. Now the only time I felt really happy was when I was lost in solving a math problem.

One important lesson I learned at that time was that mathematicians do not really solve problems. Instead, what a mathematician actually does is discover, prove and publish theorems. Mathematicians publish about two hundred thousand proofs per year. Most of the proofs do not discover new theorems, but are important because they are deemed more elegant than earlier proofs. Someone who took a different approach was David Hilbert, one of the great mathematicians of the 20th century. Believing that the search for elegance should be left to fashion designers, he focused exclusively on theorems that never have been proven.

There is a big difference between a math teacher and a mathematician. An instructor of math is one who teaches the findings of mathematicians. What Farago published every month were little theorems, and we submitted proofs of the theorems. Therefore in our proofs, we were functioning as mathematicians. (Much later I discovered that real-life mathematicians, who help people solve real-life problems, are not like theoretical mathematicians.)

I also learned other weird things about math.

For example, I recall the frustrating experience I had when I was fifteen years old and my instructor, Gyula Neukomm, quoted Euclid: "The sum of the angles of a triangle adds up to 180 degrees." An inquisitive student asked, "Please, your honor, what if the sum is not exactly 180 degrees?"

"Sit down, you idiot," the instructor angrily replied.

Believe it or not, this was the way students and teachers talked back then.

Neukomm followed by giving us a homework assignment that involved drawing an accurate ink triangle, measuring the angles and calculating the sum.

Being a good student, I went home and carefully mapped out the triangle. All the time I was thinking, "This is absurd. It will never add up to 180 degrees." But in spite of my doubts, I stayed up all night measuring this ideal triangle. It's almost as if I had to prove Euclid wrong and was willing to put in the extra effort.

Exhausted, the next day I went to class and turned in my results. As I feared, I got my homework back with a grade of zero.

When I complained to Neukomm, he said, "You of all people ought to know that the sum is 180 degrees, and not 180.5 degrees."

I was angry and frustrated. "What does he want me to do?" I fumed to my friends, "Lie?"

Actually, I didn't really know why I got 180.5 degrees instead of Euclid's 180 degrees. It was only much later that I understood that my instructor had no idea how math relates to the physical world. Or anything about the statistics of measurements. Or that he cared. He was merely interested in passing down abstract mathematical theorems. This was one of my first glimpses at how the "pure math" of ideas differed from the applied math that we live with whenever we draw triangles by hand.

Pure mathematicians just don't care at all about such earthly things as measuring angles. I also found out much later that most people don't understand how math relates to the real world either. Once, after I told a friend about my strange brush with Euclid, he responded bitterly, "Then why are we taught Euclid if it's all lies?"

At the time, however, I just thought there must be something wrong with me. Other experiences confirmed that feeling. For instance, I was a horrible auditory learner. Lectures are linear, and whenever I heard something interesting, I would latch on to that thought, go off on my own tangent and completely lose the speaker. (I do the same thing when I read a math article—I start at the end, jump back and forth and finish in the middle.) Modern learning theory confirms that this isn't too unusual—it's been known for some time that lectures are the least effective way of teaching. At the time I thought something was wrong with me. But with my mother's support I played hooky from school so that I could stay home and really learn.

Another thing I learned, which seemed useless until recently, was that when the Gregorian calendar replaced the Julian calendar in 1582, the new calendar introduced a few exceptions to the rule that every fourth year is a leap year. I still remember our teacher Neukomm warning us, "A few of you may be still alive in 2000, so note that it is a leap year." (Note: 1800 and 1900 were not leap years, nor are 2100, 2200 and 2300.)

Of course, because Neukomm didn't foresee computers, he couldn't forsee that when February 29, 2000, rolled in, most computers would be programmed incorrectly and switch over to March 1. The headlines that read, "Leap Day glitches cause minor hiccups in U.S.," should have read, "Programmers do not know the Gregorian calendar." I responded to the potential business disruption by celebrating that I was fortunate enough to see the year 2000—and by storing cases of Beefeater gin for future martinis.

Another lesson I learned in the lycée, however, had more unfortunate results. Because of my intense feelings for math, I began to resent spending time on more mundane subjects such as foreign languages and composition. In other words, I hated everything that came between me and math.

The last two years in the lycèe were the most unhappy ones of my life. I developed feuds with the instructors and, of course, I always lost. Makoldy, the history instructor, hated math and informed me in no uncertain terms that a "good Magyar" knew his history, not mathematics. But I had no interest in memorizing the coronation dates of Hungarian kings and the battles they purportedly won or lost. I concluded that I would never be part of the "good old Magyar club."

When it came to foreign languages, I wasn't any better. French and German were my Waterloo, and I was told by my unpleasant teacher that I had absolutely no talent and would never master a foreign language. Likewise, I received low ratings from my writing teacher. Despite my love of reading, I had no feeling for fiction writing. To put it mildly, I was a rotten student.

As for math, I didn't learn it in school because I was so far ahead of the other students. I learned from books—and I had my hump, which provided me with intuitive knowledge. Of course, for the majority of my schoolmates, math was an absolute nightmare and a total waste of time. As with Latin, math was taught primarily for historical reasons, and it was widely acknowledged that it was useless except as an "exercise for the mind."

In the 1800s, members of the Hungarian nobility were supposed to know Greek, Latin, literary classics, history, Euclid, calculus and many other cultural areas. By the time I came around, the rationale for why one should know these things was forgotten, but algebra, geometry and calculus stayed in the curriculum. This resulted in rote learning for the sole purpose of passing exams—not for the purpose of future recall or genuine understanding. Mathematics was (and, unfortunately, remains to this day) an instrument of torture for many students, generating much suffering, anxiety, panic and grinding of teeth.

Fortunately, my father's good sense prevailed on me before I faced the Maturity Exam, which marked the end of the lycèe years. The exam tested students on six subjects. Those who passed the exam would receive a certificate and be considered "educated." Those who failed the exam were "uneducated." Only those in the first group could attend universities, or hold high level jobs or high rank in the army. Lycèe students were accustomed to hearing unhappy instructors yell, "You'll flunk out, not get the certificate and become a latrine cleaner in the army!"

◆   ◆   ◆

In the lycée, anti-Semitism was both sporadic and subtle. Some teachers didn't practice it at all, others did. Jews weren't openly held back, but Christians were definitely favored. My class was unusual because for some statistical anomaly the Jews were in the majority, so I was never aware of any blatant oppression.

Following the lycée, the first offical anti-Semitic law I encountered was the Numerus Clausus (Closed Numbers). The number of Jews admitted to Hungarian Universities was restricted to six percent of the student population. Admiral Horthy and his supporters based the law on the premise that since six percent of the Hungarian population was Jewish, only the same percentage of Jews should be able to hold intellectual positions.

Most of my Jewish schoolmates in the lycée wanted to become engineers. But this was impossible because they couldn't be admitted to the Technical University. Fortunately, most of their parents could afford to send them to Zurich, where they could get engineering degrees. After their return, they hoped to get jobs in private industry, which was not against the law.

My situation was different. I hoped to attend the university in Budapest, so I needed not only a Maturity certificate to get into the top six percent, but also outstanding grades. My scores were so lousy, however, that I had little chance of being admitted to the university.

After many discussions with my father, we cooked up a two-year plan that I would begin in my seventh grade and complete in the eighth (roughly equivalent to the eleventh and twelfth grades in the U.S.) leading to the Maturity Exam. We agreed that I would take time off from math and focus more on my other school work. I considered this a terrible imposition and waste of time, but I also realized that I needed to be practical.

Step one was to improve from "satisfactory" to "good" marks in the seventh grade. Step two was to receive straight "excellent" marks in the eighth grade. The final step was the most important of all—to earn straight "excellent" marks in the dreaded final state test, the Maturity Test. This was the thing the University Board of Admission looked at if you were Jewish. If you were Christian, they didn't bother with marks; you were simply admitted.

"Your plan is ridiculous", my best friend, Endre Kreutzer, told me at the time. "You'll never make it."

If my plan failed, I had a few other options. There was a yearly national competition in math and geometry subjects, as well as one sponsored by the Hungarian Mathematical Society. The winners would be admitted to the university whether they were Jewish or not.

Another option was converting to Christianity. I had a friend who did this and the board didn't even look at his test scores. But my father and I felt that this was a way of ducking my responsibilities.

The third possibility of getting around the Jewish quota was to ask my well-known cousin Janos Vazsonyi if he could influence the Board to admit me. This would have very likely worked, because Hungarian life was built on the practice of "protectio" and nepotism. Society was structured not so much by merit but by family and connections. My father, however, refused to consider this approach. Instead, if necessary, he said he would somehow scrape the money together and send me to Göttingen, Germany, where I would receive some "real" math instruction.

In the end, however, we decided that I would simply do the right thing. The practical thing. So I took time off from math and devoted my time to all the subjects I considered worthless and stupid. I was hell-bent on getting "excellents" in five of the six subjects of the exam. This would give me an overall "excellent" and was my only hope for being admitted to the university.

◆   ◆   ◆

In 1934 I took "The Test," which was given by a specially appointed government commission. As I joined the other candidates in the back of the large hall, the commission chairman ("His Honor") presided at the center of a terrifyingly long table covered with the official green cloth. He was an elderly gentleman, perhaps all of forty years old. Our instructors, who asked the questions, sat on the chairman's right and left.

What was interesting was that our instructors were no longer our adversaries, because while we were being tested as students, they were being tested as teachers. Were they teaching what they were supposed to teach? Were their standards up to par? Did they follow the rules? Did they cheat and tell us the questions in advance? Some tried, but it was difficult because they were supposed to provide a list of questions to His Honor, who made the final choice about which questions would be asked.

When my turn came, my teacher, Neukomm, alerted the chairman that I was a budding math genius. Because of this, His Honor posed an especially challenging question to me: "Present and prove the basic convergence theorems of calculus."

As I quickly presented the answer, the chairman, a former teacher of German literature, was properly impressed because he could not understand a word of my reply.

Of course, I had guessed beforehand that Neukomm would pose that question to show off what a great teacher he was. He also knew that I was the only student in the class who could possibly answer it.

Unfortunately, my performance on exams in some of the "useless subjects"—Hungarian literature, history, French, German and physics—fell short of the "excellent" that I needed to be admitted to the university. But I was saved by His Honor, who told the examiners, "I would prefer to grant only one 'Good.'" By this he meant that they should award me five "Excellents." Of course, his word was law, and the upshot was that I passed with flying colors. Apparently, His Honor believed that a promising mathematician could survive without being a scholar of Hungarian history and German literature.

Hours later, at home, I asked the maid to fire up one of the stoves even though it was a hot summer day. Then I gathered all the books and papers I used to study for the certificate and fed them into the fire. Our apartment became hotter than hell, but my desk was gloriously clean—only my math papers were left behind.

◆   ◆   ◆

By my eighteenth birthday, I was considered a rising star in mathematics. Back then, becoming a mathematician could be compared to being a concert pianist or composer today. The competition was tough, and for those who didn't make it big, there was no guarantee of jobs. Fortunately for me, I had discovered a new theorem, the theorem of "N Points." (Many years later the theorem, the "Weiszfeld algorithm," became a classic in the mathematics of location analysis.) Also, I understood the rules of publishing math papers: my papers would be devoid of emotion or real-world experience and only a handful of people in the world would understand them.

I felt positive that I was on track to becoming an internationally known professor of math in one of the great universities of Europe.

But for all I knew about math, I knew precious little about the world. Or the upcoming horrors of war and ethnic killing. Despite all my hopes for the future, my days would soon go from studying math problems to learning how to survive. I remember one incident from that time, something that would come back to haunt me later.

When I was a teenager, I enjoyed walking or taking the subway to the City Park in the late afternoons and ice skating at the park's wonderful open-air artificial ice rink. There was an orchestra playing mostly Straus waltzes and, most important, girls who would let you skate arm-in-arm with them.

One day at the lycée, I overheard a conversation among some of our best students. They were talking about the ice rink, and one of them, a boy named Krumpholz, said, "Yes, the Jews in our class go around with the idiotic Jewish girls."

It was one of the first times I heard someone openly utter an anti-Semitic remark. Usually, this kind of thing took a more clandestine tone.

But it triggered something deep inside me. I walked up to Krumpholz and slapped him in the face. Of course, he slapped me back and only our classmates kept us apart.

My classmates and I never mentioned the incident again, but no one forgot it either. Years later, after the end of World War II and the defeat of the Hungarian Nazis, I heard that Krumpholz had become a war criminal for killing Jews and was executed for his crimes. Someone also told me that, during the years of horror, he had been looking for me.

After I heard this, I once again experienced my nightmare of being lost and searching for something.

In the dream, I was running along the shore of the Danube River with my brothers and friends. Krumpholz was chasing us with a gun, firing at us and killing some of us. But instead of dreaming that I was searching for something unknown, this time I knew what I was looking for. My American passport.

4

I HATE NUMBERS

When Mattel introduced a talking Barbie Doll that said, among other cheerful utterances on fashion and life, "Math is hard," parents and teachers reacted immediately. Mattel recalled the math-phobic Barbie and the media had a field day with stories about how a doll could say such a thing in our modern, enlightened age.

Personally, I believe what Barbie meant to say was, "I hate numbers." Because that's exactly how I feel—my hump for math doesn't hold numbers, although it does have room for topology, an obscure corner of the math world that most people haven't heard of and was the focus of my doctoral dissertation.

As a student in the lycèe, I could never get the right answer when it came down to a simple calculation. One heartless (or so I thought at the time) instructor told me to stop working with calculus and learn how to add and subtract. Upon hearing this, I broke into tears. Later he told my mother not to worry because I would grow out of it.

I didn't.

To this day I cannot add a column of numbers. I get a different answer every time I try to balance my checkbook or figure out a fifteen percent tip at a restaurant. Over the years I've learned to cover up for this deficiency—my checking account goes into debit mode so I won't bounce checks, and at restaurants I always take twenty percent of the bill and round down for tips.

When I was solving hyperbolic partial differential equations to find supersonic air-flows in ducts for the National Aeronautics Administration in the 1950s, I worked out complicated ways to double- and triple-check my calculations. Oddly enough, I couldn't find a system to avoid making mistakes in the first place, but I could avoid errors (and disasters!) by repeating my calculations with alternate approaches.

My inability to juggle numbers is so great that I often misread numbers, such as the times jotted down in my date book for doctor appointments, which makes me arrive at the clinic an hour late. Or if someone tells me his or her phone number over the phone, I feel very stupid asking the person to repeat it five times, and even then I may not get it right.

When I do calculate numbers in my head, I do it in Hungarian. This was terribly awkward when, as a professor at St. Mary's University in Texas, I did calculations on the blackboard. Every once in a while I would find myself muttering away in Hungarian to an audience of confused undergraduates.

I don't believe I'm the only mathematician who is numerically challenged.

Paul Erdös enjoyed telling a story about Ernst Kummer (1810–1893), a German mathematician who introduced ideal numbers and extended arithmetic to complex number fields. One day Kummer was lecturing at the blackboard and needed to find the product of seven times nine. As he struggled to find an answer that most third graders know by heart, he was heard to mutter in front of the class: "The product can't be sixty-seven because the answer must be a multiple of five, and sixty-seven is a prime. The number seventy-one is too big, but sixty-one is too small. The product must be an integer."

Then he thought for another moment and said with great satisfaction, "That leaves us with sixty-nine!"

The correct answer is sixty-three. (I checked on my calculator.)

I'm afraid this lack of number sense may reinforce the popular stereotype of the absentminded professor who forgets where he parked his car or left his hat. But I believe there's another explanation for me.

When I developed my passion for math, I had an uneasy feeling from the beginning that the world of mathematics might be pure fiction, though it had a mysterious relationship to the "real world." Just like my favorite book during my teenage years, *The Count of Monte Cristo*—whose characters seemed more real to me than Emperor Franz Joseph—math also deals with an alternate virtual reality. Interestingly enough, this world frequently offers more profound truths than do experiences in the real world. For instance, if you want to understand more about dying, skip the publications issued by the Hemlock Society and read *The Death of Ivan Ilyich* by Tolstoy. In this way the mathematician and the novelist are similar—both make a living by selling fiction.

Mathematicians tell a story about Albert Einstein, who, at the age of twelve, learned about the Pythagorean Theorem. "Euclid's proof made an indescribable impression on me," he reportedly said.

Einstein wasn't referring to something that existed in the world around his home in Munich, but rather something from Euclid's fictional math world.

I was struck twice by the Pythagorean Theorem. The first occurred at the age of fourteen, very much like Einstein. But about twenty years later, when I tried to use math in the real world, I realized that Pythagoras' theorem was actually put into practice two thousand years before the birth of Pythagoras. The story is told about Pharaoh Khufu (Cheops, 2638–2613 BC), who needed an accurate square to lay out the base of the Great Pyramid. To do this he needed 90-degree angles. His gurus solved the problem in a most ingenious manner. These geometers used a long rope with twelve knots equally placed. They kept the first and twelfth knot fixed at the same place and made the rope tight by holding the first, third and seventh knot. According to the Pythagorean Theorem, they would have obtained a right angle at knot 3. They achieved an amazing accuracy: one half inch of error along one 755-foot side—about 1 in 18,000.

♦   ♦   ♦

As a passionate young mathematician, I saw mathematics as a science of patterns, structures, shapes and relations—and not as a "science of numbers," which is how Webster defines it. My work in pure math—topology and knot theory—had nothing to do with numbers.

To me, numbers were like the hammers and knives that the workmen above my father's shop used to build leather shoes. The numbers of accounting and statistics were tools that I simply never learned to use in the day-to-day world.

The math I was interested in dealt with the work of my fellow Hungarian Janos Bolyai (1802–1860), who discovered non-Euclidean geometry. Bolyai led an impressive life. His brilliant discovery was published as an appendix to his father's math book in 1823, but was never recognized during his lifetime. At the age of thirteen, he had mastered calculus, the violin and the sword. Once, he accepted three duels to be fought one after the other, but only on the condition that he be allowed to play violin sonatas between the fights.

Earlier I had learned from Euclid that if you are given a straight line and a point not on that line, you can draw only one straight line through the point that is parallel to the straight line. This makes sense to ordinary humans, but mathematicians didn't like the idea that this was a postulate and tried to prove it for the next two thousand years. They all failed. Then Janos Bolyai asked a dumb question. "What happens if Euclid's assumption does not hold? Suppose you can draw two parallels?" He thought long and hard about this and discovered non-Euclidean geometry. "I created a new world out of nothing," he told his father.

Today, there are several kinds of geometries or virtual realities of the mathematical kind. Gurus of creativity encourage you to ask stupid questions, and they claim there are no stupid questions, only stupid answers.

After Bolyai, I discovered the work of David Hilbert, the leading German mathematician of his generation. I learned that I no longer needed to know what a point or straight line was.

However, the relationship between the virtual world of math and the practical world was a puzzle to me. What is a circle? When you draw one on a piece of paper, you deposit a mess of graphite particles on the paper. This is not a mathematical circle. When I am in my world of math I know exactly how to deal with a triangle, square, cube and hypercube, but I am not clear how these objects relate to the physical world.

Even sophisticated scientists (like my hero Richard Feynman) get into dumb discussions on this subject, because they don't realize that they are talking about two different worlds. Hilbert built his theory of geometry without defining the objects of geometry. What he did was assume some properties of these unknown objects. But I learned to put my faith in axioms and laws of nature, even if there was no way to prove them. (Much later I learned from Willard V. Quine that you may prove the craziest things if your assumptions are wrong. For example, if you assume that 1=1.00000001, then you can prove that 1= 1,000,000,000,000.)

◆   ◆   ◆

Topology is a field of math that deals with weird properties of objects. A theorem in topology states that a loop cannot be *transformed* into a knot. I have often entertained my friends with the classic problem about napkins.

There is a large napkin spread out on the table. The challenge is to grab two opposing corners firmly with your fingers and make a knot without ever releasing the napkin.

You can twist and turn but you can't make a knot. However, if you make a knot out of your body by folding your arms, as suggested by the late Hungarian math genius John von Neumann, then you can make the knot by pulling your arms apart. Now there's a practical, albeit playful, triumph of topology.

Another classic problem of topology is given in "The Bridges of Königsberg." On pleasant Sundays, the burghers of Königsberg liked to stroll across the town's seven bridges. One day an inquiring mind posed the question, "Is it possible to plan the walk so that every bridge will be crossed, but only once?" Léonhard Euler, who lived in the 1700s and was one of the greatest mathematician of all times, developed a general theorem that proved such a walk was impossible.

You'll see why if you draw four dots on a piece of paper and connect every point with every other point, so that the lines never cross. Then add a fifth point. Try to connect it with each of the other four points without crossing any of the lines. Like the walk of Königsberg, you just can't do it. But if you lived on a surface with different dimensions, you could. My Ph.D. dissertation dealt with the question of those different kinds of surfaces. In trying to explain this once to my father, I used a pretzel as one example of a multi-connected, three-dimensional body. Later, I overheard my father proudly tell my uncle that I earned my doctorate in math "by discovering new theorems about pretzels."

Back then, I deeply resented it when someone asked me about my work's practical value. It was pure math—a thing of beauty! To me it had the same value as a Bach piano sonata or Leonardo da Vinci's Mona Lisa. Of course, I also recognized that since few people can appreciate the elegance of a brilliant proof, math would never enjoy the same popularity as music or painting. I agree with Godfrey H. Hardy, one of the greatest mathematicians of the century, who said in his memoir, *A Mathematician's Apology*: "I have never done anything 'useful.' No discovery of mine has made or is likely to make, directly or indirectly, for good or ill, the least difference to the amenity of the world."

Later in life I would undergo a difficult transformation from being a disciple of pure math to a practitioner of real math. But while living in Budapest I was surrounded by friends like Géza Grünwald, who spent two years trying to prove, without success, the four-color map theorem. Every week he announced that he almost had the proof, and all he needed was another week to complete the proof. I did not think it strange that he did this, because proving theorems is the essence of life for mathematicians. Sadly, Grünwald was murdered by the Hungarian Nazis. The theorem wasn't proved until 1976, and only then by a computer processing more than one thousand hours of calculations. (After reading the hundred-plus-page proof, Paul Erdös remarked, "It seems to be correct. But it is horribly ugly.")

After I moved to the U.S., I would apply my pure-math geometry skills in a way that would have been unimaginable to me five years earlier.

My wife, Laura, and I had bought property in Los Angeles, when I decided to do my own survey of the hilly lot overlooking the city. I did it mostly for the fun of it, but also to save money.

First, I marked an elaborate network on the lot, then measured the physical distances with the help of my ever-patient wife. We figured out the differences in elevations by using a clear, rubber hose filled with water. While I held one end at eye level, Laura held the other end. Each of us used yardsticks so that we could measure the elevation of the water in the hose. The difference gave us the deviation between the elevations. It was a tedious, time-consuming process. However, by making plenty of redundant measurements, double—and triple—checking the distances and elevations, I was confident that I'd get the right numbers when I laid out the network on paper.

When the builder brought me the contract to sign, he asked if it was true that I had surveyed the lot with a hose, as a neighbor had reported to him.

"That's right," I said. "Anything wrong with that?"

"I can't take a fixed fee contract with those kind of measurements," he said. "If you're wrong about the elevations, the foundation may require more concrete and work.

He continued. "Please, do me and yourself a favor and get a licensed surveyor like your neighbor did."

"Never mind," I said. "Put in a clause that says if I'm wrong, I'll pay the extra cost."

He didn't like it, but he finally agreed to humor me.

After the foundation was poured, the builder called me.

"It is beyond me how you did it," he said, "but you were right within an inch."

He went on to say that my neighbor had troubles. His surveyor, using a transit and trigonometry, had made a mistake during his calculations.

◆　　　◆　　　◆

Nowadays, thanks to the calculator and the spreadsheet, it's much easier for number-hating folks like me and talking Barbie (first edition) to live in peace. When I need to multiply seven by nine, I recall the Kummer story and do it on my calculator. Anything more complicated requires a spreadsheet. My computer is always on, always ready to serve me.

"But what if your computer fails?" critics ask.

"Then I use my calculator."

"But what if both fail?"

My fall-back plan is simple. "I drink a martini and go to sleep."

When I first began teaching real-life math in the classroom, I must admit that I failed to take into account how much my students' math-phobia resembled my number-phobia. Just as I went numb when using numbers as tools for adding, subtracting and dividing, my students would go rigid at the thought of using an algorithm to solve a simple decision-making problem.

I fear that math-phobia is rampant in our society.

◆   ◆   ◆

Math-phobia

General description: Excruciating angst and terror of mathematical equations and formulas. General disorientation and mental paralysis in response to any attempt to learn mathematics.

General occurrence: Very common.

Symptoms. Glazing of eyes when formulas are presented. Breaking out in sweat and general nausea when such words as *formulas, mathematics, statistics, algebra, algorithm or calculus* are mentioned. Extreme anxiety at the mention of mathematics.

Etiology: Unpleasant memories of uncompleted math homework, failed math tests and undecipherable math word problems. Mental pictures of incomprehensible math lectures and fighting unsuccessfully to stay awake in class. Terror of failing the class and having to repeat it. The threat of being unable to graduate because of incomplete math requirement. Feeling dumber than the average person because of inability to do math. Having a limited choice in college curricula because of lack in math skills. Admitting that math is important but feeling deficient and inadequate.

Prognosis. Cautiously guarded unless early treatment is administered.

Treatment. Introduce computers and replace symbolic algebra with rhetoric and syncopated algebra. Use tables of numbers, and such geometric tools as graphs, flowcharts and influence charts.

◆   ◆   ◆

In the best-selling *A Brief History of Time, from the Big Bang to Black Holes,* Stephen W. Hawking writes:

> "Someone told me that each equation in the book would halve the sales. I resolved therefore not to have any equations at all. In the end, however, I did put in one equation, Einstein's famous equation, $E=mc^2$. I hope this will not scare off half of my potential readers."

A classic example of math-phobia involved Denis Diderot. After the French literary genius completed his celebrated Encyclopédie in 1772, Catherine the Great, the empress of Russia, appointed him librarian for the rest of his days. In St. Petersburg, her court received the learned man with great honor and warmth.

However, he quickly got on Catherine's nerves once he began converting her courtiers from their Roman Orthodox religion to atheism. Not wishing to renege on her promise, she devised a plan that would lead Diderot to voluntarily pack his bags.

So she invited Léonhard Euler, the most prolific mathematician in history, to be her guest. Euler is revered among knot theorists like me.

Diderot didn't have a chance against Euler. In a session attended by the entire court, Euler advanced on him with a parchment containing one single equation that had nothing to do with anything:

$$\frac{a+b^n}{n}=x$$

Then he raised his voice and triumphantly proclaimed, "Sir, hence God exists."

As Catherine suspected, Diderot was terribly math-phobic and met Euler's attack by being totally dumbfounded. After a long silence, the courtiers' laughter filled the court. It wasn't long before the humiliated Diderot bid adieu and made his way back to France.

◆   ◆   ◆

The cure for math-phobia is the same one I use to treat my number-phobia. Computers. Through the use of programs like Quicken and spreadsheets like Microsoft® Excel, millions who wouldn't touch an algorithm with a xy^2 pole can solve real-life math problems such as income tax returns, home loans, saving and retirement plans, insurance options, financial investments, health care planning, etc.

Computers have the potential to turn the biggest math-phobe into a math user, if not a lover. That's an exciting thing for a mathematician like me who is interested in seeing people use mathematics in making day-to-day decisions.

It's just a shame that Mattel didn't re-program Barbie to say, "I love computers."

5

THE GATHERING STORM

Among the many adjustments I needed to make when I settled in the U.S., one stands out. In Hungary, I received an intellectual upbringing—my family emphasized matters of the mind above all things. I was encouraged to spend all my time in my studies, mostly math. Learning was placed on a pedestal above everything. Perhaps this still occurs in some American families, thought not as often as educators would like.

The disadvantage to this upbringing was that I was discouraged from doing anything with my hands. I remember the time my father brought home a coconut. It was an exotic treat for us children, but we had no way to open it—no hammer, mallet or hatchet. Using tools was something best left to those who produced goods. Finally, my father saved the day by kicking the coconut against the wall where it shattered into edible pieces.

Once, while working for my master's in engineering at Harvard, a professor explained the three-dimensional coordinate systems using the analogy of a screw. I understood everything but his example. He said the right-hand side is similar to putting a screw in, the left-hand is like pulling a screw out. Because I had never used a screwdriver before, I had no idea what he was talking about.

In the U.S., unlike my handy neighbors, I was the anti-do-it-yourselfer. I couldn't perform even the simplest task around the house. I broke so many dishes that my wife finally stopped asking for my help in the kitchen. Fortunately, over the years, I have made some progress. I have learned to make toast, tea and instant coffee and soup. Furthermore, in November 2000, I was forced to learn how to operate a microwave oven and can now warm up a frozen dinner.

My university years were also quite different from the typical American experience. Most people look back at their college days and see how certain classes or ideas changed their lives. But when I look back, I see how my life was saved. Literally. If it wasn't for my academic work, I would have certainly stayed behind in Hungary like my brothers and thousands of other people who were killed during the war years. As it was, I barely got out in time.

I attended the Pázmány Péter University in Budapest, named after the 16th century Jesuit cardinal and writer. Like a foreign embassy, the university had extraterritorial rights—even the police could not enter the campus without first being invited by the rector. In fact, prior to the 20th century, the university had its own legal system with the right to find people guilty and chop off their heads.

The rector was the head of the university, elected for a limited time by the deans. Only the king of Hungary and the university rector were entitled to use the royal plural. "We, the king of Hungary, and Emperor of Austria, by the grace of God," was the way the king made a proclamation. "Nos Rector, lecturis salutem" ("We, the rector, greet the reader") was the way the rector introduced himself on my Ph.D. diploma.

Professors were appointed for life and were highly respected members of society, the equals of diplomats and ambassadors. They were to be addressed "Your Excellency." Their sole duty was to lecture, but they could not be asked to lecture for more than 100 hours a year. There was an immense difference between the words *teacher, instructor* and *professor*. On the bottom of the highly structured hierarchy was the little appreciated *teacher*. He taught *pupils* in the four-year elementary school, a compulsory school for all. The *instructor* was a step higher in the hierarchy. He taught *students* in the eight-year elitist lycèe. Then came a huge gap, followed by *His Excellency*, the university professor, who lectured to the *attendees* of the university. In the U.S. we talk about a *chaired professorship*, but in Hungary the highest position for a professor was the *katedra*, reminiscent of the bishop's cathedra. There were only three *katedras* in math in Hungary.

As for the attendees of the university, they were accorded more independence than their counterparts in the U.S. "Hearkening to" lectures wasn't mandatory for students. They were required only to pass their tests; no one cared if they actually attended and soaked up lectures.

In my case, since I was aware of the course material from the syllabus and knew the subjects from my personal studies, I attended only the weekly seminars of Professor Lipot Fejér. He was internationally known for his discovery of a famous theorem about the summability of the Fourier series. His original name was Weisz, but in the same spirit of political correctness that had changed my name from Weiszfeld to Vazsonyi, he had revised his surname to Fejér.

Fejér knew me as an up-and-coming mathematician. But to my other professors and fellow students, I was a stranger except on those days when I dropped by to take tests.

◆   ◆   ◆

How did I get my Ph.D. in math? There was no way to "work" for a Ph.D. In my case, after submitting a paper for publication in the *Hungarian Acta Matematica*, I approached Fejér and said, "I would like to submit this for my dissertation, too."

"Okay, let me read it," he replied.

A week later he told me that he would accept it. He didn't even have to read it, because it had already been accepted for publication by Professor Frigyes Riesz. Riesz had the reputation of having very high standards, and so it was obvious that the paper would do for the doctorate.

Does this sound too easy? Perhaps it is in light of today's Ph.D. requirements, but the most important criterion was being creative at math. As for the printing of the dissertation, all the publisher had to do was renumber the pages from the *Hungarian Acta Matematica*. So the printing was practically free.

The university granted only Ph.D. degrees, and because few people qualified, there was an alternate plan for getting a degree. Integrated with the university was a teacher's college that gave you a certificate to teach in the lycée. For two years I took courses and tests for the teacher's certificate, but the whole thing became a nuisance. Finally, my father told me to drop the certificate program because he knew I would rather be a professor than a teacher. It wasn't such a terrible sacrifice because no Jew could get such a teaching position anyway.

Altogether, the dissertation took me three months to write. Most of that time I spent sitting and staring into space. My parents would often ask me how I was doing. My standard reply was, "Fine."

"How many pages do you have?"

"None," I would say.

Then one day I sat down and wrote the final copy of my dissertation. And that was that—no editing required.

My working habits were often the subject of concern and sometimes even irritation. When my cousin Edith needed a quiet place to study for her Maturity Exam, she asked if she could join me in my room. Thirty minutes later she quietly left. Afterwards she told her family that my study habits made her nervous.

"Bandi [my Hungarian nickname] would just sit there gazing out the window, doing nothing," she said. "Finally, I couldn't stand another minute of it."

Another time I was working on the porch at Sárospatak, in the home of my Uncle Miksa. He was the government circuit doctor of Sárospatak, and there was a steady stream of patients going through his office. (Hungary provided medical benefits to the entire resident population, financed wholly by taxation or in part by social insurance contributions.)

My mother told me later that Uncle Miksa looked out between patients and saw me sitting there doing nothing.

He thought to himself, "I have never seen anybody so lazy."

Later he looked out again and saw me pulling out a scrap of paper from my pocket and making a few notes.

"Ah," he realized. "Bandi is working on his math."

◆   ◆   ◆

There are two kinds of mathematicians: algebraists and geometers. Algebraists are well known for their intimacy with numbers and formulas, and most people think all mathematicians are algebraists, but this isn't so. Less widely known are geometers, who are intimate with points, lines, circles, triangles and shapes.

I was a geometer. The first theorem I discovered dealt with a problem in geometry. I was sixteen when I became intrigued with the following problem involving N points:

> Consider N points and one more point, X. Measure the distances between X and the given points, then add the distances. Find point X so that this sum is the smallest possible.

For three points, as in a triangle, the solution was well known. But nobody was sure how to find point X for more than three points. I found the point X by using an infinite, recursive algorithm, a most unusual solution (then) for a problem in geometry. You start with a point X0, anywhere, and search for a better solution. My algorithm specified how to find a new point X1, for which the sum became smaller. Then you apply the same procedure to X1 and you get point X2, which is even better. And so on. After infinitely many steps, you find the solution point to the problem.

I published the paper in a Japanese math journal, under the name Weiszfeld—this was before I changed my name to Vazsonyi. But to my disappointment, nobody paid any attention to it. I remember my good friend Paul Turan, who was an outstanding mathematician, telling me in 1938, "Forget about it, Andy. Work on something that interests people—not geometry."

Forty years later, however, a management scientist colleague called me on the phone and asked for a pointer on convex programming.

"I know nothing about it," I said.

"I suggest you read Chapter Seven in your book, *Scientific Programming in Business and Industry*," he replied.

For a moment, I felt embarrassed because I couldn't remember my own book, but I didn't say anything about it.

We chatted for a while longer and before he hung up, he said, "I'm glad I could get better acquainted with the guy who has done such pioneering work in location theory."

Again it was my turn to feel absentminded. "What's that?" I said.

He explained. "Suppose we have a bunch of factories and want to build a warehouse in a central location so the transportation costs are minimized."

"That's a tough nonlinear programming problem," I said. "But I've never worked on it." Actually, I felt relieved now because it was clear that I wasn't having a memory lapse.

"I must be confused," he replied.

There the matter rested until a few months later when I ran across a reference to a paper in a production control article: "New developments on the Weiszfeld algorithm."

Well, Weiszfeld is a very unusual name. To my knowledge, there was only one family in Hungary with the name. So I ordered a reprint, and to my amazement I learned that my paper, published in the distant past, had used a "long-step algorithm" (which I have never heard of!) and was considered a new approach to the location problem.

After reading more, I discovered that a well-known mathematician, Harold W. Kuhn of Princeton University, had given a talk in Budapest on his discovery of an algorithm to solve the location problem. After the talk, a former colleague of mine walked to the blackboard and wrote "VAZSONYI."

"Who is that?" Kuhn asked.

"The Hungarian mathematician who discovered your algorithm thirty years ago," my old friend said. "He lives in the United States but published his revolutionary approach under the name Weiszfeld."

Later I told the story to Paul Turan.

"See, I told you to forget about it," he said. "You had to wait thirty years for recognition."

◆   ◆   ◆

My paper *"Sur le point pour lequel les sommes des distances de n points donnés et minimum"*, published in Japan in 1937 under the name Endre Weiszfeld (*Tôhoku Mathematical Journal*, Vol. 43, pp. 355–386) became a classic in the mathematics of location analysis. Today, the essence of the paper is referred to as the "Weiszfeld algorithm." It finds the point that minimizes the sum of the distances from N given points. In the year 2002, I searched for references to the algorithm on on an Internet seach engine (Google) and discovered over 170 hits, mostly referring to English articles, though some were in German and Spanish.

Location analysis goes back to the influential book of the German industrial author Alfred Weber (1909). A simple example is the following. A firm wants to locate a factory so that the transportation costs to the warehouses is a minimum. Mathematically speaking, the problem is to find the unknown point that minimizes the sum of the distances from N given points.

Mathematicians have been fascinated by the problem ever since Pierre de Fermat (1601–1665), author of the celebrated "Fermat's Last Theorem" (proven only in 1994 by Andrew Wiles, an English mathematician), solved the problem for three points, that is, for a triangle. However, for more than three points there has not been any progress until the 1960s, when the issue of the location of site facilities in diverse environments became important and computers allowed the practical execution of algorithms.

When in the 1930s, at the age of 16, I became interested in the problem, I did not have in mind to calculate the coordinates of the unknown point, but I was searching for a theorem to be proven. I hit on a bizarre idea of searching for an iterative process to find the point, which I found. (The word *algorithm* was unknown to me and to most mathematicians.) Here was a theorem to prove: does the process converge? Yes, it does! And that was what the Tôhoku article was about. Unfortunately, no mathematician was interested and the paper was forgotten until the 1960s when it was rediscovered and recognized as the key algorithm needed for location theory. Many computer programs were developed to perform the actual calculations. Thus a pure mathematical effort, a gleam in the eye, became a practical managerial tool. To my great chagrin, nobody knows that Weiszfeld is around and kicking, or that Vazsonyi=Weiszfeld.

◆   ◆   ◆

At one point my future seemed so simple. I would receive my Ph.D., then go to Gottingen, Germany—the Mecca of mathematics at the time—for postdoctoral work and receive a professorship somewhere in Germany. By 1936, however, Hitler began excluding Hungarian Jews from teaching in German universities.

My next choice was emigrating to the U.S., but that seemed hopeless. First of all, I needed a passport. It was relatively easy to get a passport to a European country, but extremely difficult to get one from Hungary to the U.S. Besides that, the Hungarian government had plans for me. As a student I had been forced to swear into the army to fight for the Regent Admiral Nicolas Horthy. The army expected me to become a first-class artillery officer. (Little did they care about my lack of practical skills, not to mention allergies.)

Nevertheless, I spent my time learning English and waiting for a break during the years between 1936 and 1938. My parents were supportive, but my brothers ridiculed me, saying that I was wasting my time and would never make it.

When I heard that the Hungarian government had an agreement with the Institute of International Education for a student exchange, I thought if I could get a fellowship, perhaps I could win a one-year grace period before my induction into the army and receive a student passport valid for the U.S.

An opportunity arose when Otto Szász, a Hungarian mathematician who was on the faculty at the University of Cincinnati, came to visit his family in Budapest. I went to see him at his brother's apartment, a sumptuous place on Andrássy Avenue. Szász was very supportive and, thanks to him, a few months later the University of Cincinnati granted me a fellowship. I was deliriously happy as I looked up Cincinnati, Ohio, on a map. I didn't really care where it was as long as it was located somewhere in the U.S.

On the basis of that fellowship, I was granted a student passport in 1938 that was valid for the U.S. Now it seemed that everything was falling into place. But at the American Consulate I learned that my visa to the U.S. was good only for one year. After that, I would be required to return to Hungary and join the military.

When I asked for an immigration visa that would allow me to stay in the U.S. indefinitely, the consulate staff person flatly refused. Instead of accepting that as the final word on the subject, I snuck into the office of the American consul, Richard Reynolds. Fortunately, my English was good because the elderly consul didn't understand a word of Hungarian.

I blurted out my request. "Can you give me an immigration visa?"

Instead of throwing me out, Reynolds smiled and looked over my papers.

"You have only a student passport," he said. "According to Hungarian law I can't give you an immigration visa."

"But what do you care about Hungarian laws?"

He could have taken offense, but to his credit he must have known I was in a state of high excitement.

"I'm a guest here," he said. "I must honor your laws."

He indicated that our talk was over.

"But suppose I go to Paris, have my papers transferred and apply for an immigration visa there?" I asked.

He looked rather surprised.

"Son, I have no way to tell. But the consul in Paris would not know a thing about Hungarian laws. All he would see is a valid passport to the U.S. So, I guess, he might give you the immigration visa. You would have to renounce your right to a student visa. But I guess that would make no difference, because you could go to Cincinnati on your immigration visa."

"How long would I have to wait?" I asked.

"There's no way to tell. Possibly a few days, or perhaps weeks. But it's worth a try."

At the time, there didn't seem to be any other choice, so I picked up a visa to France at the French consulate, bought my train ticket and was ready to leave Hungary. Then Europe took another step closer to war, and suddenly the shit hit the fan.

In the middle of September 1938, Hitler declared that "My patience is now at end." He demanded further territorial rights in Europe and threatened to start another war. Patriotic Magyars were hoping to fight a war on Germany's side to avenge the loss of two thirds of their territory in World War I.

The Hungarian government reacted by mobilizing troops and closing down the border. Nobody could leave the country. Overnight the visas in my pocket became worthless. For the next two weeks I was forced to rehearse air raid drills with my family and obey a civilian-military captain who was assigned to our apartment building. It seemed like the fighting was only days or weeks away. I resigned myself to the inevitable catastrophe.

Then everything changed again. On September 29, 1938, Hitler, Chamberlain, Daladier and Mussolini met in Munich. They signed the infamous Munich agreement, which essentially gave Czechoslovakia to Germany. While Chamberlain triumphantly returned to Britain waving a document that proclaimed "peace for our generation," and Hitler was promising peace for the next thousand years, World War II was only a year away from crashing down on everyone's heads.

As for Hungarians, the agreement took away their chance to join Hitler and recover what they lost in World War I. The government sadly cancelled war preparations and re-opened the borders.

On December 1, a Thursday afternoon, I boarded a train to leave Hungary. I was twenty-two years old, leaving home by myself for the first time. Two small suitcases held everything I owned.

My older brother and mother accompanied me. He was solemn but my mother was sobbing. She was crying from sadness, afraid that we would never see each other again. But I believe that her tears also came from the joy of seeing that my dreams were about to be realized.

With my third-class ticket, I would be riding hard wooden benches all the way, but that was the least of my worries. My father had passed away only a few months earlier, and now it seemed that I was losing my mother and brothers. I would be leaving the old, familiar world and entering a world where I was a stranger at everything except math. But at least I was finally leaving the unjust Hungarian system and government.

In the evening we reached Hegyeshalom, a Hungarian border town. My heart was beating fast but I pretended to be calm as the official checked my passport. The seconds weighed heavily in the air until he handed me back the passport and continued on. The trip was like a strange dream: in Austria, the official stamping my passport with a swastika...in Vienna, reliving memories of traveling there with my father to the international fair, and visiting my uncle and cousins...in Salzburg, buying a delicious sausage and recalling a family vacation with our Vienna relatives…in Innsbruck, seeing again the fabulous views of the mountains.

I remember nodding off to sleep wrapped in the faded wool blanket that I had brought with me. Hearing the noisy brakes of the smoky steam engine. Slowing down at a station in the darkness and seeing a clock that read 2:00. When I checked my Schaffhausen pocket watch, it read 3:00. My first thought was that there was something wrong with the watch so I shook it and listened to the ticking, but it seemed to be okay. Then it struck me. I was on West European time. Hungary and Austria were on Central Time. I was in Switzerland. My dream had come true—I had escaped misery and, most likely, death.

Later that morning, I mailed a postcard to my mother with only four words on it: "I am in Buchs." That said everything.

6

ARCH OF TRIUMPH

o o o o o o o o o o o o o o o o o o o o o o o o o o o

The best laid schemes o' mice and men
Go oft astray

—*Robert Burns*

During my years in Paris, I began my true metamorphosis from the world of pure math, that marvelous fiction, to the world of harsh reality. Living in Paris from 1938 to 1940 was both an enriching and heartbreaking experience. I learned that I could survive by using my wits. I also acquired an insight into other people and their suffering that I might never have gained if I had traveled directly to the U.S. As it was, there were many times when it looked as if I would never be allowed to reach the U.S.

Upon my arrival in Paris, I was met at the Gare de L'Est by my cousin Lotte, from the branch of my family that emigrated there from Vienna. She helped me find lodgings at a cheap student hotel on the Left Bank, where I took a mansard room (a low-ceilinged attic room) on the fifth floor. The nearest toilet—which offered a lovely view of Paris out its window—was on the fourth floor. There was no bath or shower, so occasionally, along with the other foreign students, I marched down to the public baths. The French, I learned, valued their world-famous perfumes and colognes more than daily baths. (There was not a single bathroom in the palace of Versailles.)

My troubles in Paris began the first day after I arrived. I couldn't utter a single word of French. The French poetry lessons drummed into us for six years at the lycée were quite useless—another fiasco of my formal education.

On that day I took the Metro to the U.S. Embassy, a most imposing building across from the Obelisque raised by Napoleon. Once inside, I explained to a consular official that I wanted an immigration visa for the U.S.

When I was done, the official asked for my passport. The long-awaited moment had come. Would the official know of the Hungarian law that made a distinction between a limited student passport and an open-ended immigration passport? I stood there quietly, looking as calm as I could, hoping he couldn't hear my furiously pounding heart.

He turned my passport over in his hands. Examined every inch of it.

Finally, he said, "Come back in two weeks and we'll issue your immigration visa."

I left the office in a daze. Soon I would be going to America. My game plan was working. Aranka, my fiancée, had already received her immigration visa to the U.S. and was preparing to depart. On her way, she planned to join me in Paris for some sightseeing. Then she would continue to New York where her cousins were waiting for her. Soon, I would follow, we would get married and proceed to Cincinnati where I would begin my fellowship. But man plans, God disposes. The only thing that came true was that she met me in Paris, and it would be the last time we would see each other.

Those were heady days. I felt triumphant. Against impossible odds I had managed to leave Hungary and was now safe from my own government. Few of my friends thought I would make it. But I did, and now I felt as if I could hold the entire world in my hands.

When I returned to the consulate two weeks later, however, I learned that the Munich agreement had created yet another ripple effect. Because of the threat of war posed by the agreement, Hungarian Jews living in the U.S. were now applying for immigration visas to bring their aging parents to America. The U.S. quota for Hungarian immigrants was small to begin with, and parents of U.S. citizens had first priority. Within two weeks the waiting list for Hungarians wishing to immigrate to the U.S. was filled for the next twenty years.

I was devastated.

Suddenly I became a refugee. A non-person. I couldn't speak French or obtain a work permit, and I had very few relatives to fall back on. In Budapest I had lived in a world of pure math where my family took care of all the details. Now I had nobody. Pure math couldn't feed or house me, or even wash my clothes. And the thought of being separated from Aranka forever was almost more than I could bear.

In Hungary there is a term, "élet müvész," which means someone who manages to survive marginally without any visible means of support. The closest equivalent in English is an oxymoron: an honorable flimflam man. That's what I became in Paris. Sometimes I shared my misery with some Hungarians who lived nearby, although I made a rule of not joining the city's Hungarian refugee population because I wanted to immerse myself in the French life. Sometimes I borrowed money from my cousin Fritz, who was busy supporting his elderly mother and some of his sisters—all refugees from Austria. My mother regularly sent me cans of sardines and salami. Bread came free in all restaurants with even the smallest meals, although I once heard a waitress say, "Voici, les mangeurs de pain" ("Here come the bread eaters").

Fortunately, on Sundays I could visit Fritz's house for dinner with his German-speaking family. By walking across Paris to reach his house, I could avoid taking the Metro and save a few pennies. It was a lonely time. I have never felt so abandoned in my life.

Of course, on the outside, I still looked like a young, up-and-coming Hungarian mathematician who would, once this bureaucratic matter was resolved, be sailing to America. Under that guise I visited Jacques Hadamard, a prominent Jewish-French mathematician. He handed me a letter of recommendation to Baron Rothschild, the head of the French branch of the Rotschilds, the most influential Jewish family in the world. I had high hopes, but the baron never deigned to receive me.

Unfortunately for me, France was flooded with German refugee mathematicians who came loaded with professional credentials, so there was no money at all left for freshly minted Ph.D's. Hadamard did manage to pull some strings with the French government so that I began to receive a small pittance, but it was barely enough to keep me going.

Now that it seemed as if I might be stranded in Paris for the next twenty years, I worked hard to learn French. At first I scraped a little money together and tried the popular course at the Alliance Française. But the instructors focused on grammar and literature, and I wanted to speak conversational French. So instead I followed the same approach that I had used to learn English. I would take sentences from a Berlitz book and repeat them aloud until I got sick of them. I don't understand why, but the sentences and variations somehow integrated themselves in my head and soon I began speaking French. Of course, my auditory comprehension, which has never been good in any language, was another matter. When I didn't understand what someone said, which was quite often, I was either treated like an idiot or yelled at as if I were deaf.

My day-to-day life improved after I registered at the Sorbonne as a visiting student and received the same identity card as a bona fide student. The Sorbonne was somewhat of a sacred place for me. I remember one day wandering around its corridors when I came across a door with the name of Henre-Léon Lebesgue on it. I was quite taken aback because until then I had always thought that Lebesgue was the name of an integral used in calculus, not a living person.

With my Sorbonne student card, I managed to finagle a room at the Cité Universitaire. The Cité was a large complex of buildings that housed foreign students. Each major country had its own building, but there was no Hungarian House because apparently some conniving élet müvész had embezzled the building funds. So I went to live in the Belgian House.

The staff of the Cité had no idea how desperate I was—or maybe they did, because I took every job they offered. I scrubbed floors, delivered letters, addressed envelopes, hung coats in nightclubs, tutored math in French and so on. All of these things I did very poorly except tutoring math, and even my ability at that was questionable. The fact is, at that time I didn't understand the mindset of the average math student, or to what degree he or she was suffering from math phobia. This understanding came much later when I became involved in decision making.

I tried to do a little bit of pure math, but my heart wasn't in it. Jacques Hadamard suggested that I work on Géometrie Finie, which was a shrewd choice on his part. I did some research in this bygone, esoteric branch of geometry, and while still in Paris published my swan song to pure math in the *Comptes Rendus*, the most prestigious journal of the French Académie of Sciences. There was no way that I could have foreseen that my next published article would be on the subject of airflows in ducts and would appear four years later in an engineering journal.

In Paris, math became a luxury I couldn't afford. Each day was a struggle. Then came the day that made me question if I wanted to keep on living.

It was a sunny spring day in March 1939. I was standing in the student building lobby looking through my mail when I found a card from Paul Turan, an old friend in Budapest, a fellow mathematician. I'll never forget his words: "I admire you for your robust mental health and for your taking Aranka's death with such fortitude."

This was the way I learned that my fiancée, only twenty years old, had died of influenza in New York City, where we were supposed to meet and be married. Because her cousins wanted to break the news gently to me, I was told only that she was ill with the flu. If the concierge hadn't rushed up to me, I would have collapsed on the floor.

Until that moment, I had never experienced such intense grief. I went upstairs to my room but couldn't stop sobbing. In desperation, I went outside and began walking. At one point, I found myself on a bridge on the Seine River, across from the Cathedral of Notre Dame. I saw no point in going on. It occurred to me that I might as well throw myself into the river. But for one reason or other, I wandered back to the Cité Universitaire. There I burst into the room of my good friend Pista Thein and told him what had happened. He was a medical student and gave me a Nembutal to sleep.

For the next few weeks, Pista kept me going with his kind words, and by bringing me coffee and sandwiches. I couldn't sleep at night, so he prescribed more Nembutals. He also advised me to burn all Aranka's letters, papers and photos, and cauterize my heart. I followed his advice, and on smelling the smoke, a maid rushed in and asked if I was trying to burn the Cité Universitaire down. Later on, I regretted doing this and have missed these mementos all my life.

During these terrible days and nights, I felt as if I were seeing everything through the wrong end of a pair of binoculars. The world was distant and tiny. I was no longer a part of it. I performed my daily chores, brushed my teeth, ate my meals, but moved around like a zombie. As days turned into weeks and months, I buried Aranka so deeply in my memory that somehow I managed to keep on living.

◆   ◆   ◆

In September 1939, England and France declared war on Germany. Paris was evacuated. The Cité was located close to Port d'Orléans, and I watched as cars streamed out of the city, each vehicle loaded to the hilt with mattresses, baby carriages and other household goods. It was a depressing sight to see the families fleeing to safety, especially when I had no one and nowhere to go. At the Cité, most of the other students left and the rest of us stayed in a single building.

On the plus side, because there was little competition from other students, I found it easier to get odd jobs. Also, as the citizen of a neutral country, I was the envy of French students because I couldn't be drafted to fight. Hungary had not yet entered the war, though they planned to join Hitler and recover their lost territories. Many called this period the *phony war*. Hitler thought he could appease England and France by promising peace and vowing to invade Russia. In the meantime, fighting was at a standstill.

Not that my presence in Paris went unchallenged. Whenever my Carte d'Identité expired, I had to visit the Prefecture (police) and convince them to extend my card. This was a life or death issue, because without the piece of paper I would be deported. My life hung on the thin thread of my dossier—just as it did for the main character, a German refugee, in the novel *Arch of Triumph* by Erich Maria Remarque (later made into a fine film starring Charles Boyer and Ingrid Bergman).

I always appeared in front of the police groomed to the teeth. I wore a fine silk tie, reserved exclusively for these visits, and my shoes always gleamed with fresh polish. My biggest weapon on these visits was my checkbook. Only important merchants and wealthy individuals had checkbooks. No ordinary *citizen* had one. The only reason I possessed one was due to my cousin Fritz, who was concerned about his funds and thought it would be a safe bet to hide some cash under the name of a citizen from a neutral country. So my checking account held exactly $1,000—all belonging to my cousin. When the police asked about my finances, a most critical issue, I drew out my checkbook. After that they treated me as if I were a Hungarian duke traveling incognito.

During one visit, however, my checkbook became a moot point when the clerk renewing my card informed me that Budapest officials had advised her office that I wasn't a real student. In other words, my time was up and I, a simple refugee, needed to return to Hungary.

I managed to act shocked and dismayed. How could the great, liberal nation of France trust the information imparted to them by the secret police of a fascist country? And on what basis could she say that I wasn't a real student?

She replied, "Because you're a member of the International Syndicate of Journalists."

Now I could breath a sigh of relief. "Please, look at the date of birth on your document."

She looked down and saw "1906."

I showed her the birth date on my passport. "1916."

"You have my cousin's file," I said. "He happens to be a journalist. Obviously the Hungarian secret police got the two files mixed up and sent you the wrong one."

In the end, she renewed my card.

Somehow my luck held out until the spring of 1940, when I received a long, official document from the U.S. consulate. I read it over a few times before it made sense. My quota number had come up. The U.S. was ready to issue me an immigration visa.

What happened to the twenty-year waiting list for the parents of Hungarians living in the U.S.? It seems that Hitler had decided to end the phony war and was ready to launch his real attack. Because Hungarian leaders were privy to his secret, they began mobilizing for the long-awaited war of liberation that would return them to their former glory. One of the first things they did was to close the Hungarian frontier again so that nobody could leave. As a result, the American embassy could not issue visas for them and my name moved to the head of the list. No one knew at the time, but many of the parents who couldn't leave Hungary would later face the Holocaust.

You can imagine my excitement after living in Paris for almost two years, never knowing exactly when this state of limbo would end, then suddenly learning that I could now continue my trip and arrive in the U.S. in a matter of weeks.

But once again, I hit another roadblock. This one was buried in my dossier. The U.S. consulate officials took one look at my passport and discovered that it had expired.

Because I thought I was out of the clutches of the Hungarian government, I had failed to renew my passport. So I ran to the Hungarian consulate to apply for a renewal.

"Did you know that your passport has a secret code?" a countryman told me. "It cannot be renewed without approval of the War Department. You are sworn into the Hungarian army."

I was back in my government's clutches. The consulate transmitted my application to Budapest. Two weeks later I learned the terrible news. The War Department had ordered my return to Budapest so that I could fight the joint war with Hitler's German forces. To that end, the Hungarian consulate wanted to confiscate my passport and give me a *Sauf-Conduit Provisoire,* good for a single entry to Budapest.

I was desperate to appeal my case, but embassy officials told me that I couldn't schedule an interview with the busy ambassador. In their words: "His Grace, the Count Andrássy, has better things to do than talk to nobodies like you."

"Never mind," I said. "Just submit my request."

I had nothing to lose. And perhaps my experiences in Paris had taught me something about not giving up.

The next day I had a most unexpected phone call. The ambassador, it seemed, wanted to see me after all.

The interview was exceedingly brief.

"Do you know János Vazsonyi?" his Grace asked.

"Why yes, of course, he is my cousin. I am in touch with him all the time," I said, exaggerating a bit.

His Grace nodded, but before he could say anything, there was a knock at the door. His assistant announced that the Italian ambassador was waiting outside, and I was ushered out and sent on my way.

I went home more despondent than ever. But a couple of days later I decided to resume the fight and went back to the consulate. To my amazement, the clerk treated me with great deference.

"His Grace countermanded the Hungarian War Department. He personally signed your passport. He is plenipotentiary, you know. He wrote to Budapest and told them that it is in the national interest for you to go to America."

And with that I watched as the clerk renewed my passport.

Later I discovered what had probably motivated the ambassador to release me. A group of Hungarian politicians, under the leadership of János Vazsonyi, were negotiating for a friendship treaty with France and England. Perhaps the ambassador entertained doubts that Germany and Hungary might win the war, and was hedging his bets. That way, if Germany lost the war, Janos might become prime minister, and he would be remembered as performing a good turn for one of the Vazsonyis. Of course, quite unforeseeable then, the Hungarian Nazis would later take control and murder Janos as well as the remaining Vazsonyis, including my two brothers.

At the time, though, all that mattered was that I was now free to complete the last leg of my journey. With my passport in hand, I ran to the steamship companies and learned that the French ports were all closed due to the war. However, if I traveled to Liverpool, I could board an English ship. So I got my visa for England and took the train to Dieppe. From there I boarded a night boat to England. After a few minor difficulties—one involved getting lost near Victoria Station during a total blackout—I arrived in Liverpool and boarded the SS Samaria.

The trip across the Atlantic took two weeks, and I was seasick most of the time. For security reasons, the boat's crew wouldn't give out the ship's location or estimated arrival. On most days I would struggle to make it to the deck, where I would lie on my back and watch the immense waves roll across the ocean. My dream of reaching America was about to realized—although it had taken quite a few strange, unexpected twists. Somehow I had managed to not only survive, but become stronger and more understanding. While in Paris I had learned to speak good, idiomatic French and become familiar with a rich culture that was quite different from what I had experienced in Budapest.

Most importantly, I had left the ivory tower of math and science, and picked up the practical philosophy that would guide me during the rest of my life. It was unheard of for a pure mathematician to switch to real-life math, but as it says in Proverbs, "It is an ill wind that bloweth no man to good."

This metamorphosis involved a long and painful change in my outlook on the world. But since risk and chance cannot be avoided, a knowledgeable person must take advantage of whatever comes his way.

One day, while lying on deck, I was startled out of my dreams when the sailors bared their guns, and the ship began zigzagging to avoid a German U-boat. I thought of dying—my friends in Paris had warned me about crossing the Atlantic. They thought I was a fool to take the risk. I paid no attention then, and I discovered then that I wasn't afraid to die.

Come to think of it, I was never afraid of anything. As a friend, Paul Csillag, one of the few Hungarians who had a Ph.D. in math, once said to me in Budapest: "You are so impractical and dumb, that you fear nothing."

On April 22, 1940, I saw the tops of immense drums on the horizon. They were Canadian gas storage tanks. I also saw birds flying over the calm seas. The ship had reached territorial waters.

Two days later I caught a sight that I'll never forget—the Statue of Liberty. I cried tears of happiness and relief. I was in America where all men are created equal, endowed with unalienable rights: life, liberty and the pursuit of happiness.

Less than two months later, France fell to Hitler's army.

7

THE STAR-SPANGLED HUNGARIAN

On April 24, 1940, our ship steamed into New York harbor after first passing the Statue of Liberty. I was twenty-four years old and bursting with happiness. Everything made a strong impression on me.

When the immigration officer on the ship asked me, "Hova metz," I was quite puzzled until I realized he was trying to ask me in Hungarian, "Where are you going?"

I told him my destination was the International House at 500 Riverside Drive. He looked at my papers and crossed out the International House and inserted the name of my cousin who lived on Columbus Circle. Apparently, while in Paris I must have told the U.S. consul that I had a cousin in New York, so his Columbus Circle address became my official destination.

There was no one waiting to greet me when I arrived because I didn't tell my cousin or anyone else that I was coming. I didn't mind because I wanted to walk up and surprise them. I still regretted that Aranka wasn't here to share my joy, but that wound, so raw only a year ago, was practically healed. (Later I would visit her cousins and her burial place in New Jersey.)

After I passed immigration, I exited the boat and stepped on American soil for the first time. In my imagination, I dropped down and kissed the ground, but actually I arranged for my suitcases to be dropped off at the International House. After that, I sat down on a bench. I was happy as a lark, blessing my good fortune, when a uniformed dock worker appeared in front of me.

Uh oh, I thought. Was I not allowed to sit here? Was he collecting a fee from sitters?

"Young man, don't sit here," he said. "See that big gate? Go to the other side and sit down there. Here you are an immigrant. Over there you are an American."

I was astounded by his attention—it was the first of many experiences that taught me how friendly and helpful Americans were. It was also a lesson for me as an aspiring American or, as I thought of myself, a "Star Spangled Hungarian" (SSH).

My next stop in was the International House. I pulled out my map of New York City and the subway, and studied it diligently. Coming from Paris, I had a lot of experience riding underground in the Metro. I walked to the subway station, paid my nickel (I had $50 total), took the train going north, then changed at the next stop from the local to the express train. When I exited the station at 125th Street and walked into the reception hall of the International House, I felt extremely proud of myself.

The entry hall was beautiful. The carpet was light blue, the room was wainscoted and the ceilings had fancy patterns. It was even more elegant than the Cité Universitaire in Paris. As I approached the desk, a girl smiled at me. At first I felt embarrassed: was she smiling like that because there was something wrong with me? Later I learned that Americans were always smiling. Happy faces were normal in the U.S.—and the exception in Paris and Hungary. It was another lesson for the SSH.

"I just arrived from Paris," I told her. "I am very tired and would like a room."

Later I discovered that this became a local legend, because most students arrived only after a lengthy exchange of correspondence and documents.

"We take only students," she said. "Which university will you attend?"

I pulled out a letter of recommendation from the Cité Universitaire. She glanced at it, but obviously didn't understand a word of French. This astounded me, because by that time I was so brainwashed in the Gallic way that I couldn't believe that any civilized human being would not understand French.

"Yes, we welcome students from the Cité Universitaire," she said with a big smile.

My room was small and located on the top floor. To my astonishment it came with a telephone. A private telephone! Plus a fabulous view of the Hudson River and the Grant memorial. I have never been happier in my life.

After resting a bit, I decided to make a surprise visit to my good friends from Hungary, the Hollo's, both medical doctors. Actually, they were quite a bit my senior, but they were the parents of my first love, Agnes Hollo, who still lived in Budapest.

They lived on 69th Street, so I confidently took the subway to 72nd Street and began my walk. I could hardly believe my good luck, to be strolling through New York City. As I walked, I discovered that all the faces of the people I saw were black. When I noticed that the house numbers were getting smaller, instead of bigger, I stopped someone for directions. He kindly explained that the address I was searching for was on the east side, on the other side of Manhattan. In the meantime, it was getting dark and it surprised me that street lights were coming on. That's when I remembered that the U.S. wasn't at war, thus there were no blackouts.

I had no concept of the size of New York, and after a very long hike, I arrived at my friends' building and rang their bell. Mrs. Hollo appeared and practically keeled over.

"Bandi, how did you get here?"

They made a big to-do over me and gave me a good dinner. When I told them about my walk, they informed me that I had taken the wrong subway. They were also shocked to find out that I had walked through the all-black neighborhood of Harlem.

"You took quite a risk," they said.

I had no idea what they were talking about because no one told me that I was supposed to be afraid of dark-skinned people. This was another lesson for the SSH—that Americans paid attention to different skin colors.

That was my first day in America, which to me seemed like a day of great success.

On my second day I decided to visit my cousin Lajos, on my father's side. I had never met him or his wife, Boriska, and felt the need to say hello and reassure them that I would never sponge off them. To prove that I was a proper, resourceful man, before the visit I had my shoes polished at a bootblack.

We spent a pleasant afternoon together, and later Lajos told me that he had been concerned that I was going to be a economic burden until he saw my polished shoes. He owned a very elegant nightclub and later hired me to help in the coatroom. I made a few dollars, the same pay as the girls in the coatroom, but he never gave me any money that I didn't earn.

One of the first things I did in the U.S. was check in with the New York branch of the Jewish Committee to get help. They could not understand where I came from because they had no record of me. Apparently their Paris office had failed to notify them. But they accepted me and agreed to give me a tiny allowance so I wouldn't starve. In this way, my precarious existence from Paris was transplanted to New York. But the big difference was that I didn't have to worry about being kicked out of the U.S. I was a future citizen.

There was only one thing I had to hide. Before I left Paris, my cousin Fritz handed me a thousand dollars to squirrel away in America. Even though he knew that I would have financial problems, he also knew my father's reputation for honest and trusted that I wouldn't spend his money.

Within days of arriving in New York, I met with a few successful, older mathematicians who had managed to get jobs. I attended a seminar at New York University by Professor Courant, known worldwide for his accomplishments in calculus. I hoped to make some contacts, but it didn't work. Abraham Wald, another Hungarian refugee, told me that when he couldn't find a job as a mathematician, he turned to statistics and received a position at Columbia University. Interestingly enough, Wald became a world-renowned statistician before his unfortunate death a few years later in an airplane accident.

My best chance at finding work was through my Parisian mentor, Jacques Hadamard, who gave me letters of recommendation to some famous mathematicians at the Institute for Advanced Study in Princeton. This was a dream location for mathematicians—no teaching, no strings, just plenty of pure math. The institute was endowed to the tune of $5 million. I didn't bother applying because I knew I couldn't compete against the best mathematicians in the world.

I wasn't the only mathematician with money woes. Even a recognized scholar like Paul Erdös had funding troubles. He worked at the institute in his own peculiar style, that is, by wandering around and never sitting for long behind the desk in his office. Like a true Bossu, he carried his hump with him and worked wherever he went. During the one-year period of his funding, Erdös produced more research papers than all the other grantees combined. But the institute didn't renew his grant because they found his work style and behavior objectionable. (So much for the objectivity of scientists!)

Erdös had not changed at all since I first met him six years ago in my father's shop. He still didn't care about anything besides math. One day while I was visiting him in Philadelphia, we went for a walk. I pointed out that the lining of his overcoat was hanging out and sweeping the sidewalk.

"Vazsonyi," he said, "your powers of observation of trivial things are remarkable."

But even without official support, Erdös managed just fine. He borrowed money from friends and could always camp out in Fine Hall at the institute, which was never locked and had quite comfortable couches to sleep on.

During my first visit with Erdös in Princeton, I missed out on the opportunity of a lifetime. The night before my visit, Erdös had spent the better part of the evening with Albert Einstein. If I had arrived a day early, I could have joined them. So I missed being with, as Erdös called Einstein, "a nice old uncle."

As for math jobs, the news was discouraging. With so many Ph.D.s arriving in the U.S. from Europe, especially Germany, there were fewer opportunities than ever for young academics like me. Somehow I scraped by with the tiny allowance from the Jewish Committee and occasional work at the nightclub.

During this time, I picked up a little book at the International House library that would make a big impression on me: Dale Carnegie's *How to Make Friends and Influence People*. According to Carnegie, you could willingly change your ways and become a better person (and, by extension, a practical man). Until then, it hadn't occurred to me that such a thing was possible—or desirable. It seemed like a revolutionary idea.

One point he emphasized was that you should treat other people as if they were important. Another radical concept! I had never heard anyone suggest such a thing in Europe. I studied the Carnegie book carefully—so did millions of other Americans—and began putting some of the advice to good use. For instance, when I began praising other people, I noticed that my relationships with them improved greatly. The Carnegie book also started me on my lifelong study of self-help books.

Of course, my scholarly friends never shared my admiration for Carnegie, Anthony Robbins or other self-help gurus. In their words, Carnegie was "obnoxious," "arrogant," "insincere" and "hypocritical." They considered all "inspirational literature" nonsense. But from my pragmatic point of view, I didn't care. If it made me feel better, if I got more enthusiastic, if I developed stronger emotions for my work, then I figured that it was worth reading. But I vowed never to mention Carnegie again.

◆   ◆   ◆

A few days after my arrival I used my room phone to call Annuska Boros, a Hungarian girl studying at Columbia whom I had never met before. She, too, was living at the International House, and joined me downstairs in the great hall. Unlike today's coed world, boys and girls were strictly separated and room visits were forbidden. Annuska and I became great friends, and she introduced me to American ways. I asked her to have dinner with me, Dutch treat, but she said she could not because she had a "date" and was "going out." It took me some time to understand what she meant.

To my delight, however, I learned that the rules for seeing girls in the U.S. were more flexible than what I was accustomed to. In Hungary, meeting girls was a clandestine business. Fathers were absolutely wild about protecting their daughters from any "damage." In the U.S., girls could go out on dates. And just because a boy had a "girlfriend" didn't mean they were sleeping together. I much preferred this open system and adapted quickly. It was another lesson for the SSH.

I learned other things from Annuska. When she kept talking about "going to school," I finally asked her, "But aren't you going to Columbia University?"

"Yes, yes," she said.

Slowly it dawned on me that going to the university in the U.S. wasn't the same as attending the university in Hungary or at the Sorbonne. It was more like going to the Hungarian lycée, where you attended regular classes and had homework assigned to you.

From Annuska I also heard a horrible rumor—that the Germans were building gas chambers to exterminate the Jews.

"That's just war propaganda," I told her. "It's ridiculous. I can believe they want to kill the Jews, but they can just shoot them."

One day some guys told me that Kudirat, a beautiful young Nigerian woman who was studying French literature at Columbia, wanted to see me. So I called her on my phone, and she agreed to come down and meet me. Her French was flawless, and we had a great time drinking Cokes. After she went back upstairs, my friends, who were watching, admitted that they had played a practical joke on me. Kudirat was famous for being unapproachable, and my friends thought she would never meet me downstairs, and they would have a great laugh at my expense. From this experience I learned that Americans were great practical jokesters, and they learned that Hungarians who had French manners (and possible Bossu lineage) were great charmers. It was another lesson for the SSH.

A few weeks later, Kudirat told me that her uncle was visiting in New York. She asked me to accompany her to the Nigerian embassy. There I discovered that her uncle was a prince and that she was a princess. Our friendship developed, and some time later, one of my friends asked, "Why do you eat lunch exclusively with blacks?" I was surprised because I never noticed. But it was true, and I discovered that white Americans didn't normally mix with blacks. (Another lesson, this one on racial prejudice, for the SSH.)

Many of the residents at the International House were actually Americans studying in New York, so I became familiar with another breed of U.S. citizens from far-away places—non-New Yorkers. My first American love, Becky, was a graduate student of economics at Columbia University. She was very smart, attractive and affectionate, but couldn't believe that I was Jewish. In those days Jews were much more isolated from non-Jews, and while she had nothing against Jews per se, she had a totally false image of what a non-practicing Hungarian Jew would be like.

◆   ◆   ◆

One day I discovered that room prices at the International House varied, and that the smiling girl at the desk had given me the most expensive room. So, I started my descent to cheaper rooms, and ended up in the basement. However, I thought that pricing rooms differently was unfair and saw no reason why a wealthy student should receive a better room. Students in Hungary or France wouldn't have put up with it! After all, the International Houses were publicly funded and all students were created equal.

As I was complaining bitterly to Becky, she said, "But aren't you glad that you could get a much cheaper room? The only reason that's possible is because some people pay more than others. The average rent keeps the House going."

I had never thought of that—it was another lesson for the SSH, this time in capitalistic economics.

◆   ◆   ◆

Since there was no Margit Sziget, a somewhat exclusive park that attracted young couples, I took my girlfriends to the Palisades, on the Jersey side of the Hudson. One time, I went with Annuska. After a long talk, she told me that our friends thought we went there to neck. "Why would a boy just talk?" she wondered out loud.

"But you have a boyfriend and I have a girlfriend," I said.

I was always a one-woman man—I also had certain traditional ideas about marriage. I knew a Dutch girl whose family was very rich. Apparently she loved me, and a friend suggested that if I married her, I'd never have financial problems again. But I couldn't marry a girl I didn't love.

◆   ◆   ◆

During my first year in the U.S., I sought out opportunities that would show me what life was like beyond New York City.

My first chance was as a counselor at a YMCA camp in Hartford, Connecticut. During my first summer in the U.S., I spent four weeks camping out on the shore of a picturesque lake. It was a delightful experience, even though our young campers showed very little interest in the workshops we held for them. All they wanted to do was stay in their tents and read comic books.

That fall, I took another break from New York and accepted an invitation to attend a year-long workshop in Haverford, Pennsylvania. The Quakers were sponsoring the retreat for "distinguished" European scholars who were interested in learning American ways. At the age of twenty-six, I would be at least fifteen years younger than anyone else in the group—and by far the least distinguished looking. But this was an incredible break for me—free room and board for a year. All I had to do was study. Still, I was reluctant to leave Becky, but she urged me to attend, saying that I took our love affair too seriously. This ended our relationship and I never saw her again.

In Haverford, I boarded with a friendly couple, the Yarnells, elderly members of the Society of Friends. During the day, my fellow scholars and I would attend lectures and practice English at a large house called "The Commons." We also had access to libraries at Haverford and Bryn Mawr. I spent most of my time in the Bryn Mawr library for research and other obvious reasons—girls, girls and more girls!

We had English language courses, and here I got another break. They divided us into three groups: beginning, intermediate and advanced—based on how well we could read aloud a poem by Longfellow. Because I could never read aloud in any language, I landed in the beginners' group. Whereas the other groups averaged about twenty people, in our group there were only four; the other three couldn't speak English at all. The result was that we "beginners" received quite a bit more attention, and I got the bulk of it because the others didn't care to learn.

Our English teacher, Mr. Severinghouse, was a pronunciation guru and later became nationally known. I became his prime guinea pig, a Hungarian Pygmalion. One big problem for Hungarians is differentiating between words like "bed" and "bad." So I designed and read little sentences like, "The red rat was a bad rat and slept in a red bed." Severinghouse trained me to say it right. As usual, I refused to pay any attention to grammar.

We were also assigned tutors, and I was lucky to receive help from a Bryn Mawr coed who was majoring in English. When we met the first time, she took a hard look at me and said, "You don't look like a distinguished European scholar."

"What did you expect me to look like?" I asked innocently. Since I was the youngest in the group, the Quakers called me Benjamin, after the youngest and most beloved son of the Old Testament patriarch Jacob.

"I expected you to have a beard and look at least fifty years old," she said.

After a few lessons, the coed gave up because my English was too good. When I tried to give her a goodbye kiss, she didn't go for it. (A lesson in virtue for the SSH.)

We were allowed to take extension courses at the local high school for free. Following my natural inclination toward girls, I joined the dancing class. Later, I was painfully embarrassed when the director of the workshop found me capering with high-school girls

◆   ◆   ◆

In the morning and evening, everyone helped with the daily tasks. I worked in the kitchen where my inexperience was appalling—my peeled potatoes were the size of golf balls.

As an aspiring American citizen, I also learned that my knowledge of American history, literature and other subjects was sorely lacking. So I began studying everything that, as a young math prodigy, I had previously turned my back on. I found myself fascinated by the classics, and was delighted at how fast I could learn. Francis Bacon was absolutely right when he said, "Studies serve for delight, for ornament and for ability." I found that I was curious about everything.

From my host family, the Yarnells, I learned a great deal about the Old and New Testament (to their credit, and typical of Quakers, they never tried to convert me). I also discovered reference books: dictionaries, thesauruses, books of quotations, encyclopedias, Latin dictionaries, etc.

I even found it worthwhile to read materials I didn't necessarily agree with. After all, I reasoned, the person who wrote something that I disagree with is probably not an idiot and must have spent the same amount of effort working out his thoughts as I did on mine (at least, I hope he did).

At Haverford, I found myself increasingly drawn to the subject of philosophy. I became impressed with pragmatism, in particular, the work of John Dewey and his *Logic: Theory of Inquiry,* published only four years earlier. I liked Dewey's criteria of such merits as usefulness, workability and practicability. Ideas, according to Dewey, were essentially instruments and plans of action, enabling a person to cope with the problems of living, and were to be judged by consequences alone. Years later I would be influenced by Ludwig Wittgenstein and Willard Quine, and would develop my personal philosophy about the controversial and fuzzy concept of being a rational person.

In brief, I feel that a person has the perfect right to set personal goals, as long as these goals don't harm others. In other words, humans don't need to choose a particular goal merely because it is the most rational. If someone wants to climb Mount Everest or sit in a tree for two years, that's his or her business. However, rational people do their very best to determine their goals. They also spend a great deal of time selecting actions that will most likely lead to their goals.

To me, being rational meant that I needed to understand how the world worked. I realized that I had this unquenchable thirst to discover the answers to everything around me. When I read that Leonardo da Vinci questioned everything he saw, I felt a close kinship. Why does one find sea shells in the mountains? How do they build locks for dams in Flanders? How does a bird fly? What accounts for cracks in walls? What is the origin of winds and clouds? Da Vinci would find an answer, write it down and perhaps draw an illustration.

I reconsidered my views of Sigmund Freud. Budapest, a satellite of Vienna, was a hotbed of psychoanalysis. Freud was the prophet, though I had reservations about his *Interpretation of Dreams*. Now I totally rejected his analysis. At that time, I still believed in the Old Testament: that Joseph predicted seven years of plenty throughout Egypt, followed by seven years of famine. But as I extended my scientific view to all matters of the real world, I considered this hogwash.

When I was a mathematician, my passion was searching for proofs. In the U.S., I experienced a kind of intellectual rebirth. I became an American version of the "educated man." I felt passionate about posing questions that dealt with the real world and uncovering the answers.

Benjamin Franklin's autobiography became a life-long inspiration to me. He was a man dominated by a rational approach to life. All his life, Franklin sought to improve his "virtues," especially after he learned that others regarded him as proud, overbearing and insolent. Because I felt people might also see me that way, I tried to follow his example and improve myself by acquiring the virtue of humility. I especially liked his following words:

> I cannot boast of much success in acquiring the reality of this virtue, but I had a great deal with regard to the appearance of it. I made a rule to forbear all direct contradiction to the sentiments of others and all positive assertions of my own. I soon found the advantage of this change in my manner. The modest way in which

I propos'd my opinions procur'd them a readier reception and less contradiction...

Later I also learned that Franklin had specific ideas on how to make decisions and discovered tradeoff analysis, a most important current approach. Thus he became to me a sort of a model and hero of the cognitive, rational style of living.

◆   ◆   ◆

While living in Haverford, I also kept looking for work. But for a long time there were no openings anywhere for a young refugee mathematician. Then a new angle came up.

The workshop leaders had contacted an internationally known Austrian scientist and professor of engineering at Harvard, Richard von Mises, who offered me a fellowship as a graduate engineering student. This was quite a come-down after obtaining a Ph.D. in math, but the plan was that I would pretend to be interested in engineering, while actually searching for a job as a mathematician. This would give me a grace period of one year. As a Harvard graduate student, I would be closer to the academic action.

The only drawback was that the Jewish organization that was giving me a small living allowance decided that it wasn't in my best interests to become a full-time engineering student. They felt (rightly so, as it turned out) that I would never get a job as a mathematician and insisted that I take a job as a shipping clerk. For obvious reasons, this did not appeal to me all.

After two years in the U.S., I felt that I had done my homework. I knew enough to feel comfortable living in America and felt confident that I could take control of my life. I realized that it was hopeless to get a job as a mathematician. Besides, I had lost interest in pure mathematics. I needed to do something else; the only problem was that I had no idea what. I saw very clearly that the future in America was not cast in concrete as it was in Europe. It was open and unbounded.

So in the fall of 1941, I said goodbye to my Quaker friends and benefactors, my living allowance and my math Ph.D., and hitchhiked to Harvard. As the European war waged on overseas, I would wage my own personal campaign to reach the American dream.

8

THE HARVARD MASQUERADE

In the fall of 1941, I arrived in Cambridge to accept the Gordon McKay Fellowship at Harvard's Graduate School of Engineering. The atmosphere of the American university, as I would soon discover, was nothing like its European counterpart. On the first day one of my professors remarked that students would receive "credit for homework." In Hungary, this kind of talk might be heard at the lycée, but never at the university level where students attended lectures at their pleasure and showed up to take tests. Was this a graduate school? I couldn't believe it. I also learned that whereas professors in Hungary were treated like minor royalty, in the U.S. they rubbed shoulders with students.

The only professor who ran his class in the European mode was Richard von Mises, (the worldwide authority on the foundation of statistics) who had helped me obtain my fellowship. If a student had the insolence to ask him a question about a complicated equation, this professor of aerodynamics and applied mathematics would simply stare at the guilty party and say, "To understand you must be born smart." Then he would continue his lecture. After the first few times, students learned to stay quiet.

In the beginning, I went through the motions of pretending to be interested in weird subjects such as machine design, heat engineering, aerodynamics and structures of airplanes. After all, I was taking graduate-level classes without the benefit of undergraduate studies. The only reason I had accepted the fellowship at Harvard was so that I could make contacts for a math job—not to become an engineer. But soon my curiosity got the best of me. A course on internal combustion engineering taught by a young professor, Howard Emmons, really impressed me. I appreciated the way he would interrupt his lectures to work out a problem on the blackboard. This gave me a window into how his mind worked.

Emmons' way of thinking was totally different from mine. Yet he had a deep intuitive feel for the physical world that I identified with because it was similar to how I approached the fictional world of math. I once saw him react to a report by von Neumann, possibly the greatest living mathematician, who claimed that he had discovered a fundamentally new phenomenon in a photograph showing boundary layer separation in a supersonic flow. Emmons took one look at the report and said, "I don't see what von Neumann sees." Later von Neumann admitted that he was wrong.

When I told von Mises that I intended to drop my pursuit of a math job and change my career to engineering, he tried to talk me out of it.

"You are a good mathematician, and you already have your Ph.D," he said. "Why waste your talents on a subject you know nothing about and probably have no talent for?"

But I was beginning to feel that I could make a contribution to engineering. I knew that I could never comprehend the physical objects of the world the way Emmons did, but I also knew that I could apply math to engineering in a way that he couldn't. Two of von Mises' courses—one on the theory of elasticity, the other on aerodynamics—contained so much math that most students considered them to be the hardest engineering courses at Harvard. I thoroughly enjoyed them.

Little did I know that my new feelings would put me on shaky academic ground. At the time, the fields of engineering and mathematics stood far apart. Most academics would have agreed with the views of David Hilbert, the greatest pure mathematician of the early 1900s, who said, "The mathematician and the engineer have nothing to do with each other and never will."

It seems obvious now, in the age of computers and space travel, how closely integrated math and engineering are. But in 1940, few engineers used math. Back then, engineering was more of a trade than a science. When you told people you were an engineer, they assumed you were the guy who kept the locomotive on the tracks.

Hilbert once gave a lecture in which he derived the differential equations governing the slide of an avalanche. But a student interrupted the lecture to point out that his equation had a plus sign instead of a minus. Hilbert, who wanted people to view him as a practical mathematician, hesitated a moment. Then he said, "These equations refer to two avalanches sliding down the opposite sides of a mountain connected with a rubber band."

◆ ◆ ◆

My first months in Cambridge were busy ones. The fellowship covered only tuition, so to make ends meet I found a job as a tutor for an eight-year-old boy. In return for helping him with his studies and occasional babysitting, I received an attic room and meals. Also, Von Mises arranged for me to grade the homework of students as long as they were not in my own class. I had barely enough money to keep the wolf away from my door.

Of course, the war and my family in Hungary were never far from my mind. In the fall of 1941, before the U.S. declared war, the Germans seemed unbeatable. Hitler's army occupied all of Europe, and it didn't seem as if the British could hold out much longer. A Nazi victory would have meant the end of the world for me, as it already meant the end of the world for many of my Jewish relatives. Around this time, the American Nazis were also quite active in the U.S. and only President Roosevelt's delicate handling kept them under control.

On December 7, 1941, the Japanese attacked the U.S. and the Americans declared war on Germany and Japan. Roosevelt's decision lifted my spirits. With the U.S. gearing up to fight, I felt sure that Hitler would lose.

When the U.S. military draft started, my number came up in the first round of the lottery. Because I wasn't a U.S. citizen, however, the draft board deliberated for a while on what they should do with me. Finally, my work at Harvard was deemed necessary for the war effort and I received a deferment. For the second time, I lucked out and avoided the military.

About this time, I came across another book that would greatly influence my life—*Mathematical Methods in Engineering,* by the Hungarian-born scientist Theodore von Kármán (published in 1940, and coauthored by M.A. Biot). Von Kármán was a pioneer who dedicated his life to applying math to engineering, and he became my inspiration during a crucial time. After reading his book, which became my new bible, I fully understood how useful math could be when applied to engineering.

My friends at the nearby Massachusetts Institute of Technology had a very low opinion of von Kármán and the Harvard Engineering School—they thought we were impractical because we were so obsessed with theory and math. One of their leading professors of aerodynamics called von Kármán a hopeless theorist. To illustrate his point he drew an illustration of an airplane on a piece of paper.

"All airplanes look the same," he said. "What good is a mathematical theory?" However, von Kármán became my new hero, hero of engineering, and joined my honor roll: Paul Erdös of math, and Benjamin Franklin of rationality.

It wasn't long, however, before von Kármán demonstrated in public the importance of math theory on the practical world.

About a year earlier, on the morning of November 7, 1940, high winds destroyed the Tacoma Bridge, a long suspension bridge across the Narrows of Puget Sound that connected the Olympic Peninsula with the mainland of Washington.

Nobody could explain why the bridge collapsed. Engineers said the bridge was designed properly, so it must have been a freak accident. The governor of Washington announced that an identical bridge would replace it.

When von Kármán heard about the collapse, it occurred to him that the villain was the Kármán vortices, a theory he had developed to explain some of the aerodynamic features of airplanes. Von Kármán, who was at the California Institute of Technology, thought that the high winds blowing on the Tacoma bridge that morning may have been like the air sweeping by a moving airplane. If gale-force winds had generated the same type of vibrations described by nonlinear differential equations that cause airplanes to vibrate, he wasn't surprised that the bridge collapsed the way it did. And it would be a matter of time before a replacement bridge would do the same thing.

When a federal committee was assigned to investigate the bridge collapse, von Kármán took a leading role on it and suggested that aerodynamic tests be made on the replacement bridge before it was built. Of course, the bridge engineers on the committee felt that an aeronautical engineer should stick to airplanes. One of the experts commented acidly, "You don't mean to say that you are going to build a wind tunnel big enough to test a bridge in?"

But after many meetings, von Kármán's argument and his Hungarian charm won the day. Engineers redesigned the replacement bridge to counteract the effect of high velocity winds. After that, the plate girder approach used in suspension bridge design was abandoned.

At the time that the Tacoma bridge disaster and von Kármán were making news, I didn't know him personally, though I had heard about him from his niece, a former girlfriend of mine in Budapest. Born in 1881, he was a child prodigy at math, but turned to engineering under the guidance of his father, a university professor. When he left Budapest to work in Germany, he added the "von" to his name to make himself sound more distinguished (as did John von Neumann). In 1930, when he arrived in the U.S. to escape from Hitler, he became director of the Guggenheim Aeronautical Laboratory at the California Institute of Technology and quickly turned it into a mecca for aeronautical sciences.

When I heard that von Kármán had read my paper on compressible fluids in 1945, I was delighted by his comment that I was "a true European scholar, in the classical style." He said this because of my originality and because I had put theory first and practice second, as well as made extensive references to German and French articles.

I would finally meet him in 1946 while I was employed at North American Aviation. Von Kármán had a very strong accent, but as he once said to me, "my emphaaasis is very good." He wore hearing aids in both ears and explained to me the advantage. "When a lecture is boring, I just turn them off."

One day I was visiting with him in his Pasadena office. I noticed that he had a telescope set up at his window.

"What can you see, Professor Kármán?" I asked.

"Let me show you," he said.

After a few adjustments, he smiled and said, "Look, Andrew."

I looked through the lens and it was as plain as if I were looking into the next room. A pair of hikers, a man and a woman, were kissing on Mount Wilson.

Kármán's discoveries rank among the greatest in U.S. history. His research, which made possible supersonic flight and the U.S. space program, led him to being called the "architect of the space age." Shortly before his death in 1963, President John F. Kennedy presented him with the first U.S. Medal of Science.

◆   ◆   ◆

After a year of hard work at Harvard, I did manage to get some feel for engineering. However, laboratory work was not one of my strengths. Before you could take any measurements, you first needed to calibrate the instruments, which always took a few hours of tedious work. As my classmates soon discovered, I had a touch that would cause the calibration to go berserk and make everyone start over. Soon, students were begging me not to touch anything in the lab.

Professor Emmons admitted that in the beginning he was baffled by some of the strange things I did. For example, when I plotted the test results of the old Dodge engine, I used a weird scale that made no sense to anyone else. There's no doubt that part of my problem was that I had never taken undergraduate engineering courses. Emmons considered flunking me in the first term, but gave me a break because he knew that I was a mathematician. After a while, he began to forgive my odd ways, especially when he saw some merit in them. For example, all the other students solved problems by trial and error, while I solved them by equations. Occasionally, I even pointed out flaws in Emmons' own thinking.

At the end of the year, I received my master's degree in mechanical engineering. I may be one of the few persons still walking around with an engineering degree from Harvard. You see, the Harvard faculty despised the engineering school. The only reason they put up with it was because the late Henry Lillie Pierce gave a lot of money to establish the school. Later, the Fellows of Harvard University changed the name to the Division of Applied Sciences. This made the Pierce estate very unhappy, and Harvard ended up paying millions to settle the matter and keep the new name on their letterhead.

Before I could decide on my next step, Emmons invited me to accept a teaching fellowship. I would be assisting him with his teaching and research for the National Aeronautics Association.

I was delighted to accept his offer (at the magnificent salary of $200 per month). The fellowship gave me a chance to learn even more about Emmons' way of thinking, even though I still clung to my own mathematical ways.

◆   ◆   ◆

While my career was headed in an unexpected direction, so was my personal life. I had met a young woman named Laura Saparoff at the International Club, a place where foreign students could meet and socialize. She was quite a forbidding person. Her full name was the Baroness Laura Vladimirovna Saparova, a true Georgian baroness. She was born a subject of Tsar Nicholas II, in Tiflis (Tbilisi), today the Republic of Georgia. I liked her and her family's European ways—they were poor materially, but rich culturally. Apparently, Laura had no boyfriend because she considered it beneath her dignity to chase after boys.

Laura sprang from an adventurous family with interesting European connections. In 1887, her mother, Margaret Burns, was born to a Canadian mother and Irish father in Somerville, Massachusetts. At the age of eighteen, Margaret told her parents that she was going to visit her aunt for the weekend. Instead she boarded a ship for France. In Paris, she was taken in by a shoemaker and his wife, who took care of her until she finally received money from her aunt. Next she traveled to Brussels to study music and she ended up meeting Vladimir Saparoff, a friend of Vladimir Ilich Lenin, the future Russian leader. (One of Laura's prized possessions is a postcard from Lenin to her father, saying thanks for putting him up on the sofa for one night in Brussels.)

Margaret and Vladimir traveled to Tiflis (Tbilisi), where they married and started a family. After the 1917 Revolution, they fled from Russia with their three children (Laura was six years old) and settled in the U.S. Like me, Laura was raised in the classic European style. Her family spoke French at home, she studied the piano as did her mother, attended Radcliff University, and was a budding concert pianist.

After only seven weeks of courting and applying Hungarian charm, Laura and I decided to get married. Our wedding took place at the office of a justice of the peace. As a joke and a pointed reminder that my bachelor days were over, Laura's brother showed up with a shot-gun.

Laura's family wasn't totally enthralled by the prospects of their future son-in-law. Unfortunately, I had failed to make a good first impression on my mother-in-law the winter day I entered her apartment and forgot to remove my hat. She never forgave me for that breach of manners. Laura's father, on the other hand, was more concerned about my Jewishness. In his words, "No advantage, but if you love him go ahead."

At first Laura moved in with me. I had the largest room in Cambridge—the entire attic of a rooming house, which was usually occupied by three students. Because we didn't have a kitchen, we ate all our meals at restaurants. Of course, we didn't have a car, so Laura took the subway to work, and I still walked.

When it came time to look for a new apartment with a kitchen, there was hardly anything available because of war-related housing shortages and rent control laws. Finally we lucked out and found an apartment on Massachusetts Avenue, walking distance from both Harvard and the subway.

We managed quite well on my Harvard fellowship and Laura's income—she made $17 a week as a secretary for the Family Welfare Society. Our prospects seemed even brighter when Laura took a job as an editor of Russian books, popular during the war, at the splendid salary of $28 per week. Eventually, I was even able to repay Laura the money she had advanced me to buy our wedding rings.

As we settled into our first year of marriage, I found new challenges at Harvard. In 1942, the subject of supersonic aerodynamics, which was used in developing ballistic missiles, was generating a lot of excitement among scientists and Pentagon warlords. Emmons developed his own theory about shock waves and received a grant from the National Advisory Committee on Aerodynamics. After I read his proposal, however, I sensed that something was wrong.

It was true that Emmons knew more about aerodynamics than I did, but I knew more about elliptic partial differential equations. When I discovered an error involving a crucial part of his theory and pointed it out to him, I was concerned about how he would react.

However, after two years of working together, he trusted my opinion and said, "Okay, Andy, we'll do something else."

> *One day I overheard an argument between Emmons and another assistant, Al Convisor, across from our offices in Pierce Hall. I didn't pay any attention until I heard Emmons calling for me.*
>
> *As I walked into his office, he turned to me and said, "We have a disagreement about a mathematical problem here. We're talking about a number system with the following property..."*
>
> *And he proceeded to rattle off: "0+0=0, 0+1=1, 1+0=1, 1+1=0."*
>
> *"What's the problem?" I said.*
>
> *I watched Emmons grin at Convisor, whose mouth was wide open.*
>
> *"Al said this is nonsense," said Emmons. "So I said we should ask you."*
>
> *"It's not nonsense," I said. "You're talking about Boolean algebra."*
>
> *It was a reminder of how far I had traveled in my intellectual odyssey. Starting from the island of pure math, where Boolean algebra was a creative fiction, I had reached the shores of the pleasant and practical world of engineering. And so, Howard Emmons joined Erdös, Franklin and von Kármán on my honor roll of heroes.*

So we tried a different approach. My work on the shock wave theory would occupy my attention for the next few years. At times the work was extremely tedious, but what made it rewarding, besides knowing that we were closing in on an answer, was working with Emmons and learning to combine my mathematical thinking with his engineering outlook. Our work was quite successful and was put to good use later in the design of supersonic planes and missiles.

Of course, the math I used during this time wasn't as beautiful as the pure math I was mesmerized by as a young man in Budapest. It was the math of statistics and numerical analysis, the math of Newton, who spent a good part of his life calculating the trajectories of planets. In fact, to a person who hated numbers the way I did, it was ugly math. But its virtue, which I grudgingly learned to respect, was that this math produced satisfying answers to practical, real-world problems.

In all my life I have heard of only one mathematician who really changed from a pure mathematician to a practical researcher: S. M. Ulam, who worked on the atomic bomb.

In those days, before personal computers, everyone did their computations manually. But we were fortunate enough to receive an electro-mechanical calculator made by the Friedens Corporation. In 1942 this was one of the wonders of the day, and because our work was deemed vital to national defense, the National Productivity Board allocated one to Harvard University.

The Friedens calculator could only add, subtract, multiply and divide. But it sped things up considerably. It was terribly expensive, as large as a typewriter (remember them?), and rattled out answers quite noisily on a corner of my desk. It was probably a hundred times slower than today's pocket calculator that you can buy in any drugstore. But this primitive machine spared me long hours of doing "ugly math." In a way, it also prepared me for the computer age; early on I understood how computers could function as math machines.

I was also impressed by a dinosaur of a computer lurking in the basement—the Mark I, which belonged to Professor Howard Aiken. The Mark I (51 feet long, weighing 35 tons) could perform complex calculations automatically by using "programs" on a paper tape. It was a practical reincarnation of the first automatic computer, the analytical engine of Charles Babbage. This English mathematician (1791–1871) was a true genius who discovered and built the first programmable computer. It was electro-mechanical and in theory it was fine, but its use was based on electronics that were not yet available. Babbage was a hundred years ahead of his time, and his work was all but forgotten until Aiken made it relevant again in the 1950s.

For reasons I never fully understood, Aiken stayed busy calculating Bessel functions and publishing voluminous papers with the results. At the time, he predicted that electronic computers would never work because electron tubes were fundamentally unreliable. In this respect he was right, because no computer using tubes was ever successful. Only the invention of the transistor made computers practical. Today, all his results could be reproduced in seconds.

◆   ◆   ◆

One day Emmons approached me and said that Pratt-Whitney Aircraft had asked him to look at a problem that involved calculating air pressure losses in a complicated air-duct system. Because he didn't have time to do it, he proposed that I take a stab at the consulting job.

"But I don't know anything about such problems," I said.

His diplomatic reply was something like: "Just get busy, Andy, and do it."

I started with an extensive literature survey of thirty or so articles, most of them in German. Because air pressure loss was a common problem, I found many experiments devoted to the subject. But none addressed Pratt-Whitney's troubles. I was beginning to feel that the situation called for a statistician, somebody who could organize the data, but then I had a brainstorm.

No theory could predict the pressure losses accurately, but it seemed like the "math of physics" could at least provide approximate answers. By combining empirical results with mathematical equations, surprisingly, I came up with a breakthrough approach—and, more importantly to Pratt-Whitney, a solution to their air pressure problems.

Later, I presented my findings to the American Society of Mechanical Engineers, who published the article—which became a classic—in the *Transactions of the American Mechanical Engineers* (April 1944). I felt triumphant. The experience confirmed my decision to go into engineering. I was going to make it after all!

9

THE GALLOPING FIGHTER PLANE

During my third year at Harvard, I realized that I would need to spend a few years working in industry if I hoped to land a first-class teaching job. In early 1945, I became a U.S. citizen and, with Dr. Howard Emmons' help and my wife's support, I began looking around.

Because of the war effort there were unlimited opportunities for engineers. Pratt-Whitney Aircraft, who was impressed with my earlier work on air flows in ducts, offered me a job. But it was a giant manufacturer, where I would most likely be tucked into a corner with limited contact and responsibilities. I preferred something smaller where I could become acquainted with experienced engineers from a range of backgrounds. Eventually I chose the Elliott Company of Jeanette, Pennsylvania, a small firm that manufactured pumps.

In the spring of 1945, Laura and I had our furniture packed and shipped, and left Cambridge on the train to Jeanette. Laura's family thought we were crazy to give up our apartment and leave Boston. If we had any idea of the troubles we were about to face, perhaps we would have stayed.

As in Cambridge, housing shortages and rent control meant that there were no apartments or houses to rent. For the first three months Laura and I lived in a hotel and ate in restaurants. Our furniture stayed in storage for the next year. On my first day at work, I also learned that my new company didn't have an office—or desk—for me because of explosive war-time growth. In fact, my new employers were hoping that I might work from my hotel room. But I had different ideas. I looked around and eventually found a table and chair, and created my own work space.

Early on at Elliott, my immediate boss, Herman Sheets, tested my Harvard-based credentials. Sheets was a Czech engineer, a brilliant designer of pumps, and he had the kind of educational background that made him comfortable talking about mathematics. He also had a secret formula to determine pressure losses that he wouldn't share with anyone, this formula assuring his competitive position in the industry.

Of course, when Sheets gave me a little test to see what Harvard-trained engineers were being taught, he didn't mention the formula. The problem involved calculating the flow around a sample blade. I went back to my table, worked out a solution with the help of elliptic partial differential equations, and in less than an hour dropped by his office with the answer. After he pulled out his secret formula and made his calculations, his jaw dropped when he saw that his answer matched mine. I guess I passed the test because after that, Sheets and I got along just fine.

The Elliott Company had plenty of difficult blade design problems for its small staff of research engineers, and I did creative work, all alone, on the mathematics of the hydrodynamic flow around blades. But I never gave much thought to where our pumps were being used until the draft board granted me another deferment for my contributions to the war effort. Years would pass before I learned that the pumps we manufactured were intended for the diffusion process in the atomic bomb.

◆   ◆   ◆

When we heard that General Jodl signed an unconditional surrender of all German forces in Reims on May 7, 1945, pandemonium broke out at Elliott. We all headed home to celebrate, drink champagne, dance and be deliriously happy. Many people stopped at gas stations on the way home to fill up their tanks in the hope that gas rationing was a thing of the past.

As soon as the mail began flowing through Hungary again, I received terrible news. My oldest brother, Karcsi, the poet of the family, and his wife were murdered by Hungarian Nazis. Russians imprisoned my younger brother, Pityu, the inventor of the family, and starved him to death. My famous cousin, János Vazsonyi (son of Vilmos), the statesman, congressman and Jewish leader, also starved to death in a concentration camp. And the list went on. The bombing of Budapest destroyed many apartment houses, but in the cellar of one of them my mother had managed to survive. As the news began to filter out about the true extent of the Holocaust, I realized for the first time what an incredible tragedy had taken place—and how fortunate I had been to escape.

Around this time, however, I began to suspect that my value at the firm wasn't based totally on my actual work. For instance, whenever an important customer visited the firm, the vice president of engineering would call me in and ask me to explain my research. Of course, the customers couldn't understand a word of my mathematical explanations. But that was exactly the desired effect—smoke and mirrors. Instead of doing real engineering work, I was being used as the frosting on the cake. So I talked it over with Laura and we decided it was time to look for a new job.

Laura needed little convincing to move. Jeannette was a cultural desert. By now we had relocated from the hotel to a rental house and reclaimed our furniture. But Laura couldn't drive our dilapidated Oldsmobile (one of the back doors was tied shut with string) and felt isolated. She knew she was in trouble the first day she went to the public library and the librarian enthusiastically showed her around by saying, "To the right are the westerns, and to the left are the mysteries."

It wasn't long before an opportunity came up during a trip to Washington, D.C. I was giving a talk to the American Society of Mechanical Engineers about my work, "On the Aerodynamic Design of Axial-Flow

Compressors and Turbines." During the conference, I ran into William Bollay, one of my professors at Harvard. Bollay was now in private industry, setting up a new laboratory to build supersonic missiles for North American Aviation in Los Angeles. Apparently, my work with Emmons impressed him.

"Traditional engineers haven't the faintest idea how to build a supersonic missile," he said. "Your knowledge of solving hyperbolic partial differential equations would be invaluable."

It was like music to my ears. When I came home and told Laura about Bollay's offer to work with him, she was disappointed about the prospects of yet another cultural wasteland. Only after I reminded her that California didn't have winters—she disliked the bitter New England cold—did she reluctantly agree.

◆   ◆   ◆

We stored our furniture and started the long trek from Pennsylvania to California in our oil-burning Oldsmobile. Taking the opportunity to see more of the U.S., we first drove through the South, touring spots in Florida and stopping along the way in New Orleans and San Antonio.

We were totally amazed at the disappearance of snow and winter, the sight of palm trees and other tropical marvels and the stupendous size of the country. We had a nice visit with Laura's sister, Julia, in San Antonio. Dr. Judson Brown, her husband, was a famous experimental psychologist who served as a captain in the U.S. Army. At his lab, sponsored by the military, we had fun watching rats scurrying through mazes.

◆   ◆   ◆

At North American Aviation, the first thing Bollay wanted me to do was get on the payroll.

"Are you a Mathematician 'A' or 'B'?" the personnel manager asked. I told him I didn't have a clue.

"Mathematician 'A' determines a formula," he explained. "But Mathematician 'B' takes the formula and calculates the values."

Then he looked over my offer from Bollay.

"You can't be a mathematician at all—you make too much money. So you must be an aerodynamic engineer."

So now it was official. My days of calling myself a mathematician were over. Also, for the first time in my life, I punched a time clock.

Laura and I took temporary refuge at the Biltmore Hotel in Hermosa, a fifty-year-old beach resort that had seen better days. On some nights, the waves from the Pacific Ocean crashed over the rocks with such a deafening roar that we woke up thinking our room would be flooded. Otherwise, I loved being near the beach, especially on those weekends when we could take long walks. We arrived in winter, and I could hardly wait until summer when I could battle the big waves of the Pacific.

Bollay placed me in charge of aerodynamic design. He wanted to start where the Germans left off. My first job was to study a collection of German documents on microfilm and microfiche that he had obtained from Peenemunde, Germany, the center of German missile research. Because I was the only engineer who could read German, it was my job to spend the next few months in a dark room, nearly going blind reading all the documents. In the process I also discovered that the Germans were way ahead of us.

When I finished studying the documents, Bollay decided to duplicate the Germans' pride and joy, the Wasserfall missile. He asked me to verify the supersonic flow calculations. To help out, he gave me a staff of five engineers. That's how, overnight, I became a manager without knowing the first thing about management. But I enjoyed working with people and took pleasure in planning and organizing the work.

As for the Wasserfall project, Bollay thought that the missile was too bulky. He now proposed building a supersonic missile, called the "Native," which would be half the size of the Wasserfall. Because aerodynamic flows are controlled by linear differential equations, which can be scaled up or down, we were certain that the German findings would hold true for the first American supersonic missile of whatever size.

I agreed with Bollay that we could handle the aerodynamics side of the new missile, but I had doubts about controlling its trajectory. After all, we were talking about a guided missile that would require an automatic control system. It would be more like flying an airplane than simply firing a shot from a gun.

I took my concerns over to the guy in charge, the head of the Control Section. But within a few minutes he was telling me to mind my own business.

One of his assistants, Roy Knudson, was more responsive. After some prodding, I learned that he and others on the team were concerned about the section head's competence. They didn't think the control system for the Native was adequate—and the head wouldn't listen to them either. So I took it upon myself to dig into the mathematical theory of control, a subject unknown to me and to most traditional engineers.

With the help of Paul Erdös, who had an excellent fellowship at the University of California in Los Angeles, I contacted Norbert Wiener, the internationally renowned mathematician at MIT. Wiener was developing a radically new mathematical theory, cybernetics, a term he coined from the Greek word that referred to the helmsman of a boat—hence, something that controls and communicates. (In 1948 Wiener would publish his book, *Cybernetics,* to much critical and popular acclaim.) He was quite interested in our practical problem and made some helpful comments. It seemed to me this was exactly what we needed for the Native missile.

Thanks to Wiener, I came to the conclusion that the control system under development would definitely not work. So I developed a set of differential equations of motion for the control system that would serve.

Bollay grasped my approach perfectly when I shared it with him. The next time the section head refused to listen, Bollay dismissed him and appointed me to lead the Control Systems unit. Now I faced a true challenge—I would need to organize a group of 43 people on a subject quite new to me.

My first staff meeting started off on a memorable note.

Roy Knudson began by saying that I had to make an urgent decision on ordering some electrical components for testing that had been turned down before.

But he questioned how could I approve or disapprove the order if I didn't know anything about it?

A long silence followed.

I turned to someone in the group whose opinion I respected. "What do you think?"

"I agree with Roy."

"The purchase order is hereby approved," I said.

That's all it took to win the group over. Somehow I knew enough about management to understand that I needed to delegate responsibility. And it certainly didn't hurt that the first decision turned out to be a sound one.

Before I could settle in, however, Bollay and I reached an impasse on a crucial design matter. When Bollay scaled down the Wasserfall by a factor of two, he also scaled down the ailerons—the movable flaps on the wings—by the same factor. For a linear system like the aerodynamics of the Native missile, this made perfect sense. But when you try to apply this scale to a nonlinear system like the ailerons (or, for that matter, a human being), you can get weird results. My math showed that the proper scaling for the flaps wasn't two, but thirty-two. I checked my calculations at least ten times and felt sure I was right.

But when I shared my results with Bollay and others, they laughed.

"You want to control the heavy Native with flaps the size of postage stamps?"

I tore my hair—back then I had plenty—but didn't get anywhere. They were good engineers, but they didn't understand the differential equations of Newton's laws well enough. In the end, Bollay refused to go along with my change.

The design of a missile is done, as with all complex machinery, in two steps. First, the research-oriented engineers design a preliminary version. Second, the production engineers design the final version. In this case, after our initial design was completed and the production engineers took over, I took it upon myself to submit an engineering change that would scale down the ailerons to the size I thought they should be. Because it was a "minor" change, Bollay didn't need to sign off on it.

Was I taking a big risk? Yes, but a few months earlier I had applied math to another practical problem. This one involved an experimental fighter plane.

The chief engineer of the P51, the Mustang, heard about my mathematical prowess and approached me with a problem he had. "Some of our test pilots report that occasionally the P51 starts to shake violently, galloping up and down," he said.

"They're scared stiff that it's going to fall apart. I think it's a bunch of nonsense. But the test pilots refuse to fly the plane. So how do I convince them that the plane is sound?"

I said the first thing that came to mind: "I don't know anything about airplanes—why are you asking me?"

But apparently my argument wasn't persuasive enough. The chief engineer believed in the magic of math. Soon I found myself trying to track down the mystery.

First we went over the test sheet, and I saw the engineers had checked out everything. Then we went to the shop to take a look at the monster. The P51 towered over us in the hangar. I climbed the long, skinny ladder and sat down in the cockpit. It was my first time behind the control stick of a fighter plane, and there wasn't much I could do, so I began jiggling the stick that made the rudders, ailerons and flaps move.

That's when I remembered the story of the Tacoma bridge collapse, and how von Kármán came along and explained how the gale-force winds caused the galloping of the suspension bridge to increase until it was shaken apart. It seemed that the same thing might be happening here. The nonlinear differential equations of the system could cause the wild oscillations. Knowing the mathematical theory also gave me a way to test my hunch.

I slipped off my shoe, which had a rubber heel, and pounded it against the stick. Suddenly the P51 erupted in a fit of shaking that made it feel as if the monster was going to fall apart. It was the same sensation that the test pilots felt, only they were a few thousand feet in the air when it happened. (This was formerly known as "self-excited oscillation," in which a small disturbance creates a catastrophic effect. Today, it goes under the name of chaos theory.)

While this was going on, mechanics in the hangar began running towards the plane as if it were going to take off with me, the helpless mathematician-engineer, trapped in the cockpit. But gradually the oscillations damped out, the plane calmed down and I climbed out.

My hunch turned out to be correct. The hydraulic lines were introducing delays, which led to positive feedback in the form of jarring vibrations. After the engineers shortened the hydraulic lines, they banged the stick as hard as they could and nothing happened. The reassured test pilots began flying the airplane again.

Three months later came the biggest test of my chosen career to date. It was time to fire the missile in Santa Susana in the desert testing ground. We gathered in the pit to watch the test through binoculars. When Bollay saw my last-minute design change, he leaned over and whispered, "You're fired."

When the Native missile was launched, we watched as it gracefully followed its trajectory, accomplishing its mission perfectly. The postage-stamp-sized ailerons guided the missile just as Isaac Newton's math said they would. Bollay, as the designer of the first supersonic guided missile, became a hero. I felt triumphant, too. But my relationship with Bollay never healed, and soon afterwards I resigned without ever being fired.

◆   ◆   ◆

On the domestic front, Laura and I bought our first home—a tiny 840-square-foot cottage in the boondocks—for the princely sum of $6,500 (we swung the deal with help from Laura's mother). Unfortunately, our new house came with a hitch. The army veteran who was renting it from the previous owner refused to move out, and due to rent control laws there was nothing we could do about it. While the laws protected him from a raise in rent, it caused us much hardship. So, during our first year as homeowners, we rented a basement apartment with no kitchen. When the veteran finally did move out, our little house was in terrible condition. The yard was a wilderness refuge for gophers, and Laura was crying her eyes out for the streets of Boston.

Not long afterwards, I made final plans to bring my mother over from Hungary, which was still ravaged from five years of war. After a few years of bureaucratic hassles and logistical problems, I was happily reunited with my mother. When I met her at the L.A. airport, I was shocked at how tiny she was—only 4'8"—almost a midget in the U.S.

In her letters to us, Hermine had expressed her fond wishes to follow the old Hungarian custom in which one's elderly parents slept in the kitchen. But after she looked around our house, she finally understood why we said this was impossible—the kitchen was hardly big enough for her to stretch out in.

Hermine was enthralled by California. The palm trees took her breath away. She loved the geraniums that flowered year-round. The

Pacific Ocean mesmerized her. She was astounded at the sight of so many black people in downtown Los Angles—in Budapest, I don't recall ever seeing more than two persons of African descent.

But the living arrangements quickly became a nightmare. Because Hermine couldn't speak English and Laura couldn't drive, they felt like prisoners in the tiny house. I wasn't much help because when I came home from work I was usually too tired to have conversations in two different languages.

Fortunately, Laura has always had a sixth sense about communication and managed to talk to my mother, but all the conversations were one-sided. One particular incident still stands out. One day Laura found a big toad in the yard and pointed it out to Hermine, saying, "Toad."

Hermine replied, "Not tot," using the German word for "dead." Then she grabbed a shovel and destroyed the harmless toad.

What made things more frustrating was that Laura and I had enjoyed an active social life with my colleagues at North American, and my mother somewhat dampened our fun. For her part, she felt isolated in the U.S. because she was so far from friends and the place where she was often the life of the party. But we struggled to make her days as pleasant as possible.

◆   ◆   ◆

As my frustration with North American grew, I turned to teaching an evening engineering course in control theory at UCLA. By now the word was out that I had developed a new mathematical theory for guided missiles. So on the basis of that and good luck—one of my students was a high-ranking civilian in the Navy—I was asked to head up a new guided missile division at the U.S. Naval Ordnance Station in the Mojave Desert. But rather than move my family to the barren desert where missiles could be safely tested, Navy officials agreed to set up my new division in Pasadena. The new living arrangements in a rented apartment were much better for Laura and Hermine because they had more space and were closer to downtown shops and restaurants.

When I reported to work in the fall of 1948, I was ranked as a P7. There are eight ranks in the civil service, so only the rank of P8 was above me, which made me one of the youngest P7s in the entire Navy. With great enthusiasm, I began recruiting engineers and setting work schedules, doing everything that goes with starting up a new major organizational unit.

I was doing fine until I collided with the captain in charge of funding our project. All I knew about Captain Kirk Mota was that he was a terror. Even so, when I showed up at his office in Washington, D.C., I was unprepared when he began ranting that he had never authorized setting up a Guided Missile Division. Not only that, he said, but my job didn't even exist.

His blitzkrieg attack stunned me. The civilian director of the naval station had already approved my budget. So here I was, caught between the civilian and military sides of the Navy.

After catching my breath, I finally spoke up.

"Captain Mota, I realize that without your authorization we can't do anything. So with your permission I would like to leave."

"Why?" He seemed taken aback by my quick surrender.

"Captain, it is 4:30 here. And 1:30 in Los Angeles. I made a number of offers to engineers to head up the sections of my division. They are just returning to their current offices from lunch, and I want to contact them. I seem to have different ethical standards than the U.S. Navy—I made offers to these people. Now I must tell them that the deal is off. That's the least I can do for them."

Clearly the captain wasn't used to such a direct approach. He leaned back in his chair and thought it over for a moment.

"Can you wait until tomorrow morning?" he said. "That will give me time to check with the admiral."

I had a sleepless night, wondering if I had made a terrible mistake. But the next morning, Captain Mota was quite calm.

"I studied your plan and talked it over with the admiral," he said. "I've decided to go along with you."

When I returned to Pasadena, I didn't tell my civilian bosses about my meeting with the good captain. They knew Mota well enough to know that he had tested me. And somehow I had passed the test.

◆   ◆   ◆

On October 23, 1948, Laura gave birth to our daughter, Beatrice. As a devoted reader of 14th century Italian literature, Laura borrowed the name from Dante. But twelve years later, she was overruled when our independent teenager changed her name to Bobbi.

The birth day was truly memorable. After the call came from the hospital, I jumped into the car with my mother and Laura's mother, who was visiting from Boston. We met Laura just as she was coming out of anesthesia. She was fine. The baby was 9 lbs. 5 oz., the biggest in the hospital. Big and beautiful, breathing heavily, her belly button poking out far. The grandmothers and I were nearly delirious with happiness.

When we went home with the baby, however, the fun really began.

Both grandmothers had servants helping them when their children came into the world, so they didn't have a clue about what to do with a newborn. With good intentions, they ran around, wringing their hands, driving everyone crazy. Finally, I hired a nurse for a few days and things settled down as Laura gradually took charge.

But the domestic situation with my mother finally became intolerable. While Laura was taking care of the house, Hermine spent all her time playing with Bobbi. One of the toughest decisions I ever had to make was when I decided to send my mother back to Hungary. It caused us much sadness, even though it greatly improved our living arrangements. In the long run, it also turned out best for Hermine. In

America, she was virtually a non-person, someone who didn't quite fit in. But in Hungary she basked in glory as the mother of a successful son in the U.S. She also had a treasure chest of first-hand stories about America. She became the life of the party again.

For a few years after Bobbi's birth, if the truth be known, my new daughter didn't have much of an impact on me. Being a typical European male of that generation, I found babies boring. But when she started to grow up, her life profoundly changed mine. We did a great many things together. We hiked, rode burros, ice skated, swam, bicycled, just to mention a few. Also, I realized to my amazement that children (and my child, in particular) had brains. One day I was in the TV room with Bobbi and I lowered the Venetian blinds to make the room darker. But when the reception became fuzzy, she walked to the window and pulled up the metal blinds against my will. Immediately the reception improved because we were in direct line with the TV station. Watching over her, being with her, became one of my top priorities and joys.

◆   ◆   ◆

After six months of organizing the guided missile division—my first taste of high-level managerial work—I was hardly prepared for what happened next. Because of budget cuts and thanks to Captain Mota, our department was one of the first to go. But we didn't go far. Under a new plan, our team merged with a small group of engineers working on torpedoes.

Apparently, the Navy brass believed it was high time to modernize the design of torpedoes. Because the technical problems of air missiles and water torpedoes were similar, and because the mathematical equations for the flow of air and water were identical, I was chosen to direct the new project.

One of my early challenges surfaced one day while I was having lunch with Commander Arthur Maggio in Washington, D.C. He told me that a research division of the Navy was designing a new torpedo, but the torpedo often missed its target during tests. The engineers attributed the failure to Maggio's crew. He asked if I wouldn't mind looking into the matter.

When I visited the engineers, they showed me the careful test results of the pendulum that controlled the path of the torpedo. They also brought out the pressure gauge, which determined the depth of the torpedo's path. The problem, they said, was that Commander Maggio's crew was not following the new and complex firing procedures accurately.

After returning to Pasadena, I went through the test results in my mind and realized that the pressure gauge was tested under static conditions. But as the torpedo moved at high speed, I knew mathematically that it might read the wrong pressures and this would cause it to misjudge its depth in the water. Later I confirmed my guess with some hydrodynamic calculations, and called Commander Maggio with the results.

A month later, the commander called back with some interesting news.

Maggio had instructed his men to hang some large fishing nets between motor boats and fire dummy torpedoes into the nets. When they pulled up the nets, they verified that the torpedo holes were about ten feet lower than where they should have been. He turned his findings with my comments over to the engineers, who then made some dynamic tests that confirmed my calculations. By introducing some correction factors to the depth prediction, the problem was solved to everyone's satisfaction.

Except for such times as that when I could directly apply my math and engineering skills to a complex situation, I mostly spent my days making managerial decisions. This caused me to have doubts. Did I really want to spend my life as an executive?

I made a careful analysis of the pros and cons. (Later I discovered that I was using the rudiments of the balance sheet approach to decision making.) As an executive, my future seemed clear. I would move up, step-by-step, to higher jobs, better pay, prestige and all the privileges that go with high-level jobs. But on the negative side, I had less time for technical work and was growing bored with the administrative side. Executive life also interfered with my family life. I wanted to spend more time with my daughter, but my work commitments wouldn't let me. However, when I began looking around for promising technical jobs, the future looked fuzzy. Few people advanced very far in industry by doing technical work.

Fortunately, while visiting von Kármán at Cal Tech, I met someone who was sympathetic about my personal-professional dilemma.

Dr. Si Ramo had just left his job at General Electric so that he could form, with Dean Wooldridge, another well-known scientist, a new research division at Hughes Aircraft. Ramo was a strong proponent of the belief that in our technocratic world, technical work is of the greatest importance. After hearing my qualifications, he invited me to work with him as a consultant. Later he offered me an excellent technical job.

Now I stood at another crossroads.

My friends urged me to keep my job with the Navy. They argued that my job as a civil servant was about the most secure position one could find. If I stayed at my current job and merely coasted along, I would continue to receive pay raises, vacation time, health care and early retirement at high pay. If I waited only another six months, I would qualify for permanent status and the retirement plan. They made a good point. As a refugee with a family to support, I questioned why I should give up that kind of stability.

But something inside me told me not to wait. Just as I knew when it was time to leave Hungary, I knew it was time to take another chance. So in 1953 I decided to accept Ramo's offer and join Hughes Aircraft. Little did I suspect that the last engineering work I would ever do would be for the Navy. Soon, at Hughes, a career in the new field of managerial decision making would open up for me.

10

LIFE WITHOUT COMPUTERS

o o o o o o o o o o o o o o o o o o o o o o o o o o o o
There is a tide in the affairs of men, Which taken at the flood, leads on to fortune.

—*Julius Caesar, Shakespeare*

Once, a colleague of mine, Gene Grabbe, appeared on Groucho Marx's program, *You Bet Your Life*. When Groucho asked him what he did for a living, Gene said that he worked for Ramo-Wooldridge.

"What do you do for the dime store?" Groucho asked.

Gene told him it was not a five and ten cents Woolworth and gave a brief explanation about his work in the decision sciences. Groucho waited until he was done, then looked Gene squarely in the eye.

"Do the police know about this?" Groucho asked.

Whenever someone asks, "What exactly is decision sciences?", I always squirm, as do many of my colleagues. People outside our field usually don't have the foggiest idea about what we do. Friends and families may know that we teach in a college or work in the production department of a large corporation—that we are math guys and computer nerds, but they don't really have a clue about what we actually contribute to the world.

My own daughter, Bobbi, who has assisted me with my memoirs, recently tried to explain my curious career to a friend, but finally gave up. The next day she called and said it might be nice if she had a five-minute example of decision sciences that she could use the next time the subject came up.

I told her of an article about customer waiting lines that I had recently come across in *The Wall Street Journal*. Fast-food restaurants, supermarkets, airlines and banks were debating the issue of whether customers should be forced into multiple short lines, or a serpentine single line. Multiple lines created more stress in people; on the other hand, single lines appeared more intimidating. It was an interesting article; however, the writer failed to mention the vast amount of research done by decision scientists on mathematical queuing theory, and by the use of computer-based simulation. He also ignored the subject of how customers measure time, which isn't always by the clock but sometimes by subjective feelings. As Albert Einstein once replied to a nine-year-old letter writer, "Time is relative. Flirting with a pretty girl for 10 minutes goes by fast, sitting on a hot stove for 10 minutes feels like an eternity."

The journalist's lack of awareness about our field didn't surprise me. While there are thousands of success stories about using decision sciences in real life, the discipline has only been around a few decades. Those who have benefited from decision sciences often do not know that they are using it! They are like computer users who don't have the foggiest idea that they are using, for example, the portfolio management theory of Nobel Laureate economist Harry M. Markowitz.

The terms "decision sciences," "management sciences," and "operations research" have been around only for a few years. The first edition of the *Encyclopedia of Operations Research and Management Science* was published only in 1996. The *Encyclopedia Britannica* does have something, although quite misleading, about operations research in the context of industrial engineering, but it has absolutely nothing about the others. A field like physics has been around for thousands of years, but decision sciences started around 1940, barely giving it a historical background of barely sixty years.

When I took up the subject of applying science to management in the early 1950s, I stumbled along and learned things on my own until I started finding textbooks and associations devoted to the newly emerging field, and even helped launch one association myself.

◆   ◆   ◆

For the last eight years I had applied math and engineering towards improving the performance of pumps, guided missiles, aircraft and torpedoes. But when I joined Hughes Aircraft in 1953, I soon learned that Dean Wooldridge, the vice president of the electronic research division, had ideas about going into the computer business. He thought that once we found out exactly what was needed, the company should develop computers to sell to industry.

Wooldridge's first problem, however, was trying to find someone on the engineering staff who was interested in the new field of business computers. Most technicians had a very poor opinion of business applications and customers. But something about it caught my eye. Maybe I was tired of masquerading as an engineer or was simply curious about a new and interesting challenge. Whatever the reason, I volunteered for the computer project.

With my math and engineering background, I thought I could work out a way for computers to perform engineering calculations. When I mentioned this to Wooldridge, he said that he had a better idea.

"This country spends billions of dollars on IBM punch card machines. Our goal should be to replace them with computers."

My heart sank. To me, a punch card was the same as a time card. All it did was keep track of hours worked. John Doe worked 38 hours, made $2.00 per hour, so he received 2 times 38, or $76.00. What's the big deal?

The payroll group straightened me out. Suppose John Doe punches his time card in the morning when he starts working. He drills some holes in a plate and marks the start and completion times on the card traveling with the plate. Then he goes to another location and records his times on the card traveling with that job. He does this all day long, until he punches out in the evening.

The payroll system was then responsible for taking all this data—for 20,000 or so employees—and finding the pertinent record for each employee, applying different pay rates and calculating gross earnings. The system also figured out taxes, dues, etc. before printing out a paycheck. And that was just the tip of the iceberg. The cost accountants wanted to know all the charges made against the plate, as well as the cost of the assembly requiring the plate. Moreover, all sorts of tax reports and union dues reports were printed weekly, monthly, quarterly, yearly.

Of course, the system was also a terrible mess—expensive and unreliable. At Hughes, hundreds of typists keypunched the data onto IBM cards—each card with 80 columns for numbers 1 through 10, a little hole by each number and two holes for each letter of the alphabet. A row of noisy printers rattled out cards all day. Employees carried around huge decks of cards, which were occasionally dropped and scattered to the four corners of the plant.

After watching this for a while, I realized it was utter chaos. But I felt that it might be possible to manage the turmoil by using math—only what kind of math I didn't know.

When the payroll people heard about our plan to replace their punch-card nightmare with a fully automatic computer, they were understandably skeptical. How would a computer know how much overtime to pay John Doe for his evening work, let alone calculate his additional union pay if he worked on a high scaffold on a holiday night? With the punch card system, these kinds of situations would be sorted out and the payroll people would manually adjust John Doe's salary.

I realized now that if the computer was to be successful, it would need to focus more on processing, rather than simply calculating, data.

A computer is a math machine, and it didn't occur to me previously that processing data was a proper subject for math.

Perhaps I should have known better. A few years earlier I was visiting the office of John von Neumann, the Hungarian mathematician who is now called the father of the electronic computer. We were in sitting in his office at the Institute for Advanced Study when I noticed some paper lying around that he had scribbled on.

"What are these funny symbols?" I asked.

"You see, I can solve complicated math problems with the computer," he said. "Partial differential equations are no problem. But I am trying to figure out how to sort records. These symbols form the computer program that tells the computer how to sort."

At the time I didn't think much of it. But now I realized how far ahead he was. He foresaw computers being used for data processing, and he was developing a new kind of math that could handle these such problems.

I don't have a copy of von Neumann's program, but in my 1970 book, Problem Solving by Digital Computers with PL/I Programming, *I had a program to sort 400 numbers. Here is the core (the math) of the program*

```
DECLARE KAR(400)
DO I=1 TO 399;
DO J=I+1 TO 400;
IF KAR(I) <=KAR (J) THE GO TO LABL;
L=KAR(I);
KAR(I)=KAR(J);
KAR(J)=L;
LABL:;
END;
END;
```

Sorting was a major breakthrough in the field of data processing. Suppose you wanted to line up the twelve children of the Gilbreth family by height. If you made cards that contained the height of each child, you could easily sort the cards in your hand. But what if you had thousands of records? That was the problem that punch card machines solved when they were invented in the 1890s by Herman Hollerith. The machines were so handy for sorting records that the U.S. census director immediately put them to use for processing census data. Operators punched raw data onto cards, then fed decks of these cards into the machines. As cards traveled in the machines, they dropped into pockets sorted digit by digit.

At Hughes, if you wanted to get the records, say, of those people who worked on Project 317b last week in order of seniority, you could sort through thousands of cards and produce a tidy stack with the pertinent data in the proper sequence.

When I reported back to Wooldridge, I told him that I thought we could develop computers that would sort, update and modify payroll records. Not only that, the computers would do it faster, better and cheaper than the current method. Magnetic tapes would replace punch cards. All the processing would be performed automatically except for the truly weird cases, which the computer would flag for manual processing. My biggest concern was reliability—an issue that plagued computer systems then as it does now.

I also pointed out that I thought computers could do a better job of handling production control on the shop floor. After all, if computers could process most of payroll's operations, it made sense that computers could do a better job of creating production schedules that involved sorting out different machines and parts for use at different times.

With that in mind I spent a few weeks hanging out on the Hughes Aircraft manufacturing floor. After a few noisy days, I noticed something very peculiar. By the time production control people handed out schedules to foremen, the schedules were already out of date. For instance, a fellow might pick up instructions that gave him all the information to begin making a precision volt meter on May 23, but it would be June 6 before he first saw the schedule. So he would have no choice but to ignore the dates and do the best he could. Of course, the scheduled machines would be unavailable because they were busy with some other foreman's out-of-date schedule. So everybody waited their turn, work backed up and the production people kept on scheduling more work. It was crazy.

This made a huge impression on me. When I went back to the production control people and told them what I saw, they were defensive. And for a good reason. Nobody ever told the control people that things were running behind schedule, so they assumed everything ran like clockwork. Uncertainty dominated the whole process.

In his book on cybernetics, Norbert Wiener wrote about how pilots steer ships by applying the rudder when they sense that the boat is going slightly off course. The problem with the "pilots" in production control was that they never got a response from the shop floor that indicated they were veering off course. They received no feedback. The punch cards that followed the jobs around tracked only cost data, not scheduling information.

The next time I met with Wooldridge, I told him what I had seen on the shop floor. Replacing the punch card machines with just a computer wouldn't help production, I said. What we needed was a computer system with built-in feedback that would improve the production schedules. But there was one problem. This was a management problem that I didn't know anything about.

With Wooldridge's encouragement, I began researching textbooks on management techniques from the business school at the University of Southern California. What I found was encouraging. Complex mathematical processes were involved in the manufacturing planning process. By using math models with a computer, we could solve the kind of scheduling problems that foremen faced on the shop floor.

A new kind of math was needed—a combination of traditional calculations and data processing—what would later become known as "information management." Something else was also needed—an approach that focused more on uncertainty and conflict.

It was an exciting challenge. By applying both my math hump and engineering experience, we managed to develop and install both better payroll and production control systems. Afterwards, I felt that I had contributed something to the world of business. Fortunately, it wasn't long before I came across an announcement about the first meeting of the Operations Research Society of America. Their goals included the use of math to improve business management. Little did I know how quickly this would become one of my life's goals.

11

MY METAMORPHOSIS

When I first started attending meetings of the Operations Research Society of America (ORSA), I was happy giving talks about my production experience at Hughes. After all, my last six months of working in the factory with production people, as well as my years of industrial experience applying math and science, gave me insight into the operations research field that few others had.

I enjoyed some success with my presentations, especially with members more interested in practical matters. The central feature of operations research was the mathematical model, and I began developing some new models for production control. Eventually, academics started to pay attention. To them, I was still an industrial idiot, but I knew my math.

Once I became more involved with ORSA, I learned more about the history of the field itself. Operations research as a discipline got its start during WWII. British physicists and mathematicians began working with the Royal Air Force to improve the efficiency of radar to detect enemy aircraft. This led to joint efforts by researchers and the military to improve the entire system of early warning and coordinated defense. By the early 1940s, efforts were expanded throughout the British armed services to evaluate, test and maintain military systems.

In 1942, U.S. military groups became interested in operations research as they geared up to enter the war. Six years later, the Massachusetts Institute of Technology offered the first course in military operations research techniques such as how to use radar, anti-submarine warfare and anti-aircraft problems. In 1950, ORSA was established as a result of organizing efforts by Phil Morse, a highly respected physicist and senior professor at MIT. Morse was experienced in military operations research and under his leadership, the business community was soon paying more attention to ORSA.

From my point of view, however, Morse and his disciples seemed too far removed from the day-to-day world of American business. A sense of academic hubris pervaded the sessions. Because many of the speakers lacked practical business know-how or an understanding of using computers in management, the ORSA meetings became less informative, more frustrating.

One of the organization's most obvious flaws came out during a speech I was giving at an ORSA plenary session. Someone stood up in the crowded room and asked if I was a full member of the association.

I knew what he was getting at. When ORSA was founded, the leadership drove an elitist wedge into the association by creating two classes of members. Full members were only those theorists and mathematicians certified by the core group. Associate members were riff-raff from the real world—guinea pigs from business who could try out the full members' theories. This undemocratic system reminded me of the good old days in semi-feudal Hungary—I thought it was nonsense and ignored the whole thing.

But on this day I addressed the issue head-on. When the silence in the room became unbearable, I answered with as much humility as possible, "I am only a lowly associate member and do not belong to the inner sanctum."

I received a standing ovation.

Later, during the intermission, Morse approached me.

"Why aren't you a full member?" he asked.

"I have never applied and never will," I said.

"We must do something about that," he said.

Afterward, I became a full member of ORSA, one of the few who never applied for it. I thought about declining the upgrade, but then again, didn't want to waste my time on such political nonsense.

◆   ◆   ◆

Around this time, I discovered another group of interesting scholars. Economists. They represented a new scientific field with a relatively short history.

Starting with Adam Smith's *Inquiry into the Nature and Causes of the Wealth of Nations* (1776), economists assumed that the world was governed by monetary matters, which is an idea that became an important factor in my work. However, some advanced economic thinkers were taking a hard look at behavioral decision making and psychology, and came to the revolutionary conclusion that economic theory should also take into account flesh-and-blood humans.

As I became interested in the research and started learning some of the math of economics, I began meeting others with similar interests, including some people in business. Before long, I had developed my own personal network of people, and we decided to start our own association.

In August 1953, I drafted the following manifesto.

ROUGH DRAFT
A. Vazsonyi
August 10, 1953
ANNOUNCEMENT

During the last two decades, and in particular, since World War II, the problems of modern management have increased in scope and complexity. A need now exists for systematic research which can evolve new and effective instruments for dealing with these problems. During the same period, a growing number of workers have produced a considerable amount of research in this field. A characteristic feature of this work is the attempt to deal with managerial problems by means of mathematical models. Exploiting advances in pure sciences and technology, these workers established foundations upon which a structure of management sciences may be erected.

Correspondence and communication between interested persons has made it increasingly apparent that a stage has now been reached which makes it desirable to consider founding an organization dedicated to encouraging and extending this type of work. Such an organization would, if successful, (1) establish this type of work as a field of scientific endeavor, (2) stimulate work in the field, and (3) publish a journal, convoke meetings, and adopt other suitable means of making the fruits of this work available to all interested persons.

The event was a milestone in my life. The announcement was signed by eighteen people, some of whom went on to become Nobel Laureates, and led to the founding of the Institute of Management Sciences (TIMS). On a personal level, the experience allowed me to become acquainted with Herbert Simon, a signatory and eventual Nobel Prize recipient. He would later become one of my genuine heroes in the decision sciences field.

During our first organizing meeting, I also received a rather dubious distinction. We were at Columbia University, attending to all the routine matters that go with starting a new professional organization. But we hit a snag when it came to electing officers. According to the constitution, the retiring president became the senior executive of the Institute—the chairman of the council. Bill Cooper was the elected president; however, we didn't have a past president to chair the council.

Somebody had the smart idea of abolishing the institute, then revising the constitution and starting a new organization. But it took a two thirds majority to abolish the institute, and we didn't have a quorum. In desperation, we went for a coffee break. Then somebody had a brilliant idea—"Let's elect Andy to the position of past president."

That's how I became the first and only past president of the Institute of Management Sciences who never held the office of president. At the first annual conference of TIMS, I opened the meeting and introduced the new president, Bill Cooper, assuring members that he would be continuing my policies. Following that, I assumed the role of the top executive of the Institute and sat back to rest on my fictional laurels. (On November 19, 2002, in San Jose, California, the Institute for Operations Research and the Management Sciences held a 50-year anniversary party and dinner for past presidents. I was proud to be invited as the only past president who was never president.)

As for my legacy as chairperson for the first year, West C. Churchman, our in-house philosopher and journal editor, reportedly said: "When the going gets tough, Andy pulls a flask of brandy out of his pocket, takes a good slug and resolves the issue promptly."

◆   ◆   ◆

As the years went by I managed to develop a reputation as a drinker. This was pure myth because in real life I get sleepy after a single drink. But I didn't discourage the rumor because it helped create the image that I was more than just a rational mathematician. In fact, I made a point of carrying around a flask and taking it out at opportune moments. Mike Stone, of John Wiley & Sons Publishers and editor of my first book, began the myth based on an incident in 1957.

I wrote half of my first book on airplanes while traveling to various meetings. Because I enjoyed taking shorts naps, a nip of brandy would help me fall asleep. Unfortunately, one time the brandy spilled and saturated my manuscript. When I got to the hotel, I spread the manuscript out on the bed to dry. The lines on the page disappeared, but my notes remained. When Stone visited my room later to discuss the manuscript, he was met by the smell of brandy fumes and the sight of pages scattered across the bed. Through his eyes, I must have looked like a hard-drinking writer.

Another time, a colleague and I were in Sacramento making a proposal for some computer work for the Department of Motor Vehicles. I asked a secretary to book our flights to Los Angeles and promptly forgot about the whole thing. When the meeting was over, my colleague and I stopped at a bar on the way to the airport to kill some time. Suddenly the secretary appeared with our tickets. I thanked her profusely.

"But how on earth did you find us?" I asked.

She replied that her boss had told her to go to the nearest bar, and that was where she would find Dr. Vazsonyi.

◆   ◆   ◆

TIMS opened up a new, exciting chapter in my life. I had always wanted to make a living as a mathematician. But doing research in pure math didn't work out because of the war and political disruptions, and using math as an engineer wasn't my cup of tea—I didn't have the same intuitive feel for engineering that I did for math. Now a new market appeared for *real-life math,* using math and computers to manage business, industry and the public sector. Something about it struck a loud chord with me.

Thanks to TIMS, I now had new friends who shared my interests. Most importantly, I had a platform to develop and spread my ideas on using real-life math. During this time, I studied subjects as far-ranging as economics, psychology, sociology, statistics, probability, chaos theory, computer science, philosophy and visual arts. And it wasn't just for my own personal gain, either—the results of my research could impact the lives of everyone around me. With much enthusiasm, I became an activist for real-life math.

Little did I know that ORSA and TIMS would merge in 1995 to become INFORMS, which now has a membership of over 15,000. Today, the application of the techniques envisioned by us forty years ago has an impact on practically all phases of our lives, all over the world. INFORMS has sections devoted to the usual suspects (accounting, computers, finance, management), but also looks at issues as wide-ranging as natural resources, healthcare, telecommunications and transportation. Practically all business schools teach many of these topics, and other organizations like the Decision Sciences Institute (which

I joined as a founding member, and now has over 2,500 members) have sprung up to address educational issues. However, much to the chagrin of its officers, INFORMS is still relatively unknown in the business world.

◆   ◆   ◆

As a young mathematician, I wrote articles without notes. I simply thought long and hard about the theorem and the proof. When I was ready, I sat down and wrote the paper. After I gave up math, I didn't write again until I became an engineer at Harvard and began publishing articles on topics such as the flow of air in ducts. Later, in private industry I wrote a bunch of papers on aerodynamics and control systems, as well as many tutorials for internal use. However, my method of writing did not change.

I modified it only when I became involved in the decision sciences. Now I was dealing with a wider range of issues, so I began a life-long habit of keeping journals, or what I call "aid-memoirs." I found that if I could record my thoughts and hold conversations with my alter ego (and my heroes), then I could effectively think through a topic.

As a result of my journal-keeping, I compiled quite a few notes on the subject of using math in operations research and management science, much of it dealing with linear programming, a highly esoteric mathematical field and popular topic in its day. Linear programming was introduced in the late 1930s by the Soviet mathematician Leonid Kantorovich and the American economist Wassily Leontief. During WWII, it was used extensively to deal with transportation, scheduling and allocation of resources. In the 1950s, linear programming became one of the most important techniques of quantitative decision making. The current theory and practice of investment is based on quadratic programming, an extension of linear programming.

With the help of these notes, I was ready for the day in the fall of 1956, when John Wiley, founder of John Wiley & Sons Publishers, walked into my office.

Wiley asked me point-blank, "What are you working on?"

I showed him my aid memoirs on linear programming.

"Dr. Vazsonyi, I'm interested in publishing your material," he said. "There's only a short paperback on the market by Charnes and Cooper. It's all math and incomprehensible to the layman. Can you humanize it?"

I told him I'd give it a try.

Writing *Scientific Programming in Business and Industry* was a breeze. I prepared notes wherever I was—at home, in hotels, on airplanes, because I did an awful lot of shuffling between parts of the country for various business meetings. My writing method involved an extra step because I had never quite mastered written English. I dictated the text based on my notes into a tape recorder, and my secretary transcribed it. Next I edited the rough draft, and she wrote the final copy. There was no formal peer review, and Wiley's technical editor made only minor editorial changes. She did tell me, however, that whenever she tried to reword my tangled Hungarian English, the sentences would start losing their original meaning. So eventually she decided to leave my "quaint" English alone.

By the way, Hungarian is said to be one of the world's most exasperating languages to learn. In Hungarian, it makes perfect sense to write something like, "This model requires two equation," because Hungarians don't use a plural after a number—I guess they figure the reader should be smart enough to know that a quantity of more than one implies a plural noun. Also, in Hungarian there is no way to tell genders apart. To this day, I interchange he/she and her/his. Frequently, when I tell a story, people look puzzled and ask me who I'm talking about. My wife, Laura, exclaims, "Are you talking about a man or woman?"

I thought about calling my first book *Mathematical Programming*, but after a lot of head-scratching (there was less hair to pull in those days), I changed it to *Scientific Programming in Business and Industry*, which didn't really mean anything or receive general acceptance. But it was one of the first books on operations research and became very successful. It was translated into German, Japanese and Russian and brought me international attention.

Although the book sold well in foreign countries, those markets paid only tiny royalties, perhaps a few hundred dollars. All except Russia, which ignored copyrights and paid not a penny. At the urging of a Wiley editor, I wrote a letter of protest to the Russian government. Six months later, I received a one-page reply, all in Russian. Laura studied the page for a few moments. When I asked her what it said, she solemnly answered, "Nyet."

◆　　　◆　　　◆

Scientific Programming in Business and Industry was a serious book about a serious subject. In contrast, I always made sure that my lectures were spiced with humorous anecdotes, such as the one about the head of operations research who was conducting an inspection tour with the commanding general. In the cafeteria, the executive pointed out the shortened lines in which the soldiers waited for their dinner. "Put the old system back," barked the general. "The long lines strengthen the calves of the solders."

After my colleagues and a publisher encouraged me to compile the light material in a new book, I wrote a manuscript entitled *Facts and Fables of Science and Computers in Management*. Unfortunately, this publishing experience had a sad ending. A technical editor revised the text so much that it lost whatever charm it had and became a dry, lifeless textbook. It wasn't a total loss, however. After I disowned it and lost interest in trying to publish it elsewhere, I managed to rescue many of the anecdotes for later use. It also taught me that all publishing experiences were not alike—my first one with Wiley was excellent, but in the future I would need to be more careful.

◆   ◆   ◆

My whole life didn't revolve around work. Far from it. As our daughter, Bobbi, was growing up, Laura and I spent more time doing the things that young parents do (or should do). Previously, we had kept more or less to ourselves, except for a few close friends. But with Bobbi, we became involved with other children and their parents, picnics, cook-outs and weekend trips. We often visited our friends, the Ulmers in San Fernando Valley. He was a photographer for *Life* magazine, and his wife was a hefty Hungarian woman who made us sumptuous Hungarian dishes like chicken paprikash. We often took weekend trips to the beach or the desert. During trips to Palm Springs, when Bobbi was three, I started teaching her swimming by tying an inflatable frog around her, the way I learned. While she floated on the water, she was free to move her arms and legs, and I taught her how to paddle around. Later she graduated to an orange life vest and soon she was diving in and swimming like a fish. She still swims several miles a week in a public pool.

We always shared the house with Bobbi's pets and, occasionally, the animals would hit the road with us. I recall one trip in which we smuggled a baby duck into the closet at the Casitas del Monte, an exclusive Palm Springs hotel. Everything was fine until the bellboy started to put away the luggage. When the duck let out a loud quack and charged out of the closet, the bellboy shot out of the room like a human cannonball.

In Hungary, the land of Magyar cowboys, I had never tried horseback riding before. But I learned to ride in California, and my daughter and I would go for long rides in Canoga Park where they filmed westerns. Oftentimes I felt like Palladin himself, riding through the authentic-looking Hollywood movie sets.

An enthusiastic ice skater in Budapest, I took Bobbi to the rink, and like a good European father, I made sure she had skating lessons with a professional.

Because Laura and I had different family backgrounds, we sometimes disagreed about how to raise Bobbi. I was all for bringing her up with little supervision and lots of self reliance. But Laura favored a more protective, sheltered upbringing.

The best example of my "childhood management technique" came up when I learned that my eleven-year-old angel had been caught stealing nail polish from a drugstore. My first reaction was to get very agitated—after all, I was fastidiously honest and we had a thief in the family! But before I started to raise my voice, I remembered reading somewhere that stealing is not that uncommon among pre-teens.

With some self-control, I asked Bobbi for the facts behind her crime. It seems that she was in the drugstore with her best friend, and they decided to see what they could get away with. They had the money but wanted a quick thrill and bragging rights. They were also so inept that the store detective caught them in the act. He then ushered them to a back room where he gave them a stern lecture and threatened to call the police. When Bobbi finished telling me her story, I said, "How could you be so stupid as to get caught?" I also said that stealing was wrong, but I think she already knew this. To her surprise, I added that the clerk acted wrongfully, too. "We have laws to protect us, and he violated your rights."

"What rights?" she asked.

"You better get it straight from an expert. Let's go see my attorney."

Laura was flabbergasted as she watched me call our attorney to set up a meeting. Before we met, I told him that I was bringing Bobbi to see him not only to show her how serious her actions were, but also to address how wrong the clerk's actions were. And so it went. Bobbi thought I was a pretty cool dad, and I ended up with a small legal fee, which was worth every penny.

This was a busy time for me—I was keeping many balls in the air—but I never let my career dominate my family life. I never worked in the office late in the evenings or weekends, although occasionally this involved making professional sacrifices.

My true love, my ruling passion, was being an author. Although my day-to-day job was in the Hughes laboratory, I used that time to learn, test and implement my theories. Most of the time I felt that I had to hide my mathematical side—the work environment at the time favored practical engineer types over egghead mathematician types.

Once a close colleague told me, "Andy, nobody ever knows what's on your mind."

That was because I was never interested in solely being a professional man. My goal was to always develop and apply my intellect. Thus, the story of my professional life isn't only about the sequence of jobs I held, but how I used those experiences to further my intellectual aspirations.

"What a handsome baby," my father exclaimed. Naturally he could not see my math hump. Here I am at the age of one with my mother, who was thirty-three years old. (1917)

My grandparents on my mother's side and myself (1921).

My family in 1924. The kids from left to right: Pityu (5), myself (8),
and Karcsi (12).

Pityu on the right, myself on the left, in a small wooden cart my
mother used to pull to the side of the Danube where we spent the
days during summer vacations. The sign says: Long live Daddy.
(1924)

I am taking a loathed piano lessen from Kornélia. The lesson killed
my interest in music for thirty years (1924).

"The Three Musketeers" vacationing in Zell-am-Ziller in the Austrian Alps. Karcsi is on the right, Pityu on the left, myself in the center (1925).

Father and the three boys. From left to right: myself, Karcsi, and
Pityu (1927).

Students finishing the lycée in 1934 and their teachers. "We will meet in 1944." I am the second in the third row from the left.

The banquet celebrating our passing the Maturity Exam in 1934. I am on the far right (the only one who does not wear a tie).

My 1938 "Carte d'Identé" in Paris. This document was the life-line
of every refugee in France.

My Hungarian passport enabled me to escape in 1938 to travel to
France and later to America.

My doctorate, received in 1938, was written in Latin, the official
language of Hungary until the revolution of 1848. Academia is slow
to change.

Taking time off from my kitchen duties at the Quaker Retreat
(1941).

The Baroness Laura Vladimirovna Saparova before she became Mrs. Andrew Vazsonyi in 1942.

Relaxing with one-year-old Bobbi. Before I went on my lifelong diet and exercise regime (1949).

Explaining the Gozinto theorem to Hughes executives (1953).

MODEL

for a

SOLUTION

--------→ *Today the trend is strong toward increasing use of mathematical solutions to complex problems of business and industrial management.*

On such problem of long standing is that of determining parts requirements to meet given shipping schedules. This involves processes of listing and scheduling the many components that go up any complicated assembled product.

At HUGHES this problem was recognized and studied as part of a continuing program of research in advanced management sciences. The result was development of a mathematical model formulating the problem with the aid of a single matrix equation, as follows:

$$[X] = \frac{[I]}{[I] - [N]} [S]$$

key:

[I]   Unit matrix
[N]   Next assembly quantity matrix
[S]   Shipping requirement matrix
[X]   Total parts requirement matrix

Dr. Andrew Vazsonyi, Head of Business Applications Section, Advanced Electronics Laboratory, discusses use of the matrix equation with Raymond H. Peterwest (extreme right), Vice President in charge of Electronics Manufacturing Division, Joseph Frederick (left), Production Manager Dr. D. R. Swanson (center), member of Technical Staff.

BUSINESS
APPLICATIONS
SPECIALISTS

Hughes activities in the field described here are creating some new positions. Required are scientists with advanced educational backgrounds, and experience or interest in business, to apply their talents to the solving of business management problems.

This equation allows computation of parts requirements from the shipping schedule. The vast amount of computations to be carried through in applying this formula to produce computing thousands of parts requires new types of electronic digital computers.

The Hughes electronic equipment to fill this need, specifically designed for such business data processing, will afford solution to an area of complex control problems now facing business and industry.

Scientific and Engineering Staff **HUGHES**

RESEARCH AND DEVELOPMENT LABORATORIES

Culver City, Los Angeles County, California

Assurance is required that relocation of the applicant will not cause disruption of an urgent military project.

LA R-307 ~ 7" x 10" ~ Trade Magazines, 1954 ~ 9

Hughes advertising the Gozinto theorem in 1953.

Paul Erdös said: "Sam and Joe went up the hill." Bobbi, my daughter, corrected him. "No, Erdös, Jack and Jill went up the hill." Tommy and Judy are the epsilons of my Hungarian mathematician friend Béla Lengyel (Pacific Palisades park in 1954).

The thirty-nine-year-old industrial tycoon relaxing on the Santa
Monica Palisades (1955).

"Get well" card from my co-workers at North American Aviation in 1966. The picture refers to the diagnosis of my illness by my physician Dr. Thomas L. Stern.

After mastering the art of skiing in the basement, I am ready for the great cross-country race in Rochester (1972).

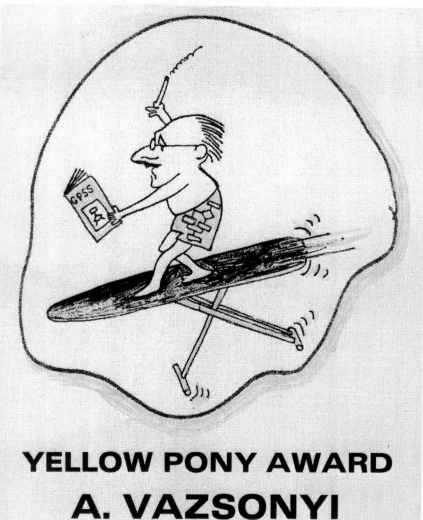

YELLOW PONY AWARD
A. VAZSONYI

Students at the University of Rochester gave me the "Yellow Pony Award" in 1975. Surfing on the ironing board refers to simulation.

I used to smoke cigars when I gave talks, lectured to my class, and chaired professional meetings. I finally stopped because the ashes made too many holes in my shirts.

$$\frac{3}{5}$$

$$\frac{7}{10}$$

$$\frac{10}{14} = \frac{5}{7}$$

$$\sqrt{2} = \frac{a}{b} \qquad \left(\sqrt{2}\right)^2 \cdot \sqrt{2} = 2$$

$$\left(\sqrt{2}\right)^2 = 2$$

$$\frac{a^2}{b^2} = 2$$

$$a \quad a$$

$$a^2 = 2b^2 \qquad 6 \qquad 15$$

$$a = 2x \qquad 3$$

$$2x \cdot 2x = 4x^2 \qquad 20 \qquad 30$$

$$4x^2 = 2b^2 \qquad 10$$

$$2x^2 = b^2 \qquad b = 2y$$

$$a = 2x$$

$$b = 2y$$

$$\underline{\mathcal{E}. \mathcal{O}}$$

$\mathcal{O}$ Erdös (p.g o n a.d) explains to
Laura Vázsonyi that $\sqrt{2}$ is irrational
Gainesville Florida 1979 I 13

Paul Erdös explains to Laura that the square root of 2 is irrational
(1979).

Here I am with Carol Latta, executive director of the Decision
Sciences Institute, after being named a Fellow of the Institute
(1981).

Discussing plans with Dean Robert C. Howe at St. Mary's University
at San Antonio, Texas (1982).

My colleague at St. Mary's University, Irwin Goldberg (left) and myself surrounded by four beauties. Compare the way we are holding the girls (1985).

Demonstrating how I practiced plinking in San Antonio (1986).

Paul Erdös delivers his lecture at Trinity College, University of
Cambridge, upon receiving his honorary doctorate (1991).
(Photo of Paul Erdös by George Csicsery from his 1993 documentary
film "N is a Number: A Portrait of Paul Erdös." All rights reserved.)

Cartoonist's vision of myself at a Santa Rosa fair (1994).

Bobbi and myself in the Oakmont hot tub where I get most of my first-hand, verbal information about the world (2000).

12

FALL OF EXACT SCIENCES

o o o o o o o o o o o o o o o o o o o o o o o o o o o o o o

The most decisive conceptual event of twentieth century physics has been the discovery that the world is not deterministic.

—Ian Hacking, in The Taming of Chance, 1990.

I was feeling pretty smug about my book *Scientific Programming in Business and Industry* and about my role as a contributor to the decision sciences, when suddenly I got a whack on the head that changed everything.

It was around 1956. I was having lunch with Ron Howard of Stanford University, an up-and-coming guru of decision making. I knew Ron from the summer he did some inventory control work for me while he was still at Stanford working on his Ph.D. His dissertation on dynamic programming and Markov processes—a topic about which I knew nothing—had made quite a stir in academic circles.

Ron started off by asking, "Suppose you play heads-or-tails in a bar with a dubious-looking character. He wins twenty times in a row, tossing heads each time. What do think his twenty-first toss will be?"

"The track record has nothing to do with it," I said. "So the probability of tossing heads is one in two." I said it with confidence, relying on good old statistical probability.

"You obviously don't know anything about gambling in bars, subjective probability and predicting the future," said Ron. Did I forget to add that he was also known for his directness?

"The twenty-first toss will very likely be heads because this character is cheating."

I retreated with somewhat hurt feelings, but later thought a bit more about this particular coin toss. Naturally, I assumed fairness on the part of the coin flipper, so I had looked only at the simple probability question involved. But in a real game, after ten or twenty tosses, surely I would have suspected that the game was rigged. In fact, if I was playing against my brother-in-law, Judson, an amateur card shark and practical joker, I might have thought something was up after the first ten tosses.

This was my wake-up call to look deeper into the subject of *subjective probability,* which I came to know as future-oriented probability, or personal probability. This meant that as the events leading up to a certain conclusion change, so does the probability of the future outcome change. If I'm asked, before the first coin toss, to figure out the probability of flipping a coin thirty times and getting heads each time, I might answer it one way. But if I'm asked after twenty tosses—and after seeing the coin come up heads each time—then I definitely should reconsider my answer in light of this new information.

At the time, this concept of subjective probability was quite alien for a person like me, a refugee from the cut-and-dried world of pure math and engineering. It introduced a new way of looking at the world and making choices. As someone who thought math was the skeleton key that opened all doors, I knew I had to explore the subject further, either to reject it as academic nonsense, or accept it and make it part of my one-size-fits-all key.

◆   ◆   ◆

While working in the physical sciences, I always believed in the philosophy of determinism, which says, quite simply, that the present state of the universe is caused by events leading up to it. The element of chance doesn't really figure into the deterministic scheme of things. A true determinist would not admit chance and random events as causes in his analysis. He would blame uncertainty on lack of knowledge.

Of course, humans have always known that the future is shaky. But rather than let that uncertainty get the best of them, most ancient cultures built a solid place for uncertainty in their belief systems. The Greeks and Romans had the goddess of chance, Fortuna, who was known to be rather capricious in the way she handed out good and ill fortune. Not surprisingly, Fortuna often appeared wearing a blindfold, which meant that if you were on the receiving end of bad luck, you shouldn't take it too personally. (Perhaps the modern equivalent of this is the bumper sticker that says, "Shit Happens.")

Just as Fortuna stood for uncertainty, chance and probability, Apollo was the god of prophecy—in other words, god of the sure thing. Apollo came by his powers because he was the well-connected son of Zeus, the powerful patriarch who ruled over all in Olympus. Luckily for humans, Apollo was more accessible than Fortuna—you could reach him on a dedicated line via his oracle at Delphi, or by the gift of prophecy that he occasionally handed out to deserving mortals. Through Apollo, many Greeks and Romans felt they could control their fate by prayer, offerings and the predictions of soothsayers—the ancient equivalent of today's psychics, astrologers and stockbrokers.

The philosopher who laid a solid groundwork for future determinists was Baruch Spinoza, who in 1677 wrote his famous expression, "Nature abhors a vacuum." In other words, there must be a reason for all things. If you find out what led up to the existence of something, then you'll know with certainty what that thing is. Chance has nothing to do with it.

Pierre Laplace (1749–1827), the great French astronomer and mathematician, epitomized the deterministic spirit when he wrote in his *Philosophical Essay on Probabilities*:

> If a superior intellect in any given moment knew all the facts that animate Nature, this intellect could condense into a single formula the movement of all the bodies of the universe. For such an intel-

lect nothing could be uncertain, and the future just like the past would be known.

This sums up the view of the world that many mathematicians and scientists, including myself, inherited from our academic forbears. The more I started thinking about it, however, I realized we were acting out the same primitive fears that humans have always felt when facing the unknown. Modern people are desperate to understand and discover the reason behind seemingly random events in their lives so they can have more control of their environment. Pick up the newspaper and you'll find a crew of analysts and pundits trying to explain why something happened the way it did. Flip to the business section and you'll see quickly how many people make a good living by explaining yesterday's erratic ups and downs of the Dow Jones average, but fail to predict the future.

The result of all this personal inquiry was that I deliberately began to include chance and probability in my professional and personal life. I even found a counterpart to Spinoza who could guide me.

Blaise Pascal was a seventeenth-century mathematician, physicist and philosopher who may have been the first person to actually measure probability and chance. It was Pascal who proved in a celebrated math case that an honest person would need to throw a pair of dice twenty-five times to have an even chance of getting a six on both dice. Pascal also laid the foundation for modern risk analysis by noting that, "Fear of harm ought to be proportional not merely to the gravity, but also to the probability of the event." He gave as an example the probability of getting hit by lightning, which is small, but noted that "many are excessively terrified when they hear thunder."

◆   ◆   ◆

Psychological tests have shown that small children and adults in some cultures have no sense of probability. For example, when they have a choice between two chances in ten or two in five, they show no preference for the latter. It's a difficult subject to master—one isn't born with the ability to perform calculations with probability. Over the years, I applied what I learned about probability until I was fairly comfortable with it—comfortable enough to make a recommendation on treating a medical problem that I was facing.

In 1946, while working at Jeannette in the Pittsburgh area, I became allergic to ragweed. I suffered terrible hay fever with runny nose, congestion, sneezing and the threat of asthma. Laura tried to help me by keeping the rooms extra clean, washing the floor and the walls, and keeping a "clean room" in which to sleep, but the only result was that I was driving her crazy. I took many shots, some intravenous, but nothing helped. Finally, when we moved to Los Angeles a year later, my symptoms disappeared. To my great delight, I learned that ragweed doesn't grow in Los Angeles.

Now let's fast forward twenty-five years. In 1972 I landed a tenured professorship in management and computers at the University of Rochester in New York, and we moved back to the East Coast. Prior to the move, I consulted a specialist in California who tested me for allergies. He concluded that I was still sensitive. Because I would arrive in Rochester at the height of the ragweed season, I started a six-month program of shots to build up my resistance.

After the move to Rochester, I was fine. But I was still under the doctor's orders to continue monthly shots; he shipped the serum to a local doctor who poked me with the needle. To make matters worse, whenever I traveled during the time of the month when I needed a shot, I had to pack the serum in a thermos, store it in a refrigerator wherever I was staying and search for a doctor to administer it. The whole ordeal lessened my hay fever symptoms, but made me feel like a drug addict. Nevertheless, I didn't dare stop taking the shots because I was afraid of the consequences.

Finally, after three years of this, I went to see the department head at the university's medical school and asked for his advice. After hearing the particulars of my case, Dr. Smith, as I'll call him, felt that I should continue taking the shots. In his opinion, scratch tests for allergies were not accurate enough to predict if I was still sensitive to ragweed. Also, since I was doing well with the shots, he didn't see any reason to quit.

I wasn't satisfied with his conclusions, however, so I began to think like a decision scientist.

"Sounds like I have two alternatives," I said. "Either I continue taking hay fever shots or I don't. If I discontinue, I may continue being sensitive or I may have no reaction. What are my chances of having no reaction?"

He said he didn't know. All he knew was that I was sensitive in the past.

"Based on that," I said, "let's make it fifty-fifty. Fifty percent probability that I'm sensitive and fifty percent probability that I'm fine."

"If you put it like that, I'd say it's more likely that you're not sensitive, probably more like a 30 percent chance."

"And if I am reactive, what's the chance of a severe reaction like I had before?"

"Probably one in three," he said. "But that's just a guess."

"What's the treatment in each case?" I asked.

"If you have a light reaction, I'll give you a few antihistamine pills and build up your resistance over three months. If it's more severe, you'll get a series of shots over a period of three to six months."

As he said this, I was doing the math in my head. "So the probability of a severe reaction is two times one in three," I said, "which equals one in nine, or a little more than ten percent."

He looked at me kind of funny. "Are you sure? You multiplied the one in three chances—aren't you supposed to add them?"

"Trust me," I said. "You're the doctor, I'm the decision specialist. And I believe I can risk a ten percent chance of discontinuing the treatments, getting a severe reaction and a three to six months treatment."

He hemmed and hawed, shook his head, then finally deferred to me, the senior professor colleague. As it turned out, three months later I showed no sensitivity to ragweed and would never again need allergy shots. And I was thrilled because I actually used decision sciences to make an important choice about my health.

◆   ◆   ◆

Because of my pure math and engineering background, it was hard for me to understand that probability is multi-faceted, both statistical and subjective, just like Janus, the Roman god with two faces looking in opposite directions.

Public opinion polls, for example, use statistical probability. Before the vote, pollsters may learn that 55 percent of voters are opposed to Proposition 205, with 5 percent confidence. Yet, the proposition could still easily pass because the poll measures only what people thought when questioned—that is, what they planned to do. Thus, the probability would be high that they would vote against the proposition, but not certain. How high? Nobody knows; it is subjective probability. Polls do not take into account how people change their minds at the last minute. The expression "5 percent confidence" is confusing.

Dr. Smith did not make a statistical study for the probability that I was sensitive to ragweed. He did not think the data was significant. He guessed. He formed an opinion by using subjective probability.

Subjective probability comes closer to dealing with the fluctuation of personal beliefs and opinions. It measures an individual's state of mind—which hardly seems scientific, but that's life. It is more like when the physician asks you to rate your pain on a scale of one to ten. On statistical probability there are no disagreements, but subjective probability is strictly a personal opinion.

For instance, you could be sightseeing in New York City and decide to visit the roof of the Empire State Building. You arrive early in the morning before the visitors' platform opens and stand in the growing line of tourists. By counting the people in line, you figure you'll be going up on elevator 5.

But wait. The loudmouth guy behind you is explaining to his cousin from Des Moines that there are problems with the elevators. It seems they frequently get stuck. So now you wonder about the probability of elevator 5 becoming disabled.

Of course, you tell yourself not to worry. The guy is probably just showing off. A big tourist attraction like the Empire State Building wouldn't have crummy elevators. Surely you'll reach the top on elevator 5. In your mind you have an imaginary *histogram*, the statistical evidence of the past, that says elevator failures are extremely unlikely.

Then the first elevator starts up and, behold, it gets stuck. You hear the emergency bell ringing away in the shaft.

Now what do you think about the probability of a smooth ride in elevator 5?

Especially with the loudmouth guy behind you saying, "See, I told you so. Happens all the time."

Still, you're not worried. Not until you see that elevators 2 through 4 have developed problems and have stopped moving.

At this point, you quickly revise the probability of elevator 5 breaking down and take off for the next stop on the sightseeing tour.

Has there been any actual change in elevator 5 from the moment you stepped in line until now? That is, has the mechanical or electrical equipment in the elevator been altered in any way? No. The only thing that changed was your mind—subjective probability represents the state of mind that you use to predict the future. Because of new information, you changed your opinion of the future. Your new opinion combines your past history with elevators and the current breakdown of elevators 1 through 4, as well as the loudmouth guy behind you.

But let's add another twist. Suppose your partner accompanies you and persuades you to stay and ride elevator 5. It works fine and soon you're standing high over Manhattan. Who made the better decision, you or your significant other? Guess what? There's no way to tell.

◆   ◆   ◆

When I worked in the exact sciences, answers were either right or wrong. But with subjective probability, you couldn't always say for sure. The good decision maker was the one with a good track record—which, come to think of it, is based only on past performance. It's still anyone's guess how good the next decision will be.

Part of me still wanted to put decision making on a more scientific basis. All my life I believed that the right principle could be empirically verified—I had faith in Newton's law for that reason. As I sorted out the issues involving probability, I wondered if in the future I would need to use principles that were contrary to my fundamental scientific outlook.

I also wondered if I could discover a unified philosophy that would help guide me through both my professional and personal choices.

In 1956 I was first alerted to the importance of chance, but it took many years before it had an impact on me. In my first book, *Scientific Programming in Business and Industry*, there was no mention of it. Today it has a dominant role in my work.

Many people I know are slow to adapt to the new view and want to believe that there is a "reason" for everything. There have been some changes. Insurance is an example of managing chance. Buying index funds in the stock market is an admission of the fact that the price of stock is dominated by chance.

When health care issues became critical, the following story in different versions attracted much attention.

Consider the fictitious situation of Clarence, a foreign student who is worried about contracting AIDS. Ten percent of the folks in his township are HIV-positive, and so the chance that he is HIV-positive is 10 percent. Clarence wants to know for sure and goes to a clinic to have a test. The test, which has a "90% reliability," turns out to be positive. He is, of course, devastated. But his professor, who once took a course on decision analysis in the U.S., says that the situation may not be so catastrophic, because his calculations show that the probability of Clarence being HIV-positive is only 0.5.

This story caused quite a furor in the press, and acrimonious arguments followed. The mathematical analysis was not available (and would have been incomprehensible to most, anyway) and many thought the result was ridiculous. They did not realize that the so-called "reliability" of the test referred to the probability that if someone is HIV-positive then the test will discover it, and not to the probability of someone being HIV-positive, a subtle, but most important, distinction.

◆   ◆   ◆

Around 1990, chaos theory hit the general public with the message that minor events can cause catastrophic troubles. We were told about the "butterfly" principle, according to which a little girl catching a butterfly in Bombay could trigger an El Nino in Texas.

Like other mathematicians, engineers and computer users, I was aware that small changes can lead to large problems. Also, that scientists and the general public need to be careful with such "critical points." But the advantage of chaos theory is that it called attention to the general public of this important fact of life.

This famous anonymous poem sums it up:

For want of nail
the shoe was lost,
For want of shoe
the horse was lost,
For want of a horse
the rider was lost,
For want of rider
the battle was lost,
For want of winning

the kingdom was lost.
And all for the want
of a horse shoe nail.

The columnist Dave Barry referred to the year 2000 as "The Year of the Chad" (Press Democrat, 12/31/00). Who could have predicted that these small pieces of paper would contribute so much to the election of George W. Bush as president of the U.S?

An unknown wit pointed out the approach we must take for dealing with uncertainty. He added a comment to Ecclesiastes, 9:11–12:

> I returned and saw under the sun, that the race is not to the swift, nor the battle to the strong, neither yet bread to the wise, nor riches to men of understanding, nor yet favor to men of all skills: but time and chance happeneth to all…
>
> But there's where I lay my dough.

Looking back, I must admit that it took me a great deal of trouble to move from a deterministic outlook to a point of view that accepted uncertainty. But the effort was undeniably worthwhile in that I developed a better strategy for dealing with the world.

13

ENCOUNTERS OF THE THIRD KIND

As I began to work more closely with probability theory, I could feel myself stepping away from the mindset of the exact sciences and moving toward subjects that the traditional outlook didn't considered scientific. In the process, I felt a little wobbly because I was leaving behind heroes who had given me so much support over the years—Erdös in math, and von Kármán and Howard Emmons in engineering. Fortunately, I soon found a new hero to support my efforts.

I ran into Herb Simon on the beach of Santa Monica in 1950, where we both happened to be swimming and frolicking. At the time, he was a psychologist at the Carnegie Institute of Technology and was hired by the RAND Corporation to look into forecasting theories for a paint factory. During a long conversation, Simon caught my attention when he suggested an idea that was quite different from the typical linear programming approach. After I told him of a mathematical direction I was trying, he confessed that he was no mathematician but was intrigued by the different tack. I walked away feeling very impressed by him.

We became friends and I followed his career over the years, which was highlighted by his receiving the Nobel Prize in economics in 1978. He died February 10, 2001, at the age of eighty-four.

Simon's 1969 book, *The Sciences of the Artificial*, made a big impression on me. Using straightforward language, he described how humans live in an artificial world (the subject of decision sciences in my lingo) that often affects their lives more than the natural world (the subject of the exact sciences). For instance, a dramatic change in interest rates (the artificial world) has more impact on society than does a hurricane (the natural world).

Simon also thought of cognitive science as "the domain of inquiry that seeks to understand intelligent systems and the nature of intelligence." Just as the world can be divided into the natural and artificial, intelligent systems include natural (biological) and artificial (computer-based) systems. In one stroke, Simon gave greater legitimacy to the theory and practice of decision making, and such action-oriented goals as improving production, management and educational programs.

Another powerful argument that Simon advanced in his book was that because individuals are limited in finding information and performing calculations, researchers should accept *satisficing solutions*, using *bounded rationality*. In other words, we shouldn't waste all our time trying to find the optimal (perfect) answer when what we really need is an answer that works.

After this groundbreaking work, Simon kept publishing important articles and books such as *The Shape of Automation, The New Science of Management Decisions, and Scientific Discovery and Reason in Human Affairs*. To me and plenty of others, Herb Simon was the Isaac Newton of cognitive science.

His work provided me with a framework for my journey in the decision sciences. My math fit in perfectly with Simon's artificial world, which dealt with everyday objects and situations that individuals found themselves in. But rather than call my new math "artificial math"—by the way, Simon's use of "artificial" never caught on—I coined the term "real-life mathematics."

My work was cut out for me. In order to help myself and others get control of their lives, I needed to learn how to form practical hypotheses and derive heuristics (that is, rules of thumb that make sense even if they're not scientifically proven).

What I also needed, before I could apply real-life math, was a clearer understanding of how people make decisions. I needed to find out how people received information, how they looked at the future, appraised consequences, made choices and balanced logic with emotion. I needed to discover which heuristics they used, and which ones they should be using.

To help me in my quest, I began carefully reading the daily newspapers, *The Wall Street Journal*, popular magazines and many self-help books. I was astounded at how much useful information was out there.

◆   ◆   ◆

Using the hypothesis that the world is uncertain, confusing and chaotic, I started developing practical heuristics for myself that use probability theory. Once I accepted these probabilities, I found that my life became more pleasant, less stressful. (The following examples are revised to be more in keeping with the spirit of the times.)

- When I turn on my computer, the probability that it will work is high but not certain.

- When I telephone a business that answers with a pre-recorded menu of options, the probability is low that I will ever hear a real human voice.

- When I visit a doctor, there is a low probability that my stay in the waiting room will be brief, but a high probability that I will receive the correct treatment.

- When I buy a new gadget, there is a low probability that I can follow the instructions to make it work on the first go around.

- When I imagine all the bad things that can happen to me, there is a low probability that they will ever occur.

While we're at it, let me also include my life-time heuristics for decision making:

a. Spend an inordinate amount of time listing possible actions.

b. Spend an inordinate amount of time evaluating the consequences of each.

c. Based on the above, select the most desirable, satisfying action.

◆   ◆   ◆

In the exact sciences, we can predict next month's sunrise with great accuracy, next month's tides with less accuracy and next week's weather with little, if any, accuracy. (While the laws of weather forecasting are known, the data isn't manageable.)

In the artificial sciences, however, we don't want to predict the future as much as bend it to our benefit. We want to plan—apply feedback to our environment—so that we can take hold of our lives. And we want to do this in spite of all the other individuals trying to bend the future to their own benefit.

Can math help us make a decision that provides the best consequence in the future?

When my hero Benjamin Franklin wrote a letter to a friend in 1772 describing his *moral and prudential algebra*, he was doing exactly that. He admitted that he did not know enough of his friend's problem, but he could offer *general* advice on how to make a decision. He recommended using pros and contras, and invented what later became known as tradeoff analysis and the balance sheet approach. He was some 150 years ahead of his time.

But the first decisive step for linking math and decision making came in 1928 when John von Neumann wrote a paper that dealt with mathematical games. He described games in which players handled economic and sociological issues with the aid of the theory of expected utility. His *MiniMax* theorem gave specific advice regarding what the players must do under very restricted assumptions. Game theory was born.

In 1944 von Neumann and Oscar Morgenstern published the *Theory of Games and Economic Behavior*, which created a sensation throughout the scientific and popular communities. By the time I became involved in the '50s, game theory had become an important part of the artificial sciences. The availability of computers gave a huge boost to the field.

About the same time that the technique of *simulation* started to become popular, it became my time machine. In my version of H.G. Wells' device, I could create different scenarios each time I rode into the future. The model I preferred was similar to the one Stanley G. Weinbaum wrote about in his science fiction novel *The Worlds of IF*. This model could reveal the conditional world of IF: If you had done such and such, so and so would have happened. Like Scrooge in Dicken's *A Christmas Carol*, I could see alternate futures and do something about them. Each future, however, was an uncertain, fluctuating entity. That way, even if I began my travel with the same assumptions, each time I ventured out I found new scenarios.

With my computer, I could now play simulation games against the Goddess Fortuna. I could make choices, and the computer would display the consequences. I could play the game many times, view alternate scenarios and allow variations due to uncertainty and probabilities, and the computer would automatically keep statistics on the consequences. After many trials and errors, I could find the best-looking action. (In 2000, I published a popular textbook with two coauthors about doing simulation with Microsoft Excel.)

In the 1960s Herb Simon started to use von Neumann's utility theory with a twist. He assumed that the probabilities were subjective and called this the theory of subjective expected utility (SEU). None of the equations changed, but the new interpretation of probability brought the theory closer to real life.

For example, assume you participate in a raffle and you have two choices. You can win a trip to Hawaii or the Himalayas. You prefer Hawaii. Would you take that option?

You may recall Pascal saying, "Fear of harm ought to be proportional not merely to the gravity, but also to the probability of the event." You search your mind and find that on a scale of 10, you estimate the desirability (utility) of Hawaii to be 8 and the Himalayas to be 5. But you think too many people will choose this option and the chances of winning are low. How low? You don't know; the raffle people themselves don't know how many tickets they've sold. But you think that the subjective probability of Hawaii is 0.2 and that of the Himalayas is 0.8. The SEU theory advises you to calculate the products for

Hawaii—8*0.8=.64
Himalayas—5*0.2=1.0

and select the higher value, that is the Himalayas. The equations are the same as of the classical utility theory; the interpretation of probabilities is not statistical but subjective.

This is only *advice* because, after all, no theory can mandate what you should do. However, this is a standard that your decisions ought to measure up to, and something to be aware of when you do not accept the SEU recommendation. This technique is particularly useful when you are faced with many alternatives.

◆   ◆   ◆

Herb Simon also helped me see another important side of decision making—creativity. I had always felt strongly that creativity was something you were born with, not something you could be taught. In the 1980s, when I heard that more than half of Fortune 500 companies were requiring creativity training, I thought this was perfect nonsense. Then Simon changed my mind.

In his book *Scientific Discovery, Computational Exploration of the Creative Process,* he and his coauthors presented a computer program called BACON that could discover many laws of nature. For example, after the data was input, this artificial intelligence software discovered the three laws of Kepler, Ohm's law, Coulomb's law and many others. I couldn't believe it, but after I saw the math, I could no longer deny it—given enough information, a computer program could devise a highly creative solution.

If a computer could learn to be creative, then perhaps so could humans. I already knew some of the rules of brainstorming from Alex Osborn, the founder of creativity training:

- The wilder the idea, the better.
- Abolish the word "no" from your opening discussions; wear a Green Hat, reminding yourself of the "go" street light.
- Quantity of ideas breeds quality of ideas.
- If it ain't broke, break it.
- Seek many new combinations.
- Defer judgment on ideas until a later time.

I soon learned that the creativity training people had a large bag of tricks to enhance creativity while making decisions. After trying many of their methods and finding them quite handy, I came to believe that while in the exact sciences I must operate by the laws of nature, in the sciences of the artificial I needed a bunch of practical heuristics. So I collected many of them and used them until they became second nature.

- Spend more time searching for alternatives using Green Hat thinking.
- Balance the probabilities of the good and bad consequences of the alternatives.

- Know how to turn the decision into action.

- Prepare contingency plans if things go wrong.

Working on these, revising them over the years, dropping some and adding others became a life-long effort.

During the last quarter of the 20th century an avalanche of books and articles appeared that dealt with human affairs in a quantitative manner. I diligently studied and tried to assimilate these outlooks into my mode of living. The more philosophical and increasingly scientific concepts transformed my professional and even personal life. I was emulating my hero Benjamin Franklin, who applied his "virtues" to his day-to-day life, though it wasn't always easy. As Franklin admitted: "[T]his mode, which I first put on with some violence to natural inclination, became at length natural...."

14

MARKETING ADVENTURES

In 1954, as a result of an irrevocable rift between my bosses and Howard Hughes, Drs. Si Ramo and Dean Wooldridge quit and founded the Ramo-Wooldridge Corporation (RW). Hughes tried to convince them to stay, but lost out. After the experience, Hughes said that he learned something about scientists: "They are like sheep—they follow the leader." And he was right; many of us followed suit.

RW was financed by Thompson Products, Inc. of Cleveland, an automotive parts manufacturer that had serious troubles running its factory. They contracted RW to straighten out the mess, and RW put me in charge of a consulting group to take care of the situation. I built up a group of 25 people for what would become my largest consulting job. It took us a year to straighten out their production control system, but by then their sales had dropped and they cancelled the contract.

Dr. Wooldridge thought that we should keep the group together and find other consulting jobs. However, we weren't financially successful and, logistically, we weren't a great fit as part of an electronic firm. Finally, in 1958, RW decided to disband my group and offered me an engineering job. But I had different ideas.

I felt confident that I knew enough about production and that the time had come to broaden my outlook. I figured the best way to continue my work as a management advisor would be as a consultant involved with marketing. Everything I read suggested that this field was of great importance to business.

While marketing research was widely accepted in the U.S., however, it was still viewed skeptically in other parts of the world.

I remember talking with Paul Turan in the 1950s. Paul was a noted Hungarian mathematician and a personal friend. "In a socialist country like Hungary, your work in marketing would not be tolerated," he said. "It would be seen as counterproductive—as a capitalist waste of effort."

The truth is, as a young math student in Hungary, I might have agreed with that point of view. Our country was poor and had problems simply producing goods, with little time or energy left for frills like marketing.

Of course, as a newly christened American businessman, I could only marvel at marketing's range and power. But Turan wouldn't hear a word of it until I brought up the subject of shoes, my father's trade. At this, Turan immediately began praising the excellent shoes he bought in America and how it was absolutely impossible to get shoes that would fit him in Hungary. In fact, it was a national scandal that Hungarian warehouses were overflowing with shoes that people couldn't use.

As I told Turan, it all came down to marketing. Communist party leaders thought of marketing only in terms of advertising and sales. They ignored the bigger picture, in which marketing tells manufacturers what consumers want and which innovations they are most likely to accept. For shoe makers, marketing research develops knowledge on the shape of people's feet so that manufacturers won't waste time making useless shoes. This kind of information is invaluable when competing against rival products and services. But in Hungary the government had set up strict quotas for manufacturing shoes without ever finding out what kind of shoes the people wanted.

But Turan wouldn't listen to me. He believed that the leaders of Hungary knew best and marketing was just a trick to make bigger profits. In his opinion, communists and socialists were idealists who meant to love all people and wanted to do good for them. Production was the essence of well being.

◆   ◆   ◆

In 1958, I was looking around for a consulting job when I renewed an acquaintance with someone I had met at the Quaker workshop in Haverford, Pennsylvania, during my first year in the U.S. Roe Alderson now had a marketing consulting business in Philadelphia. After learning of my work in management science, he offered me a partnership in his Philadelphia firm.

At the time, marketing seemed contrary to my "classical" European outlook and math experience—and that's probably what I found so appealing about it. After I accepted Roe's offer, I wasted no time in digging deeper into the subject, as well as related studies in psychology and sociology.

Maybe I was crazy to jump jobs like that. My friends had serious doubts about the move from California to Pennsylvania. After all, my family had spent twelve good years on the West Coast, long enough to wonder if there was life beyond California. But Laura felt differently. She never got used to the "lack of culture" in California, and while Philadelphia wasn't Boston, it was close enough. Bobbi was going into the fourth grade and we didn't think the move would be detrimental to her. As far as keeping my professional contacts with colleagues in the Institute of Management Sciences (TIMS), it meant less time spent on airplanes getting to meetings in the East.

◆   ◆   ◆

One of my first big tests as a marketing consultant was with the Seagram Company Ltd., a multibillion company and leading manufacturer and distributor of distilled liquor. At the corporate office, located in a bronze-and-steel skyscraper in Manhattan, the 32-year old president, Mr. Edgar (Edgar Bronfman, son of Mr. Sam, Samuel Bronfman), wanted us to help them find a way to make higher profits selling vodka. At the time, they were selling their vodka at the same low price as their competitors, and no one was making a decent profit. Unlike fine Scotch and bourbon, vodka was generally perceived as having no taste of its own. So it was difficult to convince the public that Seagram's vodka tasted better than the other brands.

As for pricing the vodka higher or lower than its competition, I knew from my studies of economics that as the price of goods increases, the demand decreases. I believed then—as many people still do—that the way you price a product is to add a markup to the production cost. A "fair profit" was a reasonable markup that didn't gouge the consumer. In my first months as a marketing consultant, I learned all this was wrong.

To begin with, "cost" is an accounting fiction. You price your product according to what the market will bear and still lets you beat out the competition. The relationship between production expenses and markup is practically nonexistent. There is no such thing as a "fair profit" in business. There is, however, such as thing as public opinion.

What tipped me off about the importance of opinion was Seagram's experience in selling its Four Roses brand of whisky. When Seagram decreased its price, the demand for the whisky decreased as well. The reason was obvious. People didn't buy Four Roses for its taste alone, but for its prestige—they wanted to impress their guests. When the price of Four Roses went down, so did its prestige.

Based on this, I proposed that Seagram increase the price of its vodka. At the same time, I recommended that they begin a new ad campaign promoting their brand's elegance and sophistication. The strategy worked like a charm—both sales and profits skyrocketed.

Years later, I received a related economics lesson while telling a colleague in economics that I had just bought some stock because I heard there would be a split forthcoming. "That's the trouble," he said. "According to economic theory, there is no reason for the price of a stock to go up when there is a split. But ignorant people like you, buying for the wrong reason, make the price rise and ruin economic theory."

◆   ◆   ◆

Our stay in Philadelphia began on a bumpy note. At the first hotel we checked into, Bobbi, now eight years old, refused to sleep in her bed because the springs were "floating." Being an obedient and somewhat indulgent father, I found us another room at the Sheraton, where the bedsprings were more to my daughter's liking. The next morning, to Bobbi's great delight, we looked out the window and it was snowing. To her it was a new treat, but to us it meant a quick hike through the "catacombs" (that is, underground walkways) of Philadelphia to winterize ourselves with coats, gloves and boots from a nearby department store.

Within days, we found accommodations at the Chetwynd Apartments in Rosemont, which was on the Main Line, a proper suburban commute from the office in downtown Philly. Like my neighbors, I learned to keep the new Oldsmobile in the garage while I walked to the rail station, boarded the train for the 25-minute ride into the city, exited the underground station, stepped on the elevator that rose thirty floors to my office—and reversed the sequence for the trip home.

Our new life in Philadelphia also reminded me that social classes were still alive and well in the U.S.—though not as bad as in Boston where "the Lowells speak only to the Cabots, and the Cabots only to God." At the Chetwynd Apartments, we were surrounded by genteel old ladies who were driven to the market by their chauffeurs. Once there, the drivers did double duty by pushing the shopping carts. As recent arrivals and Californians to boot, we were made fully aware that we wouldn't be accepted in a hundred years. Bobbi did manage to find a best friend on the second floor whose mother was a nurse. They walked to school together and spent hours twirling hula hoops and watching "American Bandstand" on TV.

The Chetwynd Apartments were built on a hill, and we had a charming view of the rolling woods from our ninth floor windows. During the winter, we gathered to watch a steep, icy road a few miles away. Cars would gain speed on the downhill slope to build momentum to climb the next hill. Then they would stop just shy of the top, and the drivers would have to turn around to make another attempt. Most of them crested the hill after a few tries, and we would applaud their success.

When a real snowstorm hit Philadelphia, the city practically closed down. We would hole up in our apartment, where tenants would throw open their doors and have a party. During one particular storm, Bobbi and I made the silly decision to go to the movies. We trudged down to the railroad station and, after a long wait, boarded an emergency train. We exited at the next stop where the theater was located and hiked through the snow, only to find the cinema closed. So we returned home, weary but in good spirits.

While in Philadelphia, I was happy to become reacquainted with the Quaker tradition and their quaint use of "thou" and "thee." Bobbi went to the excellent Quaker school for a while where she learned to recite the books of the Bible, sing the Lord's Prayer and make candles. Roe, my new business partner, was an elder in the Quaker establishment. I was still a non-believer, but I enjoyed sitting in the meeting house on Sunday mornings, waiting for someone to be moved by the spirit into standing up and making a declaration. My favorite activity came after the meeting when Roe would invite me back to his house for a drink of Beefeater's gin.

During the summer we swam in the apartment pool and on some weekends we went to the "shore" (not the "beach," as we called it in California). Roe had a summer place on Chesapeake Bay ("Unlike Home") and a motor boat that we piled into for long cruises. I remember one time when we anchored far from shore, and both Roe and I dived in to cool off. When it came time to climb back onboard, my overweight business partner couldn't pull himself onto the deck. (One day Roe said to Bobbi, "Little girl, come and sit on my lap." Bobbi took a long hard look and replied, "You don't have a lap.")

Finally, I went underwater below him and, placing my head under his rump, pushed up with all my might. It worked. Of course, as I soon learned, this kind of push and pull between business partners isn't at all uncommon.

◆   ◆   ◆

During my first year in business for myself, the work often involved long hours and heavy personal sacrifices—in my case, time away from my family.

One experience, in particular, stands out. The Thomas Corporation of San Francisco, which made metal parts, was having serious problems with their marketing and production systems. Because Roe was on good terms with their president, we were invited to fly out and make a sales pitch about how we were the answer to all their needs. We spent a great deal of time preparing the proposal—our largest so far—and before we left Roe warned me about two danger spots: one, the vice president of production hated all consultants, especially son-of-a-bitch consultants from the East Coast. And, two, during the presentation I should never mention math or such things as mathematical models.

Our proposal was scheduled for Tuesday at 10:00 a.m., so we worked all day Monday, then spent most of that night in San Francisco fine-tuning our pitch. In the morning we arrived at the plant early, and company personnel escorted us to a private theater where we set up our easels and charts on the stage. Of course, the stage was too formal for our taste, but we didn't have any say in the matter. When nobody showed up by 10:30 a.m., we learned that the presentation was postponed until 2:00 p.m. because the president had to deal with more pressing issues. Unfortunately, another crisis prevented us from meeting until 8:00 p.m.

By then everyone was exhausted, especially me, and I did my best to wrap up early. However, a long, heated discussion followed my pitch. As expected, the vice president of production opposed our plan with every fiber of his body. If not for that, I sensed that the president was ready to give us the nod. So I took a drastic step and began describing, in excruciating detail, a particular math theorem which, though it had nothing to do with their problem, sounded impressive.

As expected, nobody understood a word I was saying. The math even took the wind out of the VP's sails, and the meeting soon concluded on a successful note. Afterwards, I expected to find myself sleeping soundly in a hotel bed, but my partner had different ideas. For the sake of morale and being a good sport (an important asset in business), I went along with the vodka screwdrivers and steak breakfast on the waterfront. Then, at Roe's urging, we returned to the hotel, packed our suitcases and flew back that morning.

When I arrived home in Philadelphia, more dead than alive, I had serious doubts about my future as a marketing consultant. I decided a life that left little time for my family, that would likely lead to a heart attack, wasn't the life for me. Sadly, Roe died of a stroke a few years after I left.

Around the end of 1958, with a recession driving small businesses like ours into the ground, I pulled up stakes and returned with my family to Los Angles, where Ramo-Wooldridge took me back as an engineer. A few years later when RW fell on hard times and my friend and sponsor Dean Wooldridge resigned as president, I went back to North American Aviation for the second time, as an expert control engineer. I considered these to be temporary setbacks and kept my eyes open to get back to decision making.

◆　　◆　　◆

During the whole time that I was delving into marketing, I kept writing my aid-mémoirs and eventually finished a draft of a book on the mathematics of marketing. Part of the book dealt with decision making under uncertainty, which was quite different from my first book's focus on linear programming and decision making under deterministic conditions. Unfortunately, a contractual relationship with a co-author fell through and the book was never published. It wasn't a total loss, however, because I've always felt that learning new things and recording my impressions are the true rewards of writing.

◆　　◆　　◆

One thing about marketing that always stuck with me was how much attention people in that field pay to creativity—perhaps more so than people involved in finance or production. The following story is a good example.

The UNEEDA Corporation manufactures outdoor clothing made of colorful nylon cloth. The president of the corporation—a great believer in Total Quality Control—wages a continuous fight against waste. He wants to eliminate scrap, so he is especially proud of his company's elaborate cutting procedures that minimize leftover cloth.

When a consultant comes along and recommends a sophisticated computer program that will improve the cutting system even more, the president is gung ho. But a young employee at the company has a different idea. Even though he majored in business psychology and knows squat about production, he decides to use his creativity training and apply the *Crovitz relational algorithm*, an esoteric approach that very few people know about.

He looks at jackets and scrap with two simple goals in mind—increase profit and/or decrease costs. So he generates alternate ideas and approaches. (Nowadays he might use a Visual Basic program in Excel.) After looking at a number of alternatives generated by the program, he latches onto the following bizarre sentences:

Jackets after Scrap
Jackets from Scrap
Jackets through Scrap

It sounds crazy, but why not make jackets out of scrap, instead of fighting scraps? Isn't that what his wife does when she uses leftovers to make casseroles? And didn't she tell him about sustainable business when she came home last night from her evening MBA class?

When he proposes the idea to production people, they say he's crazy. But the marketing folks love the idea—it's creative! They make a survey and find that the colorful "scrap jackets" will not only sell, but sell at a premium price. The upshot is that the costly effort of minimizing scrap is scrapped, scrap increases, costs decrease and UNEEDA realizes a significant increase in market share and profit from the sale of the new jackets.

Stories like that and my firsthand experience in marketing expanded my views on management for the rest of my life. Also, as I got older I found that my early business experience—what I picked up from my father and grandfathers—and my efforts at settling my father's estate, reinforced what I was learning.

Another management lesson that made a permanent impression on me were the times when my partner and I had slow months and couldn't meet our payroll. As a result, I had to write personal checks to cover salaries.

The upshot of all these changes were more lessons in growth and humility, as advocated by my hero Benjamin Franklin. I didn't realize how much I had changed until the day I had a conversation with my editor at John Wiley. I was in the middle of proposing a textbook, when he stopped me and said, "Andy, you have totally changed your outlook."

"What do you mean?" I said.

"Well, you just asked me how you can change the text so it would be more acceptable to students. When you wrote your first book you would have said, "That's too bad for the students. They'll just have to learn.""

15

FROM PARIS TO TOKYO

○ ○
Travel, in the younger sort, is a part of education; in the elder
a part of experience.

—Francis Bacon (1561–1626)

It was the kind of moment every penniless refugee dreams of—the moment when you make your triumphant return to the city that witnessed all your hardships and, in the process, taught you more about yourself than you could ever realize at the time.

For me, the city was Paris. The year, 1956. After twelve years in the U.S., I was returning to present a talk on production control to over 300 attendees at the TIMS international meeting at the Sorbonne. Needless to say, I made the most of my opportunity. Before I began my speech, I waited long enough for the Americans to slip off their headsets that they wore to hear the translation of the previous speaker's words and for the French to adjust their headsets as they prepared to hear the interpreter's version of my speech.

Then, to everyone's consternation, I began speaking French—a neat trick for a 1950s-era American businessman. (Of course, I didn't tell anyone that I had begun preparing for this precise moment many months before.) I was chattering along just fine until I came to an expression that I couldn't translate—"but that's not all gravy"—so I slipped into English. (Later, back in the States, someone remarked that this was the most memorable part of my speech.) Throughout my speech, I focused on a pretty girl who sat in the last row knitting a sweater. I remembered from attending a few Toastmasters presentations that speakers should pick out a person in the last row to make eye contact with, so everyone in the crowd will feel your eyes on them. Personally, I believe finding a pretty girl in the last row makes for an even more dynamic speech. Based on her reaction—she stopped knitting to listen to the Amazing French-speaking American with the Hungarian accent—I judged my presentation to be a success.

It was a joy to be back in Paris under these circumstances. The last time I was there, I was a non-person refugee. Now I had my own American family and a career that I could have never imagined for myself back then—I was in charge of a consulting group at Ramo-Wooldridge in Los Angeles, California.

During the days and nights of the conference, I was able to put my previous experience as a Parisian refugee to good use.

For instance, one night a friend and I visited the Crazy Horse Saloon, a famous burlesque club. Unfortunately, the line of people waiting to go inside stretched on for blocks. But rather than quietly take a place in line, I walked up to the doorman and asked in my colloquial French if my companion and I could enter and stand at the bar. He replied, "Certainement." After a few minutes inside, I spoke to a waiter about getting a table, and in no time at all we were sharing a table with two friendly American women.

As for the show itself, it was quite different from the usual American-style burlesque. When the curtain rose, a beautiful young woman stood before the crowd in all her naked glory. Then she slowly pulled on her stockings, undergarments, dress and shoes—in other words, she performed a reverse strip tease. (To the chagrin of my friends, this is the same approach I take when reading math papers: I start at the end and go backwards.)

The champagne flowed freely that night, in fact, more freely than we realized. Because an hour after the American women left for the night, we learned that they had paid the entire drink bill. Needless to say, I received much attention after word spread at the conference about the "Vazsonyi Method" of enjoying the Parisian night life.

My other days in Paris were also filled with memorable moments. My friend Arnold Kauffman, a leading French management scientist, and I visited the Machine Bull Computer Company, where he introduced me to the president. Before I knew it, I was whisked into a big hall with a few hundred people waiting to hear me, the Amazing French-speaking American with the Hungarian accent, give a speech on decision making. Somehow I made it through and was informed later that my lecture was interesting enough to keep people from paying too much attention to my mangling of the French language.

Instead of an honorarium, the computer executives invited me to dinner at the Tour d'Argent, reportedly one of the world's most expensive restaurants at the time. (It's located across from the Notre Dame on Quai de Tournell.) Twelve years earlier, I marveled when I heard that a single lunch there cost more than all of my monthly expenses combined.

While at the conference, I also took time off to be with my cousin, who had helped me during the war years. Fritz had managed to escape the concentration camp by hiding in the country when the Nazis occupied Paris. After the war, he resumed his successful career as a lingerie manufacturer and was currently enjoying his days at his country home in Le Vésinet. When he was busy, I spent time chumming around with his 14-year old son, Alain, who is a successful dentist today.

Alain and I went sightseeing in Paris, took cabs everywhere, rode the Bateau-Mouche on the Seine, visited Napoleon's Mausoleum and the Eiffel Tower—we did all the things I missed when I was a poor refugee waiting for a U.S. visa. One day we walked past the elegant shops on the Rue de La Paix and stopped in front of a jewelry story. In the window was an immense diamond. When Alain refused to believe that it was real, I escorted him inside the store on the pretext that we were wealthy Americans. The owner proudly showed off his prized rock, saying it was only ninety-five thousand American dollars, and offered to let me leave a traveler's check so that I could take the ring to my hotel and show it to my wife. I graciously declined, saying that it might be a waste of time because my wife probably had her heart set on something better.

◆　　　◆　　　◆

Years after my lecture in Paris, people who were in the audience or had heard about my bilingual stunt were still talking about it. Some of them also picked up on a story I told that featured a certain Italian mathematician named Zepartzatt Gozinto. Over the years, it's possible that more people knew of my connection with this Gozinto character than any of my scientific work published in over 100 journal articles and eight textbooks. Let me explain.

Gozinto was born around 1956 during a lecture I gave at the RAND Corporation on the parts requirements problem of production control. The difficulty in this problem is that each assembly requires subassemblies and parts, and each subassembly may require, on its own, more subassemblies and parts. Some parts are required directly by an assembly, some indirectly. Counting the total number of parts required to meet a production schedule is a huge job. However, I was able to solve the problem by using esoteric, complex matrix algebra:

Consider the manufacture of articles A(1), A(2),…and denote by N(i,j) the number of A(i)'s going directly into an A(j). Let S(1), S(2),…denote the sales forecast and let X(1), X(2),…denote the (unknown) parts requirements. Then

. [I]
. $[X] = \dfrac{\quad}{\quad} [S]$
. [I]—[N]

where [N] is the square matrix formed by the N(i,j)'s, [I] is the unit matrix, [S] and [X] are the column matrices formed by the S's and X's.

One of my figures, which illustrated the idea that one part goes into another, was entitled the Gozinto Diagram. At the time, "Gozinto" seemed like a catchy phonetical way of getting this "goes into" point across. But after the presentation, one of my colleagues, George B. Dantzig, considered the father of linear programming, remarked that he had never heard of this mathematician named Gozinto and wondered what university he was associated with.

I pretended to be surprised and thought fast. "You've never heard of the celebrated Italian mathematician Z. Gozinto?"

Dantzig shook his head.

"He's like Paul Erdös in that he travels continuously," I said. "So he's not permanently associated with any university. But you can contact him through me, because we're in touch most of the time."

"I wonder why I've never heard of him," said Dantzig. "What's his first name?"

I was momentarily stumped and said that I didn't know what the initial "Z" stood for. Later, when I returned to my office and shared the story with Bill Cooper and Abraham Charnes (both known for their work in linear programming), Cooper came up with the perfect name: Zepartzatt Gozinto.

From these humble origins, Gozinto reached a large, international audience by the time I mentioned his contributions during my talk at the Sorbonne. Later he was nominated by my good friend and colleague George Kozmetski and myself for membership in TIMS. Once his name was added to the TIMS membership, a steady flow of mail addressed to Z. Gozinto, c/o Vazsonyi, began arriving at my house.

Gozinto was quite prolific during these years. When my book *Scientific Programming in Business and Industry* (Wiley, 1958, pp. 429–438) was published, Gozinto was given his due, as was his magnum opus, "The Problem of Parts Listing: The Gozinto Theorem." Always seeking the academic limelight, he was gratified to see his name appear in the German, Japanese and Russian editions of the book. The Gozinto

Theorem was also published in *Basic Mathematics*, by Springer, Herlihy and Beggs.

With his valuable contribution to the field of operations management, Gozinto began accumulating fans all over the world. But, alas, it was just a matter of time before he incurred the wrath of professional jealousy. Of course, it didn't help that his name appeared above a few sarcastic book reviews that were published in a leading journal (with my help, of course). In fact, the furious reaction he received after one of his critiques appeared in print caused him to retreat to his native village in Italy for a few months of rest, relaxation and extra security.

Some skeptics even tried to deny his existence. When he submitted a paper, "A Queuing Model for an Inventory Problem," to *Operations Research*, the editor insisted on publishing the article under my own name. Gozinto was deeply insulted and argued, to no avail, that he was real and that Vazsonyi was actually the fictional character.

As a consultant, Zepartzatt was once offered a job by a colonel in the Air Force Systems Command, but he had to decline the offer because of travel commitments. Reportedly, the Gozinto name appears in some military secret reports because of his predilection for spending vacations in Hanoi and Saigon.

I often crossed paths with him during these days. Once, I reported to work at North American Aviation and found the vacant office next to mine bearing a bronze plate on the door with his name inscribed on it. It appears that the corporate vice president of engineering was preparing for the arrival of the celebrated scientist. Unfortunately, as Gozinto later explained, he was first detained while researching the mathematical patterns of penguins in Antarctica; he then received a better offer at a Mount Everest research station.

Another time I was at home with a slight fever and my physician, Dr. T. L. Stern, advised me, "Dr. Vazsonyi, you have a rare problem, the Gozinto syndrome." I always wondered how Gozinto contributed to the medical profession. When I recovered and returned to work, I found on my desk a card showing the good doctor telling me, "This is the first case of 'Gozinto' Syndrome that I've seen in a man this young." It was signed by a dozen or so of my coworkers.

Others have contributed information on Gozinto that deserves to be mentioned here. Dr. Stephen Vajda, a management science professor who lives in London, made a genealogical study of Gozinto's family tree. It appears that the Italian math prodigy is of noble origin and is related to both the French Cavadedants and the Hungarian Belemegyens. It is also rumored that he is a direct descendent of a Bossu who wandered into the Italian Alps while pursing romantic interests with a young Gypsy maiden.

Dr. Martin K. Starr, a management scientist and director of the Center for Enterprise Management at Rollins College, gathered information (alas, unpublished) on Zepartzatt's twin brother, Takeaparto, who may have been a double agent for the CIA specializing in secret mathematical formulas for intergalactic travel via hyperspace.

Thanks to these dedicated disciples and others, the Distinguished Fan Club of Gozinto (DFCG) was founded in 1980. Hugo Staelens of Eeklo, Belgium, is lifetime chairman and represents the Flemish Association of Mathematics Teachers. There are a few memberships still available, and if you hurry you may join at the reduced dues of aleph zero Hungarian pengös.

During his short career, which possibly ended quite tragically (more on that later), Gozinto made his biggest mark in the 1960s at an international meeting of the Institute of Management Sciences in Tokyo. As I stepped off the plane, I was met by a delegation of four professors. After deep bows, the group spokesman, Masaaki Ito, presented me with a silk scarf in appreciation for the Japanese translation of *Scientific Programming in Business and Industry*.

Later, as we rode in their car to the conference hotel, Dr. Ito told me that conference organizers were feeling somewhat anxious because they had received a cable from Professor Abraham Charnes, who was in Hong Kong. The cable advised them in no uncertain terms that they should be particularly careful about the proper reception of Professor

Gozinto. Because they couldn't find anything about the elusive Italian, they turned to me for help.

It was a real problem for me. I had been told that the Japanese had a different sense of humor, and that a joke could easily misfire and be perceived by them as a deep insult. I was upset with Charnes for putting me in this situation. At the same time, I didn't know what to say because obviously these professional colleagues of mine had already spent much time and effort in trying to locate Gozinto. Of course, nowadays the risks of using humor are even higher—who knows what is politically correct anymore?

In the end, I decided to be open with them. When I suggested, somewhat delicately, that Gozinto was a fictional character, they erupted in laughter. They thought it was hilarious. In fact, the driver was laughing so hard that I worried he might lose control of the car in the awful Tokyo traffic.

Then they launched into a spirited discussion in Japanese. After a few minutes, Dr. Ito turned to me and said, "We want to keep this an absolute secret. When we see the other conference organizers, we will tell them that Professor Gozinto is unfortunately delayed, but that he will be attending the banquet as the principal speaker."

On the first day of the conference, Bill Cooper, who was responsible for christening Gozinto with his first name, addressed the crowd. While giving an overview of the meeting's highlights, he mentioned that although Professor Gozinto's flight was still delayed, the eccentric, globetrotting mathematician would arrive on time to be the guest speaker at the banquet.

Now the only problem my fellow pranksters and I faced was deciding what to do at the banquet. Finally, we settled on this scenario: when the time came, we would say that Gozinto was expected momentarily, but that in the meantime, I had a copy of his speech which I would deliver to the assembly.

And so, after the last dish was cleared and another round of sake poured, the conference organizer said it was his sad duty to inform the audience that Professors Gozinto and Bill Cooper were in police custody because of an unfortunate altercation with several Geisha girls. Then he introduced me.

I began with a very straight face and launched into a talk that was pure nonsense.

"You realize that for years we have tried to find an algorithm to determine mathematically the highest point on the planet. Unfortunately, linear programming could not do the job. I am delighted to tell you, however, that nonlinear dynamic programming has reached the point where it can solve the problem. The place is Mount Everest, which is 8,848.653 meters high, though the last digit of three is somewhat doubtful and warrants further research."

I noticed that a few people in the crowd were beginning to look around and grin, then I reached under my table and pulled out the first of many toys to illustrate my point. (Earlier in the day I had visited a toy store and was loaded down with props.) Soon everyone was in on the joke and having a good time. Except, that is, for poor Gozinto and Cooper, who spent the evening in a Japanese jail with two Geisha girls studying combinatorial relationships between two men and two women.

Of course, I don't mean to suggest that professional conferences are all fun and games. There is a great deal of high-minded discussion and serious brain-picking on current research that leads to new ideas, new research. Looking back at a distance of some forty years, however, the fun moments stand out vividly. Like that unforgettable, deluxe Ginza bath that Masaaki Ito treated me to.

In a private, two-room suite, I was met by a young woman wearing only a bikini. After motioning for me to sit down, she first, very ceremoniously, removed my shoes, tie and shirt. By then, she had my complete attention as she motioned for me to stand. Next she proceeded to remove my pants and shorts. Naturally, I felt very uncomfortable—after all, I was brought up in the old-fashioned Hungarian way to feel embarrassed whenever naked, even if no one else was around.

But as a gentleman and researcher interested in foreign customs, I willingly followed her to the adjoining room, where I sat down on a stool and she began splashing hot water on me from a tub. After a long massage, then a leisurely bath, followed by a little time in a hot sweat box, my hostess dried me off and dressed me. By that time, I felt like a limp noodle, but it was definitely one of the most rejuvenating multicultural experiences I've ever had.

◆   ·   ◆   ◆

As for rumors about Gozinto's demise, I can only say that it is believed that the celebrated number cruncher may have perished in an earthquake in the Chilean Andes while backpacking through remote villages studying the relationship of mathematics to traditional flute music. As executor of his estate, I hope to be able to announce one day that Gozinto's collected works will finally be published, along with his definitive biography. Of course, there's always the possibility that Zepartzatt may turn up again when we least expect it. But, in the meantime, if you have any information about Professor Z. Gozinto, I would appreciate hearing from you.

As for building on Gozinto's early work, I became more involved in production systems and discovered that the what-goes-into-what question needed to be extended to include the what-comes-ahead-of-what question. For example, the builder of your house cannot install the wiring before the house is framed, which cannot be done before the foundation is poured, and so on. These questions became all-important in the management of operations, and much research has been devoted to these "beyond Gozinto" issues.

16

RETURN TO RED HUNGARY

In the mid-1960s I felt so strongly about the importance of real-life math in the artificial sciences that I decided to become more active in spreading the message. Fortunately, around that same time, a few U.S. agencies sponsored projects that sent individuals abroad to spread the word about American business techniques. To my great delight, I was chosen to be a goodwill ambassador to the Hungarian People's Republic.

According to the agreement, the International Institute of Education (with Ford Foundation money) would send my wife and myself to Budapest and I would give lectures on the use of math in management at the Karl Marx University. The institute would cover most of the expenses, while the Hungarian government was responsible for providing lodging, meals and local transportation. It was a straightforward arrangement, but I should have known that nothing moves straight through the Hungarian bureaucracy, and this was especially true during the time when the country was in the hands of communist party officials.

At the time, however, I basked in the dream of returning to my homeland as a successful American businessman with an important message to spread behind the Iron Curtain. There was even a note of intrigue about my homecoming—because the Atomic Energy Commission had once cleared me for top-secret work, I had to inform the CIA of my trip beforehand, and was even told to check in at the U.S.

Embassy in Budapest for "further instructions." During my stay, rumors did circulate in Budapest that I had ties with the CIA, but that was about the extent of my James Bond adventures.

After landing in London, I quickly became reacquainted with the strange ways and manners of the new government and people of my homeland living under the Stalinist shadow. According to the agreement, Hungarian officials were to pay our fare from London to Budapest, and I was supposed to pick up the tickets in London. So Laura and I went to the Hungarian consulate. After ringing and ringing, a grouchy guy appeared and grunted, "Go to the embassy," before slamming the door in our faces. At the embassy, another guy did the same thing, directing us back to the consulate. We were pretty mad by the time we returned and kept on ringing until an old woman opened the door. We explained that we were official guests of the Hungarian government. She diplomatically replied that anybody could say that, so why should she believe us?

After I pulled out the official document, she reluctantly opened the door, leading us into a large, sumptuous room. We were boiling mad as we waited for a consular official to finally appear. I was ready to give him hell when Laura straightened up, took on her role of the "baroness" and did it for me.

"We are honored guests of the Hungarian government," she began. "We are doing you a favor, and you are just impossible to deal with!"

I could see the wheels turning in his worried head about who we might be. After reading the invitation from the Academy of Sciences with the impressive stamps, he apologized.

"I will send my assistant to the airlines to get the tickets, and tomorrow you can pick them up," he said. "Furthermore, I will personally arrange for your visa." (If only it had been this easy back in 1938!)

I was astounded. The embassy was closed on Saturday and I couldn't imagine anything short of an act of God that would cause it to open its doors on the weekend.

But sure enough, on Saturday morning we got everything we needed. When the baroness speaks, officials jump.

We arrived at the airport early, and in the crowd I happened to see our obliging consular official. But when I approached him with a friendly smile, he turned his back and walked away. Later I learned that there were spies everywhere, and he would have been suspect for being friendly with an "imperialist" (American).

As the first people at the airline departure gate, Laura and I felt confident about getting a good seat. The ticket was for a Hungarian airline, however, which meant the protocol of waiting in line was different from the typical American one. As more and more Hungarians arrived, the crowd squeezed tighter and tighter against the gate. Two hours later, when the gate finally opened, there was an explosive rush to the plane, and we, being unaccustomed to marathon pushing and shoving, arrived last. By the time we reached the cabin, we could find no adjacent seats.

As we waited inside the plane, it began to get hot and finally someone opened the doors to give us some air. However, as we began to taxi down the runway, the doors were still open. The plane was actually in the air before the flight attendants finally closed the doors. Hungarians apparently have different ideas about safety, because there were no seat belts either. I am thankful to this day that I was not sucked out the door by the low pressure generated according to the aerodynamic laws of Bernoulli.

As the jetliner approached Budapest, I began to feel nostalgic at the sight of the bridges over the Danube, the parliament building and Margit Sziget, the island in the center of the Danube. When we landed, I applauded along with everybody else aboard the plane. After twenty-seven years, it was exciting to be back. Of course, in my version of my homecoming, I imagined Laura and me checking into the first-class Grand Hotel—the hotel I often dreamed about visiting as a child. The Grand Hotel was a luxury resort situated on Margit Sziget. Guests could stroll around the little island and enjoy the sight of beautiful peacocks and exotic flowers in the park, watch the rowing teams on the Danube, or relax in one of the three hot pools.

But my disillusionment began as soon as we checked into the third-rate hotel that party officials had arranged for us. It was a dreary building in a noisy, commercial district of downtown Budapest. On our first morning there we were awakened at 6:00 a.m. by the sounds of people reporting to work. There were no sights to see, no places to walk, no peace or quiet to enjoy.

So I resolved to straighten things out. After several attempts to call out using the government's unreliable phone system, I finally reached my contact, a high-ranking government official, and asked for a room at the Grand Hotel. A short time later the phone rang. It was the hotel front desk saying that my comrade was on the line, but I needed to come downstairs because it was impossible to receive incoming calls on room phones. So I ran down four flights of stairs—the elevator was as reliable as the phone system—only to hear my comrade say the word that became a constant refrain in Hungary: "Impossible!"

Never one to be easily deterred, I met with the "porta," the major domo of the hotel, who was supposed to be able to arrange anything. When he heard that I wanted a room at the Grand Hotel, he shook his head and said, "Impossible." But then I remembered that in the old days, many things were made possible in Hungary by using the baksheesh system. I wasn't sure how the communist system had changed the old order, so I carefully slipped a $10 bill into his hand. In those days, ten dollars in American currency was a lot of money—it was also illegal for Hungarians to keep American money.

"Perhaps if you try real hard, you may be able to get us a room," I said. "And this is to help you in your work."

Twenty minutes later, the porta called my room. "Doktor Ur (Doctor Mister), I got a room for you."

When I called my contact and told him that I had managed to get a room at the Grand Hotel, he was immediately suspicious and wanted to know all the details. Of course, I wasn't about to give away my source—I'm sure the communists had a special place for those accused of taking baksheesh.

So my comrade contact said he would verify the room reservation. Twenty minutes later he called back.

"I'm sorry," he said, "but there are only single rooms available. Your wife can have a room with a bath, but you'll have to stay in another single room without a bath. You can either use your wife's bathroom, or the one at the end of the corridor."

This is one of those rare times when I lost my cool and decided to use some muscle. The fact that a party official could not get us a room with a bathroom—not to mention the pompous way that he issued this final little bureaucratic decree—was the final straw.

"Please be advised that my lectures are hereby cancelled," I said calmly. "My wife and I are taking the first flight back to California."

"What is the American government going to say about this?" he asked.

"That's your problem, comrade. I'm leaving right now for MALEV [the Hungarian airline agency]." I hung up the phone.

It seemed totally beyond his comprehension that U.S. citizens were free to do as they chose. All he knew was that if he had visited the U.S. to give a series of talks, then canceled and left, upon his return home he would have been jailed as a dissident or, even worse, would have simply "disappeared."

A few hours later, when we arrived at the airline agency to book flights for our departure, there was a message waiting from the comrade. He wanted to know if I would give at least one lecture on the next day. Since we couldn't get a flight until later the following afternoon, I asked the "clerk comrade" to relay a message saying that I would.

The next morning when I entered the lecture hall at the university, I felt a tension and uneasiness in the audience because it had leaked out that this would be my first and last lecture. After my talk, I went back to the hotel where Ferenc Forgo, a young professor who later worked with me at the University of Southern California, was waiting for me. He had good news. There was a suite at the Grand Hotel waiting for us.

It was a truly gratifying moment when we walked into the large living room that overlooked the Danube to check out the master bedroom and large bathroom that would be ours for the next ten days. We later learned that party officials had evicted a rather important Soviet comrade to make room for us. If I had canceled my talks and returned home, my official contact would have found himself in big trouble.

◆   ◆   ◆

One of the highlights of my trip was acting the part of a real Magyar nobleman. I had started preparing for the role long before we left Los Angeles, when I managed to get a book of Hungarian songs that Laura played on the piano while I croaked along. I had learned that singing Hungarian songs in Los Angeles was a great way to connect with other people. Unfortunately, I had two drawbacks: a total ignorance of Hungarian music and a voice that sounded like a frog with laryngitis. For this trip to Hungary, I listed all the words to the folk songs on 3x5 cards and, to the distress of my fellow travelers, practiced them diligently on the airplane.

My moment came when Laura and I attended a party in our honor at a first-class restaurant deep in the hills of Buda. We arrived in a chauffeur-driven limousine and joined a large crowd of mathematicians, economists and other academics who had assembled to celebrate with us in high style. As typical in most deluxe restaurants, there was an excellent Gypsy orchestra playing wonderful Hungarian songs.

In the middle of one song, the lead violinist, or "cigany primas," approached my table and began to play in my ear. Following the old Magyar custom, I did what was expected of me. I took out a $10 bill, licked it and stuck it on his forehead. Then, to the great astonishment of the restaurant patrons, I started belting out a Hungarian folksong, "Akinek a lelke beteg, gyenge szive vérzig":

> "If you are melancholic, and your heart is bleeding
> Gulp a few liters of wine daily, for a week.
> Ask the Gypsy to play the old song,
> Poplars don't grow to the sky."

The cigany primas picked up the song immediately, and I sang it with great gusto. After it was done, in the tradition of the Hungarian nobleman, I called for the Gypsies to play other songs, all the while plastering more American dollars on their foreheads.

Of course, my playing the part of a wealthy nobleman made for a great show, but growing up in Hungary, my family could never have afforded such a fine restaurant—not to mention a Gypsy orchestra. Besides, when I was younger I wasn't interested in anything outside the world of mathematics.

◆   ◆   ◆

The lectures that I gave on real-life math at the Karl Marx University went over well with managers who appreciated my avoidance of complicated math theorems. I talked about my favorite research on production control and touched only lightly on the subject of marketing, which the communist regime considered "capitalist profiteering." The best attempt at marketing that I saw in Hungary was a sign in the airport terminal that greeted us as we stepped off the plane. "Welcome in Elegant" read the sign in English. Of course, it made no sense at all until we found out later that "Elegant" was the name of a Hungarian department store. Other than that, Hungary was devoid of billboards or other signs of marketing. Once, when we dropped by a department store to buy an umbrella, nobody paid any attention to us, especially the salesgirl who continued to look bored and eat her sandwich. So much for customer service.

I followed my real-life math talks with three additional lectures on math in management, sponsored by the Hungarian Academy of Sciences. These lectures to mathematicians and scientists were a fiasco. As one friend later told me, the math I used was considered trivial by Hungarian academicians.

"I thought they wanted to hear something practical," I said.

"Yes," he replied, "but we expected you to talk about something like dynamic programming."

"The only problem with that is that I've never seen a real-life application of dynamic programming," I said.

> *I remember once asking my friend Dick Bellman, the father of dynamic programming and a brilliant mathematician, for applications of dynamic programming.*
>
> *"I spent six months inventing the term dynamic programming," he said, "and there are so many applications that I don't know where to begin."*
>
> *"Try me," I said, calling his bluff. "Just give me one."*
>
> *"Well, okay, if you insist. There is a well-known multi-stage inventory control problem in the theory of non-linear programming that nobody knew how to solve. I applied dynamic programming to this theory and solved the problem."*
>
> *From this example, I concluded that dynamic programming was popular in academia because it was a high-powered, very ingenious mathematical extension of linear programming. Today, hardly anyone remembers it.*

The Hungarian mathematicians and I ended up having a long discussion on our views of math, with others joining in. At one point, I described my metamorphosis from pure to real-life math, which involved a long, painful, confusing change in my outlook on the world. But I still shared their appreciation for the beauty of pure math. Their lament was similar to Godfrey H. Hardy's, one of the greatest mathematicians of the 20th century, who wrote:

I have never done anything "useful." No discovery of mine has made or is likely to make, directly or indirectly, for good or ill, the least difference to the amenity of the world... Judged by all practical standards, the value of my mathematical life is nil: and outside mathematics is trivial anyhow. (*A Mathematician's Apology*, 1941)

◆   ◆   ◆

After a while, I pieced together the Hungarian communist party's attitude towards mathematics. According to them, pure math was an imperialistic science to please the capitalistic elite and did nothing for the "workers and peasants." "Applied" math (whatever that is), on the other hand, fit perfectly into the Leninist/Stalinist doctrine and was pursued by the new Cybernetics Institute. Under the cloak of this institute, members cultivated sophisticated mathematical extensions of such fields as dynamic programming, game theory and input-output dynamics. These researchers didn't know anything about the practical managerial revolution taking place in the U.S. Putting aside the many philosophical differences between the private enterprise system and the totalitarian system of central control, I considered the math of the Cybernetic Institute a total waste of time because it ignored anything practical from real life.

Mathematicians who fought the party system faced harsh scrutiny by the government. Not even Paul Erdös was exempt from censure—party mathematicians reproached him for his obsession with pure math and for not endorsing "applied" math. As proof, they used Erdös' private language in which he referred to anyone (including me) who no longer did pure math as "dead." To party officials, this proved that Erdös was opposed to using math in the real world. Of course, this was absolute nonsense. He just wasn't interested in using it himself. However, officials did not bother him and, though he was a Hungarian citizen and traveled on a Hungarian passport, they always gave him an exit permit before he entered Hungary. (This way he wouldn't worry about being denied the permit after reentry and becoming a prisoner behind the Iron Curtain.) They did discourage his followers by never giving them raises or other benefits. As to the "government-approved" applied math work, I thought it lacked the beauty and theoretical value of pure math as a science, besides being ugly and useless. Moreover, I have a firm belief that science should be left in the hands of scientists, and that it is inexcusable for government officials to meddle in science.

◆   ◆   ◆

During my stay in Budapest, I didn't hear much talk about communism, or lack or freedom, perhaps because most individuals were afraid of informers.

For example, the 1956 revolt against communism and the Soviets, which caused such great excitement in the West, was not a topic of conversation. Soviet troops and tanks suppressed the insurgents during the Hungary occupation. Hundreds of people were executed, thousands more were imprisoned and about 200,000 fled the country. I tried to talk to people about their views on the real causes of the revolt but couldn't get anywhere.

Other times while traveling in Germany and Switzerland I would attempt to join a couple speaking Hungarian, only to see them stop talking and turn away until I had left. Once, after this happened, I introduced myself as a Vazsonyi.

"One of the true Vazsonyi's?" the young woman asked.

When I proved it with my American passport, her attitude totally changed. She admitted that earlier she was concerned that I was an agent provocateur.

The problems that I mostly heard about dealt with shortages of material goods and frustration with things not working (phones, elevators, etc.). Most of the complaints were that people could not buy things at any price. Lajos Biro, a high ranking official involved in production, told me that he spent a good part of his time tracking down comfortable, well-made shoes for his friends.

Laura and I experienced this during one rainy day in Budapest when we tried to buy an umbrella and learned that it was "Impossible" to find one. In grocery stores, we saw shelves that were empty, disheveled and unattractive. When we found goods that were in stock, we would first stand in line to make our selection. Then stand in another line to pay for a voucher. Then stand in a third line to present the voucher and receive the item. Self-service was unknown, the assumption being, though somewhat exaggerated, that everybody was dishonest. One Sunday we needed some aspirin and learned that in the entire city of Budapest there was only one drugstore open.

For their part, communist party members considered these problems to be just a temporary nuisance—most of the leaders were highly dedicated, idealistic and incorruptible. They wanted the best for their people and wanted to change the old, privileged, Magyar system that didn't give a hoot for the suffering of the multitudes. These communist doctrinaires, who were forced to cater to Moscow, thought they knew best. They had an elaborate secret police and informers' system, and didn't hesitate to lock up "enemies" of society, though I don't believe the Hungarians resorted to atrocities. The difficulty was that the undemocratic system they believed in did not work. In their desire for change, they proved the old saying: the road to Hell is paved with good intentions.

Occasionally I'd meet a communist who was willing to openly discuss our political differences. I remember talking with a friend from the old days, Jenö Kocsis, who had learned about my use of the baksheesh system to get a room at the Grand Hotel. He began ranting about my imperial ways corrupting his socialist community.

"Our people are not supposed to work for personal gain and be dominated by greed," he said. "They are supposed to work for the sole compensation of contributing to the welfare of our community."

As he talked, I gazed out the window and watched three workman standing around, smoking cigarettes and enjoying a long chit-chat while they were supposed to be fixing the road for the welfare of the community.

Another time, a good friend of mine from the old days, now employed by the government, invited me to his home for dinner. The minute I entered the front door, his wife confronted me without any reason, calling me an imperialist agent.

"You Americans are taking illegal measures to stifle the Hungarian nation," she said.

I tried to explain to this woman, who worked as a radio news commentator, that I didn't vote for President Eisenhower and wasn't responsible for "imperialist" policies. But she paid no attention and continued spouting the communist party line. After dinner, I finally had enough and left. My friend met me outside and apologized for his wife's behavior.

"It's okay," I said. "The breaded chicken was delicious in spite of the fact that it was obviously a communist chicken."

The next day I visited him at his office and we calmly discussed the differences between the U.S. free enterprise system (imperialist) and Hungary's socialist system. He was candid, saying that one aspect of our system that he particularly disliked was that imperialist people "worked themselves to death." He said that he had seen it first-hand during a trip he made to New York City while on a trade mission with the United Nations. According to him, U.S. employees worked day and night for the sole reason that they feared being fired by their bosses.

His lack of knowledge about private enterprise in the U.S. floored me. He truly and honestly believed that the communist government could suddenly motivate people to work for the collective good rather than for their own personal gain—a total break from the existing Hungarian culture.

◆   ◆   ◆

Fortunately, around this time I was able to leave all this political nonsense behind to attend a TIMS' meeting in Israel. Laura stayed behind to travel to Siofok, where a conference was being held on Lake Balaton to celebrate the birthday of Paul Erdös.

My flight to Israel on a Hungarian airline had one unexpected pleasure. After landing in Bucharest in the middle of the night only to learn that we had missed our connecting flight to Tel Aviv, I managed to find a nearby hotel room. The next day, relying on the TIMS membership list that I always carried with me, I looked up a certain Francis Alexander who lived in Bucharest. Although we had never met before, he knew of me and we spent a pleasant day together. Later, he accompanied me to the airport, and the next morning I arrived in Tel Aviv.

While we were going through customs, our suitcases received a most thorough search as officials were on high alert for bombs. A young woman asked me to run my travel clock, and I complied. But when she asked me to take apart my electric shaver, which I didn't know how to do, she waved me on.

The conference was held at the sumptuous Hilton Hotel. A pleasant pool overlooked the Mediterranean. A few of us sat down in the sun and enjoyed a leisurely conversation about the meeting. After the frustrating talks I'd been having in Hungary, it was a pleasure to talk about real problems—like material requirements planning, and the control of production and services.

After the conference, I returned to Budapest where, once again, I learned that nothing in Hungary is straightforward. First, my visa was no longer valid. Then I was told that because Israel was considered an Asian country, I couldn't re-enter Hungary without first being inoculated with the smallpox vaccine. Next, my suitcase mysteriously disappeared, then magically reappeared after a half hour of complaining and spreading baksheesh around. While waiting for a taxi, I was shoved aside several times in the grand Hungarian tradition, before finally managing to fight my way into one. Luck was on my side though, because I still had my room at the Grand Hotel and I was able to head straight to the hot pools.

The next morning I took the train to join Laura at the meeting honoring Paul Erdös. After attending math meetings as a young man, I should have felt at home, but I didn't. The mathematicians were as crazy as ever. Erdös was openly declaring war on Hungary because the government, in a move designed to please their Soviet masters, had refused to grant visas to the Israeli mathematicians who wanted to attend the conference. As a result, Erdös refused to return to Hungary for many years, not until party officials changed their attitude towards Israel. I agreed with his sentiment but thought he punished only his fellow mathematicians, while having no impact on the government.

When the hour finally arrived to fly home, I left Hungary feeling enriched by some of the experiences we had and some of the people we met. Visits with my family brought up sad memories of the Holocaust. However, it made me feel a little better when I saw my mother, who attended all my lectures, enjoying the attention of her "successful American son." Overall, I couldn't help but feel saddened by the country's dire economic condition and the idealistic but unsuccessful attempts of the government to improve the situation.

In 1988, I observed with delight the collapse of the communist governments, when Hungary ceased to be in the Soviet orbit. I watched with great hopes for the emergence of a totally new Hungary.

◆   ◆   ◆

Because my visit to Hungary as a goodwill ambassador had been soured by dealings with party officials, I returned later with my wife and daughter as a private citizen. We stayed, of course, at the Grand Hotel and took trips all over Budapest and Hungary in a rental car that was bigger and newer than most of the other cars on the road. We visited the old apartment house I lived in as a boy, as well my old school. We also sought out the former Vilmos Vazsonyi residence, where as a boy I had once admired my famous cousin's talking parrot and the framed document appointing him to the cabinet and the privy council of King Karoly IV. I was shocked at how shabby the buildings now appeared, but Bobbi thought they were interesting.

As "rich American tourists," we took the ferry across Lake Balaton to Siofok and got pleasantly lost many times. We visited the country town of Nagyvazsony which inspired surnames for my uncle and myself. We saw a wonderful Hungarian folk orchestra with an incredible performer on the cimbalom, the Gypsy instrument that resembles a xylophone. Bobbi enjoyed a trip to Vienna on the hydrofoil, and Laura got her first taste of Hungarian goulash, which, in its native form, is really a greasy, unappetizing soup. Later, we went to a "goulash party" where she tasted *pörkölt,* the delicious goulash made especially for tourists.

◆　　　◆　　　◆

So rarely is the Hungarian language encountered outside the country, that when my countrymen visit other places they have the habit of speaking to each other as if no one else in the world can understand them. I've often taken a kind of mischievous pleasure at listening in, then adding my two cents worth.

Once, while I was enjoying an excellent sauna in Reykjavik, Iceland, two middle-aged Hungarian men entered and, ignoring me, began sharing details of their sexual exploits, as well as their occasional impotence problems. I remained silent for a while thinking about what I could say that would blow their minds. Finally, I had it. I waited for an opportune moment and said, "Az én véleményem szerint egyen libamájat, az segiteni fog" ("In my opinion, you should eat some goose liver, that will help"). They looked at me, too stunned for words. On that note, I quickly exited.

Another time, while relaxing with colleagues by a swimming pool at a Tel Aviv hotel, I overheard two pretty Hungarian girls devise a sneaky plan to get shade without renting an umbrella. Slowly they worked their way closer to our umbrella until they were enjoying its benefits. At this point, I went to the clerk, gave him another dollar and asked him to give the girls an umbrella with a little note saying, "Courtesy of your Hungarian-speaking neighbor." They accepted my gift with lovely smiles, but as they couldn't speak English, and I couldn't abandon my professional colleagues, my act of international goodwill didn't lead to anything more interesting.

17

THE GLOBE TROTTER

As my colleagues and I spread the word of decision sciences and real-life math to other parts of the world, we were following a time-honored tradition of exporting American management techniques elsewhere. At the beginning of the 1900s, Frederic W. Taylor, an American industrial engineer who originated scientific management in business, traveled to all four corners of the globe. Around the same time, so did the managerial engineering principles of Frank B. and Lillian Gilbreth, inventors of time-and-motion study, and Henry Ford's mass production techniques. Likewise, new management theories developed after World War II soon reached a worldwide audience.

From the 1950s until 1985, I crisscrossed the U.S., Europe and parts of the Far East to talk about my adventures in decision making. (Fortunately, I could always find organizations to finance my travels.) As someone who started off as a *pure* mathematician and became a *real-life* mathematician, not to mention going from a poverty-stricken Hungarian to a star-spangled American, I shared my passion with the enthusiasm of the newly converted. I naively believed that math was destined to become the language of business, and mathematical models would form the cornerstone of all areas of management, finance, production, services and marketing.

Of course, in the process of explaining artificial science concepts to others, I began to understand them better myself. At the same time, I was always looking for ideas that I had in common with others and ways of using these ideas to improve our lives.

As a general rule, whenever I visited a foreign city, I would spend a few days giving talks and then schedule a few extra days to see places that interested me. In Athens, however, I once combined a talk with an interesting sightseeing experience. I began the evening by giving a talk in the IBM lecture hall, but my speech was drowned out by some kind of political demonstration outside. Finally, the chairman stood up and announced that it was necessary to change our venue. With the help of his colleagues, he slipped me out through a back door. I continued my presentation on the rooftop garden of a nearby restaurant, where I had a fantastic view of the Acropolis in the distance.

While in Athens, I also made a memorable impression on my guests. A colleague and I were discussing a computer program in the IBM office, when my associate looked out the fourth floor window and gasped. Apparently, he had parked his car illegally, and he saw a police car headed his way. This looked like an opportunity to have some fun so I said, "Let's run down, and I'll pretend it's my car."

When we reached his vehicle, the police were just pulling up behind it. So I hopped in and started the car. Unfortunately, it had a manual transmission, and I shifted into the wrong gear. Instead of going ahead, I backed straight into the police car. I'm sure the Greek policeman was thoroughly confused when I then jumped out and started yelling at him in English. "You have no business parking so close behind me!" Then I jumped back inside the car, shifted into first and drove away. My friend caught up with me around the block, and we both doubled over laughing.

When traveling, I always tried to make professional contacts in advance, so that I would have local guides who were glad to discuss professional issues while showing me around. Usually this worked out quite well. It also kept me on my toes. For instance, I once planned a trip to Hong Kong and exchanged letters with an ORSA member whose name I found in a membership directory. When I arrived at the airport, however, my colleague didn't show. So I took a cab to the hotel, an imposing looking Victorian building. I had just settled down in my room when the doorbell rang. When I opened the door, I came face to face with two identical-looking Chinese men. At first I thought I was dreaming, then they introduced themselves as the colleague I had arranged to meet. Because they were identical twins, they figured they would save money by getting only one ORSA membership. Afterwards, the brothers steered me to the kind of authentic Chinese restaurant that tourists rarely see. I liked the bread, a round piece of dough with a plum in the middle, and the exotic fish, though I was surprised to find a "spittoon" under the table that we used for dumping our leftover tea leaves.

> One day, I was taking a flight from New York to Los Angeles, and someone who knew I was fond of yoga wagered that I couldn't drink a martini while standing on my head. Since I was in good yoga form (and a real ham) at the time, I accepted the bet and asked the stewardess to place a martini (with a straw) in the middle of the aisle. To the amusement and wonder of my fellow passengers, I was successful on the first try. My prize? A second martini, of course.

Another time, in Berlin, I learned the dangers of traveling solo. It was in the 1960s, at the height of the Cold War, and I was giving lectures in West Germany when I decided to visit East Berlin. Because of the Berlin Wall I couldn't cross at the Brandenburg Gate, so I had to take a sightseeing bus. We passed Checkpoint Charlie and observed how the soldiers' machine guns followed every vehicle that went through the gates. The tour lasted only an hour, so after we stepped down from the bus, I told my companions that I was going back to East Berlin, this time on foot. They thought that I was crazy.

I passed through the checkpoint and had a great time walking around for a couple of hours. I was shocked to find practically empty store windows, few privately owned cars, and shabbily dressed people. Apparently not all communist countries were the same because Hungarians were much better off. I enjoyed dinner at a small restaurant. Because my German sounded like the real thing, people talked openly to me without realizing that I was a foreigner, and an American imperialist at that.

Everything was going fine until I walked back to the checkpoint. There I made the mistake of crossing at the wrong place. Suddenly, I heard soldiers from both sides shout, "Halt!"

As East Berlin soldiers aimed their machine guns at me, I stopped in the middle of the pavement. Then, not knowing what else to do, I grabbed my American passport and raised it high over my head. Luckily, no one thought I was reaching for a weapon, or I would have joined the hundreds of others who became casualties of the Berlin Wall. Finally, an American soldier walked over to my side and escorted me, a little shaky on my feet, to West Berlin.

This experience reminded me of the dreams I once had about Krumpholz trying to shoot me while I was desperately looking for an American passport. The only difference was that this time, about 20 years later, I actually had the passport in my hand.

◆　　　◆　　　◆

Here's an example of how my brain works in different countries.

One day, I was taking a nap after lunch in Munich, when the phone rang. It was R. Oldenburg, who was the owner of the publishing house that was publishing the German edition of my PL/I book. I sleepily told him that I would come down to the lobby in 10 minutes. When I met him, we started to discuss plans for the translation. We were talking in German. Suddenly, I asked him, "What language did I answer when you woke me up?"

"German, of course," he said.

When I go to Germany, France, or Hungary, after a few days of confusion, I begin talking to myself in that country's language without bothering to translate. If I stay away too long from the U.S., my English begins to deteriorate.

◆   ◆   ◆

Perhaps the most exotic trip I made was to Calcutta in the 1960s. After the plane landed and I waded into a crowd of thousands milling around the airport, I didn't have a clue what to do next. There was no one to meet me and no help in sight. Finally, when the crowd thinned out, I was approached by a young woman who introduced herself as my guide, courtesy of the Indian Statistical Institute.

Throughout that trip I was taken aback by the cultural differences. For instance, after I showered and dressed the next morning, no sooner did I begin waiting for my guide to appear, when there was a knock at the door.

"What a coincidence," I said to my two young escorts. "You came just at the moment when I was ready."

"No coincidence," said one of the students. He pointed across the room. "See that hole high on the wall? We have been watching you all morning. When we saw that you were ready, we came to your door." At first I didn't believe they were telling the truth, but they most solemnly assured me that they were.

I nodded politely, saying nothing about the loss of privacy.

Later that morning I made a huge social faux pas. I was meeting with a group of professors when I sat down on a sofa and arranged myself in the cross-legged position. I had studied yoga for a few years and thought something along the lines of "when in the East, strut your stuff." Of course, I was also the only one wearing sandals without socks. The men wore European suits, while the women dressed in Indian garb with European shoes.

They stared at me in disbelief. Finally, one of them broke the tension by confiding that no educated, upper-caste person would sit like that—it showed lack of "learning." Sure, they might sit cross-legged in the privacy of their own home, but never in public.

The next day the true impact of East vs. West arose, this time more logistical. I had asked my guide if a group of operations researchers from Calcutta would be coming to my presentation the next day.

"Unfortunately, they live too far away," she said.

"How far?" I asked.

"About a mile," she said, "but road conditions during the monsoon rains are such that the drive is impossible."

While in Calcutta, I learned a great deal from a prominent industrialist that I had met on the plane from Hong Kong. Ishwar Bairi, a traditional Hindu, was impressed by my interest in yoga—unlike my professor colleagues—and we became quite friendly in a short time. He told me that his biggest problem was motivating factory workers. After a couple of days on the job, his workers made enough money to live on for the rest of the week. Under Hinduism, this sort of attitude wasn't frowned on—unlike Judaism and Christianity, neither of which tolerates much loafing around. I added this employee motivation problem to the one I learned in Hungary, that people aren't willing to work solely for the public good or even their own long-term good.

At one point, Bairi mysteriously took me to a tailor who measured me. A day later I received a package containing a traditional white, raw silk gown, pants and long shirt, which I still treasure. I think he gave me the present in honor of my interest in yoga.

Like all good Brahmins, Bairi was a vegetarian. One day he wanted to take me out for lunch, but first we had something to eat at his house. I was confused and wondered if this was customary. I might add, as an avid carnivore, that I could not detect the lack of meat because the food was so good.

◆　　　◆　　　◆

At the end of my Calcutta trip, I went to New Delhi where I stayed in a magnificent hotel. Against everyone's advice, I accepted a lift in a three-wheeled motor cart for a hair-raising joy ride to the university at

Delhi. There I delivered a talk on production control to Professor Pankay Mittal's class. My photo was taken and, the last I heard, it is still on display with photographs of other guests from that era.

18

INVISIBLE MATHEMATICS

o o o o o o o o o o o o o o o o o o o o o o o o o o o o o o

The triumph of applied science is that it provides a cookbook for the ordinary person to use the sciences.

—*Paraphrased from Ernst Mach (1838–1916)*
Austrian physicist and philosopher

While I find it only natural to use math to figure out which direction I should take, I realize that most people don't share this view. As soon as you change the subject to numbers, graphs or equations, some people's eyes begin to glaze over, their blood pressure drops, they lose feeling in their extremities.

It took me years to realize what the problem was. Many people feel they don't need math the same way they feel they don't need classical music, medieval poetry, or Latin to get along in this world.

They are probably right.

Most folks are interested in things like insurance, 401(k) savings programs, affordable healthcare, environmental regulations, business planning, Internet-based applications, casino gambling, census data, urban planning, checkbook balancing, computer programming and so on.

So when I became more deeply involved in decision making, step-by-step, I started to hide math behind computers, which are math machines par excellence.

What I find so wonderful about computers is that although they were invented by mathematicians, you don't need to be a mathematician to use one. Stockbrokers, surveyors, writers, children, teenagers, mechanics, waitresses, supermarket cashiers and real estate agents who don't know any math use computer programs every day that contain complex mathematical recipes invented by mathematicians.

If, on the other hand, you'd like to know a few math basics so that you can appreciate how computers perform some of their little miracles, here's a little trigonometry lesson. In fact, it may be everything you'll ever need to know about trigonometry.

First, take a straight edge ruler and a protractor—if you don't have one, your neighborhood drugstore should. Draw a straight line that is 5" long.

Now measure an angle of 60 degrees with your protractor and draw another 5" line. Congratulations. You have created an open-ended triangle. If you were to measure the length of the third side without drawing it, it would be close to about 5".

Now leave that one and start another from scratch. This time draw a 5" line, only change the angle to 30 degrees and add another 5" line.

Notice how the third side (the one that you didn't draw) is a result—a **function**—of the two sides and the angle in between them? Sure, you could draw in this third side and measure it by hand, but it's not as accurate. That's why mathematicians have invented a way to calculate the third side without measuring it. They call that kind of calculation an **algorithm.** Algorithms are similar to recipes in a cookbook, because they tell you, step by step, what to do.

The third, and last, key word you need to know is **variable**. Variables are the details—like the length of the two sides of the triangle and the degrees of the angles—that you start off with.

That's all you need to know about trigonometry. Because with the help of a computer, the functions and the algorithms are available to you in spreadsheet form.

When you look at the spreadsheet on your screen, you see a giant chessboard, except the little boxes are not squares but elongated rectangles. You can think of them as matchboxes. But instead of holding matchsticks, each box contains a single variable or number, like the length of the side of the triangle or the degree of the angle between them. Then you push a button, and instantly the computer calculates the length of the third side and puts it into another box. Isn't that wonderful?

Of course, you need to know the correct variables to put into the correct boxes. For instance, if you want to calculate the third side of the triangle, you need to know the length of two sides, the angle between and where to put them. You also need to know which box to look into for the answer. But once you plug in the correct variables, the computer calculates the answer. It's that simple. The math is invisible, concealed by the spreadsheet. If you feel ambitious, you can uncover the process if you really want to. Otherwise, leave it alone and let the results speak for themselves.

◆   ◆   ◆

Suppose you own a house, and you want to sell it so that you net $150,000. If the agent takes a commission of 6 percent of the sales price, what should the selling price be?

I posed this question to my daughter, who, as I predicted, looked at me blankly, then said she had no idea. (Reluctantly, I have overcome my expectation that she would follow in my footsteps.) This "Markup on the Selling Price" problem is the hardest one to be found in my book *Business Mathematics for Colleges* (with Richard Brunell, 3rd edition, 1984). For some reason, students have a great deal of trouble with this problem.

So, after coaching Bobbi about variables and boxes, I asked her to tell me the variables of the problem.

"The input variables are the net and the percent, and the output variable is the selling price," she answered correctly.

Next I pulled out the spreadsheet that I had prepared and showed her which boxes to enter the inputs, and where the output would appear. She entered the numbers and, presto, received the correct answer of $159,574.

Then I gave her a second problem: What if you want to get a net of $200,000 and the commission is 8%. She quickly got the answer of $217,391. That's all there is to it.

That's why the cashier at the grocery store is a math wizard as she produces a detailed list of purchases, calculates taxes and totals, and, furthermore, enters the purchases into the inventory record, thereby initiating a complex sequence of actions that results in the dispatch of more trucks delivering necessary goods to the supermarket.

She may not consider herself a mathematician, but her performance is a triumph of the application of mathematical sciences and technology. Brilliant mathematicians like von Neumann were needed to invent the computer, but a supermarket cashier with no understanding of math can take advantage of its power.

◆   ◆   ◆

One thing I always felt confident about was my ability to handle any kind of math formula that came my way. I found out how wrong I was in the 1960s when I started to learn computer programming, beginning with FORTRAN (FORmula TRANslation), the first widely used programming language for scientists and engineers. I was horrified to see formulas like

I=I+1.

This made absolutely no sense to me. How could I equal I+1? But then I discovered that the equal sign meant something quite different to computer programmers. Because I like to have a good understanding of things I'm working with, I dug into the history of math, a subject that had never interested me as a young student. I discovered that the approach of pure mathematics was quite different from the math I used in real life.

The decisive aspect of real-life math is that it is a language that uses algorithms to solve specific types of problems that have numeric content. Language, which is indispensable to humans, is also the secret behind real-life math.

Back when Sumeria ruled the Mediterranean shipping lanes, Sumerian teachers spent a lot of time teaching by example the calculations required for everyday life. They did the same problem over and over again, until the students memorized the process. Later they discovered shortcuts to teaching calculations; they used words to describe various math processes and collected these examples into "math cookbooks." They also discovered that ordinary language, common prose, is awkward, confusing, inefficient and often useless. So they invented a dialect of prose, using words in a specific manner that describe and solve everyday business transactions. Over the years, they devised more shortcuts—the most important being the use of a shorthand to describe common math problems.

Using an example from today's business world, we write "TAX=0.07*PRICE." We call using words like this in a math problem *rhetorical algebra,* or *natural language.* When computers came along, program languages were invented that used natural languages, too. The most popular of these was COBOL (COmmon Business-Oriented Language). For example, in COBOL you might write: "MULTIPLY PRICE BY 0.07 GIVING TAX." Millions of people learned this language, using computers to make business calculations that the Sumerians would have been proud of.

When the Egyptians flexed their economic muscle a few centuries later, however, they felt that rhetorical algebra was clumsy and inefficient. So they introduced variables that replaced words, as well as symbols and a special grammar that took the Sumerian shorthand a step further. This *syncopated*, or *mnemonic*, algebra would later become the basis of the FORTRAN language (which, incidentally, put programmers in a straightjacket by limiting the names of variables to eight letters).

Math languages took yet another direction when some Europeans decided that the syncopated/mnemonic algebra of the Egyptians was too clumsy for their complex calculations. Brahmagupta, the most accomplished of the ancient Indian astronomers and inventor of the concept of the zero, used the first letters of colors to denote unknowns in equations in his poem "Brahma-sphuta-siddhanta" (628 AD). Franciscus Vieta (1540–1603) designated the unknowns by vowels and the givens by consonants. *Symbolic algebra*, as it is known, was recast into its current shape by Rene Descartes (1596–1650), who encoded knowns into "*a,b,c*" and unknowns into "*x,y,z*."

Unfortunately, for many school children, the "*x,y,z*" of Cartesian algebra deals a death blow to their hope of grasping basic math concepts. They become diehard math phobics.

◆   ◆   ◆

Whereas traditional math deals with exact numbers and formulas, real-life math must deal with fuzzy numbers—a shocking thing for students of classical math and the exact sciences. The following story illustrates my point.

One day I was having lunch with Kurt, a vice president of marketing, who was going on about his teenage daughter, Beth, and how she was something of a math genius. He knew I was a mathematician and wanted me to give her a math problem so he could prove how gifted she was.

Because I didn't appreciate hearing about anyone's daughter being more intelligent than mine, especially in math, I balked at the idea. I protested that my work was in real-life math, so I didn't have an appro-

priate problem for a high schooler. But he insisted and asked me to dis-
guise a problem to look like a high school assignment. Reluctantly, I
yielded and posed the following problem:

> The sum of father's age and daughter's age is about fifty-one. The
> difference between the father's age and the daughter's age is about
> thirty. Take twice the father's age and add the daughter's age and
> you get about ninety. What is the age of the father and the daugh-
> ter?

He was optimistic when he took the problem with him, saying that
this was exactly the kind of word-problem his little math genius
excelled in. But I added a warning: watch the word *about*. The problem does not admit a solution in which the equations are exactly satisfied. In real-life math, equations hold only approximately, and I
needed an approximate solution.

A couple of days later I received a phone call. Kurt was very upset.
"Why did you give my daughter an unsolvable problem?"

"What do you mean?" I said not so innocently.

"You tricked her. Beth could not solve the problem. She went so far
as to ask her teacher, and he said there was a mistake somewhere,
because according to the advanced theory of determinants, the problem had no solution."

"But, remember, I told you to watch out for the word *about*, a clue
that the problem has no exact solution. I have only an approximate
solution. Father is about forty years old and the daughter is about ten
years old."

The next day Kurt called back and said that Beth tried my solution
and it was no good.

"Why?" I asked, pretending to be surprised.

Kurt explained that if she used the figures in my solution, the sum
of the father and daughter's ages would be fifty years. According to the
original data, however, it is only fifty-one years. She was further confused because my solution met exactly the other two conditions.

"Let me ask you a question," I said. "When I prepared your sales quota last year, did you exactly meet the boss' specifications?"

"No way," he said. "I'm lucky if I get close."

"You got it," I said with a smile. "Fifty-one is close enough to fifty. My solution is practical."

◆   ◆   ◆

Do you watch your weight? I do. In 1953 I discovered to my chagrin that I weighed 167 pounds, too much for my height. This was many years before dieting became a worldwide craze. So I bought a medical scale and changed my eating habits. My permanent breakfast became a piece of dry toast and two cups of tea. Lunch, during the dieting period, was a glass of beer and four carrots. I developed a quality control chart and I watched the wiggly line on the chart until I lost 37 pounds. Whenever the chart went above 135 pounds, I put the screws on and went on my lunch diet, until I got down to 130. I never counted calories. Today, I am generally considered to be the lean scientific type.

In 1998 the government issued new federal height and weight guidelines. A journalist in my local newspaper reported that Earl, a local athlete, who was 6'2" and weighed 194.5 pounds, tested the formula and found that it was faulty.

It seems that on weekend mornings, Earl's weight was average according to the formula. But on Monday morning he was "overweight." This made no sense to Earl because he was essentially the same weight, give or take a few ounces. It turned out that Earl had had a big dinner Sunday evening and weighed 195 pounds on Monday morning. The 1/2 pound gain tipped the scales and also tipped him into the overweight category. The trouble was that formulas, like computers, obey binary arithmetic.

The tip-off point in Earl's case is 194.5 pounds. Below that weight, he is average; above it, he is overweight. This, of course, makes no practical sense, but is unavoidable when using a formula that declares you fat or not.

Engineers, of course, understand this discrepancy and always design with a safety factor, taking into account the tip-off points. They don't want bridges to collapse and airplane wings to flutter. Researchers in catastrophe theory (the theory of fractals) found very interesting tip-off points for innocent-looking formulas and experiments. For example, if you vigorously shake a double jointed pendulum, a pendulum hanging on another pendulum, you get some crazy oscillations. Binary decision making has the characteristics of the following ditty by the famous wit, Dr. Anonymous:

> You have two chances—
> One of getting the germ
> And one of not.
> And if you get the germ
> You have two chances—
> One of getting the disease
> And one of not.
> And if you get the disease
> You have two chances—
> One of dying
> And one of not
> And if you die—
> Well, you still have two chances!

◆   ◆   ◆

Paul Erdös, my math hero, introduced the following equation to calculate the age of "legal death":

Legally Dead=Your age—Your life expectancy at your birth.
For example, suppose you are 70 years old. You were born in 1927,

and the life expectancy in 1927 was about 58 years. So Erdös claimed that you have been legally dead for 12 years (70–58=12).

Erdös was joking, of course, but Dan Rather wasn't kidding around in a CBS News feature about Baby Boomers reaching the age of 50. Rather pointed out that at the turn of the century, the U.S. life expectancy was about 51 years. He went on to imply that someone living in that era who was nearing 50 was basically approaching death. He went on to say that later in the century, because life expectancy had increased to about 65 years, someone approaching 50 could look forward to another 15 years.

Unfortunately, Dan Rather totally misunderstood the statistics. In 1900–1902, the life expectancy of white males at the age of 50 was an additional 20.76, and by 1992 it increased to 27.1 years. The life expectancy in 1900–1902 of white males at the age of 80 was an additional 5.4 years; in 1992 that increased to 7.2 years. What Rather missed was the fact that your life expectancy depends on how old you already are. The older you are, the fewer number of years you have ahead of you.

If you examined the life expectancy tables using Dan Rather's approach, you would find the amazing result that all people over 60 are legally dead. To make the approach more mathematical I derived the approximate equation:

Years of being legally dead=3/2 × Your Age—90

For example, if you are 80 years old, you have been legally dead for 3/2 × 80–90=30 years.

◆   ◆   ◆

I don't like talking about Wall Street because it only leads to trouble—most investors don't want to hear the truth. They hear what they want to hear and make their decisions based on emotions, leading to dire consequences. I am a good example of someone who fell into the common pit and managed to crawl out.

One evening in 1972, I was watching my favorite television show, "You Bet Your Life," when the phone rang. It was Leonard, the investor guru who began managing my stocks after I joined the faculty at the University of Rochester.

"Did you look at the market?" he asked, his voice more subdued than usual.

"No," I said. "You know I leave all the decisions in your hands."

"You'd better look," he said.

I felt disturbed, but returned to my show and later went to bed. In the morning I reviewed my stocks in the newspaper and discovered that Leonard had lost ninety percent of my investments.

Although my jobs had always come with retirement packages, I had never stayed in one place long enough to receive any of the fruits. Social Security wouldn't amount to much; besides, after what I had seen in Hungary, I didn't have much confidence in government funding. So I was building up my own retirement fund. And that's what I had just lost in the stock market.

After World War I, most retired Hungarians with savings were ruined when the korona dropped to one thousandth of its value. The big stack of bonds my father kept in his strongbox were worthless. Unlike America, with its postwar boom, Hungary stagnated after the war. During my lifetime, not one new apartment building was built in Budapest. No bridges were built over the Danube. Only the wealthy had cars (driven by chauffeurs). Peasants and workers often didn't have enough to eat.

When the time came for me to build my retirement fund, however, I saw a completely different picture in the U.S. Every year there were more buildings, homes, roads, cars and larger factories. For the last one hundred years, America just kept getting richer and richer. So I decided to buy into the wealth of my adopted country. I pictured it as a kind of Hungarian partnership: we laugh together and cry together.

And if America got rich, we'd get rich together. The bottom line was that I trusted the U.S. and wanted to tie my financial future to Uncle Sam's. The only problem was, how would I get my slice of the wealth?

I had a vague notion about stocks on Wall Street having something to do with the wealth of America. If only I could have a tiny slice of the pie—a share of the automobile industry, the telephone business, soft drinks like Coca-Cola and 7-Up, PG&E, Safeway and so on—I would own a thin financial serving of America. The only drawback was that I had vivid memories of the crash of 1928, when I was only twelve years old. We were vacationing at Lake Balaton when the banks closed. Father had to return to Budapest, with all of us, to keep his affairs going. Over the following years, I heard plenty about the folly of playing the Bourse, the European stock exchange.

In 1971, however, I put these fears behind me and began looking into the best way to buy stocks. I talked to a number of friends who were quite successful at making money. Some handled their investments by themselves, others had reliable advisors. From the latter, I learned that unless you could take time off from your business/personal life, you should rely on experts to make smart money decisions.

My guy was Leonard. A good friend recommended him, and all of Leonard's references gave him glowing reviews. So I entrusted him with half of my savings. (Apparently I did have some common sense left.) In the first year, Leonard doubled my money. I was ecstatic at the thought of my rapidly growing nest egg. Six months later, he lost ninety percent of my original investment.

The experience did have a silver lining, though. It marked the last time in my life that I took somebody's advice without understanding first what I was doing.

What I discovered about the stock market was truly astounding. Brokers and financial advisors, I learned, had remarkably little rational basis for their actions. They made many financial decisions based on emotions, hunches, gossip and other unreliable sources. Instead of spending their time studying the market, stockbrokers were really salespeople who spent their time talking to clients and selling stock. A flourishing multibillion industry existed that was mostly based on the romance of Wall Street.

From my perspective, mathematics seemed like the best guide for future investments. Of course, stock prices go up and down based on the whims of investors (and the Goddess Fortuna), which makes the future rather fuzzy. But I also knew of ways to work with this uncertainty using probability theory.

> *Jupiter was holding his centennial executive staff meeting and was admonishing the Goddess Fortuna. "Humans have enjoyed gambling for millennia, but you need to invent something new to keep them interested. I expect you to present a new plan in our next meeting."*
>
> *At the next meeting, a century later, Fortuna presented a brand new plan. "I will start a new industry called Wall Street, a more interesting game, promising humans to become rich." Her plan was enthusiastically approved by the Olympian staff. A lot of merriment and drinking followed.*

So I reviewed everything I could find about decision making under uncertainty. This included going back to von Neumann's theory of games and checking out the work of Kahneman and Tversky, which helped me with the heuristics. At some point, I ran across a little known article that applied math to "portfolio theory." It was written in 1952 by Harry Markowitz, who was then studying at the University of Chicago and went on to receive the Nobel Prize in economics in 1990. His articles on investing and dealing with risk made a profound impression on Wall Street (and me).

Markowitz's math was fairly simple for me. He applied von Neumann's utility theory to stock portfolios, which I then applied to the idea of diversification. The most important thing I learned from Markowitz, though, was that I should stop worrying about individual stocks. Contrary to conventional wisdom that said you should ride one horse to victory, I began thinking in terms of groups of stocks, portfolios—that is, of riding a herd to victory. Now my challenge became to build a diversified portfolio that would represent the wealth of America as reflected by the Dow Jones Industrial Average.

With that in mind, I began squirreling away a small part of my paycheck so that I could buy mutual funds. My goal was to own a balanced combination of the various instruments of investing such as mutuals, cash equivalents, equities, real estate, gold and whatever looked reasonable. I figured that by purchasing a little here, a little there, my portfolio would resemble a thin slice of the Dow. As it turned out, my strategy worked. Relying on compound growth, tying my financial future to Uncle Sam's—in effect, owning shares in USA Inc.—was a sound investment strategy.

> *"To market to market, to buy a few piglets," ruminates a farmhand, as she walks to the market with a basket of eggs on her head. Her hens laid a big heap of eggs and she is planning to sell the eggs to buy piglets. She will fatten the piglets and sell the hogs. Then she will buy baby lambs, raise them to sheep, sell them and buy calves. The calves will grow to cows, she will own a daily farm and become rich. When her beau comes and proposes to her, she will say NO! So she shakes her head vigorously. All the eggs spill out and break.*
>
> *The moral is: Do not put all your eggs in one basket, as proposed in 1605 by Cervantes in Don Quixote and proved mathematically in 1952 by Dr. Harvey Markowitz.*

I never discussed my method of investing because it sounded too simple and passive. Our culture holds that there must be a way to beat the market and predict the future value of stocks, if only you have the magic word. When two people trade a stock, both believe they are clever: the seller who thinks the stock value will go down, and the buyer who thinks that it will go up. Both parties think that they can foresee the future. Trading people don't want to hear the truth. The track record shows that on the average they do worse than the market. I found it better to stay away from all explanations.

It was much later that my approach was vindicated by the random walk theory of the market and the wide-spread acceptance of index funds.

19

INDUSTRIAL TYCOON

The reason I went into private industry in 1946 was that Professor Westergaard, dean of Harvard's Engineering School, advised me that I needed a few years of industrial experience if I wanted to obtain a good teaching job. Somehow, those "few years" stretched into twenty-four satisfying ones. Looking back on all the jobs I held during those years, I must admit that my last position at North American Aviation was the best.

When I first went to work at North American Aviation in 1946, my job was designing supersonic missiles. Nineteen years later, I returned after stints with the civil service, Hughes Aircraft and Ramo-Wooldridge Corporation and as a partner of a marketing consulting firm. The circle was completed in 1965, when I returned to North American Aviation as a systems engineer to help with strategic decision making. Within a few months, I managed to get transferred to work as a scientific advisor to Elmer Woolf, corporate vice president of administration.

What I really liked about my new job was that I could pick and choose which managerial crises to stick my nose into. My authority in these matters was not unlike that of a relatively low-ranking officer in the Hungarian Army who, as a representative of the all-powerful general staff, dealt with generals on an equal basis.

My job called for developing personal relationships with top executives, and I focused much attention on Chief Executive Officer Lee Atwood. One of my strategies involved sharing lunch with him in the executive dining room. Doors opened at 12:30 p.m. sharp, but

Atwood typically showed up five minutes late. Because he had a reputation for being rather gruff and demanding, most of the executives tried to avoid sitting next to him. They would line up before the doors opened and fill up tables before Atwood arrived. Because Atwood was also an engineer who respected mathematics, I saw an opportunity to make a friend right at the top.

Once I saw how everything worked, I developed the habit of showing up ten minutes late for lunch. That meant I always found an empty seat next to Mr. Atwood. Before long, people would ask what we talked about because they always heard us laughing. I remember one day I told Atwood that I was having a tough domestic problem and would appreciate his advice.

"You see, my daughter got married, and I'm converting her bedroom into an office."

"What's the problem?" he asked.

"I can't make up my mind. Should I buy a huge, square mahogany desk for the office so that I can play corporate vice president? Or buy a wraparound desk and play corporate director?" I was referring to North American's well-known corporate policy of matching office furniture to an executive's rank on the food chain. (The commoners had gray metal desks.)

One thing for sure, the executive dining room served the best hamburgers anywhere. The chef told me his secret. By Atwood's executive order, the staff served hamburgers once a week. Because Atwood was not only demanding but parsimonious, too, the chef's way of getting even was to buy filet mignon and grind it up until it resembled ground beef.

As a thrifty person, Atwood was always gratified to see us using handmade charts during our briefings. Never mind that handmade charts cost twice as much as the standard machine drawn charts. They looked cruder and, hence, cheaper.

◆   ◆   ◆

In many organizations there are important executives who abuse their powers and enjoy bullying people. I've always thought it great fun to meet these domineering types and felt ethically justified in playing my favorite game, "I got you, you S.O.B.," with them. There was once a notorious barbarian whom I'll call Eric Stone. He had considerable clout because he was the president of the all-important space division of North American Aviation. People feared him and avoided him whenever possible.

One day Stone submitted a request for a large computer installation with a budget of eighteen million dollars—a huge sum at the time. After examining the request, however, we found Stone was missing certain justifications for the purchase. When we told the corporate vice president of research about our findings, he suggested that one of us should go over to Stone's division and ask questions.

Of course, no one enjoyed the prospect of tackling Stone. Finally, the VP said, "Vazsonyi is the only guy who is crazy enough to take him on."

Whether that bit of flattery was true or not, I was sent on my way. Stone's division was at the other end of town, so I hopped on one of the corporate helicopters and flew towards the lion's den.

When I arrived, I found Stone sitting behind his giant, custom-made table with his chief engineer beside him. Then he started a long harangue, ending with, "You guys in Corporate sit on your asses, doing nothing or worse—holding up progress. I need the eighteen million—and that's that!"

I slowly rose to my feet and imagined my phantom army, Atwood and all my colleagues, supporting me.

"You can insult me as much as you want," I said, "but I won't tolerate your insults to the corporate offices that I represent."

His eyes bulged out as if he were about to have a stroke.

"Now I'm leaving and reporting back to Mr. Atwood."

It occurred to me at that moment that nobody had ever talked to him like that before. Or perhaps he wasn't a poker player and didn't know that I might be bluffing.

Just when I thought maybe I was as crazy as my colleagues thought, he took a deep breath and asked me to have a seat. Then, in a softer voice, he repeated his claim that he must have the eighteen million.

I decided to continue playing my hand and looked him straight in the eye. "You remind me of my daughter," I said. His face turned red at this assault on his masculinity. "She says she must have a car. But she doesn't tell me what she needs a car for, or where she wants to go in the car. Likewise, when I look over your inventory proposal, I can't tell if you plan to carry inventory for spares for one week, one month, one year or a hundred years."

He turned for an answer to the chief engineer, who didn't know what to say.

Then I pulled the math card that I kept up my sleeve. "Are you familiar with the mathematical theory of inventory control?" I said.

Once again, Stone deferred to his chief engineer.

"We don't have any mathematicians on our staff who know how to do that," the engineer said.

"Okay," I said. "I'll set up a math model that you can use."

Stone, who didn't get into his position by being a complete jerk, began to act like more of a pussycat. He probably remembered Atwood's respect for math. "When can you start?" he asked.

Later, as I was about to leave, Stone turned to me and smiled like Mr. Nice Guy. "So what happened? Did you buy your daughter the car?"

"No," I said, "It turns out that she's too young to get a driver's license."

◆   ◆   ◆

There were other times at North American Aviation when knowing math saved my skin.

One day I was sitting in my office when I got a desperate call from an engineering analyst.

"We have this data from telemetering and have been trying to do a regression analysis on it," he said. "But we've tried everything, even the most sophisticated nonlinear regression techniques, and nothing works."

"Come over," I said, "and bring the data with you."

I activated my math hump as he appeared with a box of IBM cards. In those days, all data was stored on cards.

"Let's see the data," I said.

He started to hand me the box. I knew that the cards weren't going to do me any good because I couldn't read them.

"Not that. I want to see the graph."

He acted surprised. "We don't have a graph. Anyway, what would you do with it?"

I gave him a mysterious look and said, "Trust me. Go back to your office and make a graph. This is just standard practice for mathematicians."

Thirty minutes later the phone rang.

"Dr. Vazsonyi," he said, sounding happily relieved. "We made the graph and discovered that the decimal point was misplaced on one of the data points. Naturally every program blew using such crazy data. But after we used the simplest linear regression program, it worked like magic."

Another time I received a call from Stone's space division. (By now we were reluctant buddies.) A programmer needed the Gamma function, an advanced mathematical function required for an inventory control problem, but could not make it work. After he came by my office, I looked over the program and couldn't find the error.

"Where did you get this program?" I asked.

"From our bible, the IBM Scientific Library," he said.

"What value of the argument did you need?"

"Two point five one," he said.

The power series of expansion of the Gamma function—as every mathematician knows—converges very fast between 0 and 1, but it's extremely slow—if it works at all—for larger values. So it was obvious that his program wouldn't work.

"Let me write a new program," I proposed.

"No," he said. "I'll contact IBM. They'll know what to do."

I decided to write the simple program anyway and after less than an hour, I had one that he could use. A few weeks later, I ran into him and asked how he made out with IBM. Not so good, he said. After many phone calls he discovered that the programmer who wrote the program quit, and nobody else knew why it wouldn't work. At that point I offered him the program I wrote. He accepted it and of course it worked like magic.

◆   ◆   ◆

I was always looking for an application of dynamic programming, the highly touted mathematical programming technique that, as far as I could determine, had no practical application whatsoever. Then I read a news release about a mathematician in Stone's space division who claimed to have found an important application that helped with inventory management. Always the skeptic, I dug in and found that the so-called "application" existed only in the imagination of this mathematician.

A few weeks later I was talking with the chief engineer, who had become quite friendly after my encounter with Stone. I asked him about the project.

"The Air Force has been badgering me about that theory," he said angrily. "The fact is that we are on a cost-plus project and couldn't care less about saving inventory control costs."

"So what did you do about the mathematician?"

"He received a professorship at a good university and quit."

◆　　　◆　　　◆

At that time, North American Aviation was the largest IBM user in the world—our space program required nonstop calculations. As scientific advisor, I was the point person for IBM. Of course, there were certain advantages to this. When I traveled in foreign cities, IBM usually made its presence known. Once, when I arrived in Bangkok, the town was full of tourists, and I could not find a decent room. The IBM rep, who was alerted to my situation by the home office, was very influential and got me a suite in the best hotel.

In Budapest, IBM reps attended my talk and gave me a "GONDOLKOZZ!" sign. This was the Hungarian version of the famous "THINK!" sign by Thomas Watson, the founder of IBM.

Another time Laura and I were driving from Marseilles to Grenoble on the scenic Napoleonic route. We stopped at La Gaude, the international research center of IBM. When I called to speak to someone, the chief programmer came on the line and offered to take us to dinner. After he picked us up at our hotel, we were driving along and he pointed out a chateau-like place. "That's where we take VIPs," he said. I fully expected to pull in, but instead he went on to a modest-looking restaurant. The food and wine were excellent, but my feelings were hurt. The next morning, when I went to IBM, I was introduced to the general manager.

"I hope you enjoyed the restaurant," he said. "The food is much better than the tourist trap where we usually take the VIPs."

Because of my position, whenever I asked IBM a question about our computer needs, the reps jumped. One day I received a bunch of reports about their new programming system, APL, which they suggested we install.

I was interested because the author, Kenneth E. Iverson, earned his Ph.D. in mathematics from Harvard. His goal was to develop a language that dealt with math problems, theoretical and practical. At some of the conferences I attended, there was huge interest in his APL language.

Once I had a reasonable understanding of the language, I asked for more information. An IBM representative quickly set up an appointment for me with an expert in their Wilshire Boulevard building in Los Angeles.

When I arrived, the programmer received me with great courtesy.

"Have you ever been on the system?" he asked.

"Not yet," I confessed.

"Let me give you a demonstration." He clicked on his terminal and started his spiel.

As I soon discovered, he assumed that I was a mathematical idiot, matching my executive rank. So, I interrupted and told him that I knew all that and had specific questions.

This interruption, however, only made him start his spiel all over again.

After a few more starts and stops like this, I pulled out a sheet of paper from my pocket and shoved it under his nose.

"I wrote a recursive program to calculate terms of the Fibonacci series [something every mathematician knows]. Would this program run?"

He looked at the program and his chin dropped.

"You wrote this program? But you said you've never been on the machine before."

Then he typed in the program and ran it. Behold, the terminal started to type out the Fibonacci series.

"Let me save this first," he said. "I want to use it with my clients."

He hit a few more keys, then we started our dialogue.

Unfortunately, he didn't know enough math to answer all my questions, so I flew to Philadelphia to get the stuff straight from the horse's mouth.

My IBM guide escorted me to the lab where Ken Iverson worked. But as we walked in, a couple of guys were on their way out.

"Hey, you're Iverson, aren't you?" my guide called out.

"Yes," said Iverson.

"You have an appointment with Dr. Vazsonyi."

"I'm going out for lunch," he said. "I'm bothered by executives all the time."

He might as well have said "bothered by idiots."

Then he invited us into his office.

I recalled my previous experience and tried to figure out how to break the ice with Iverson.

"You know, I wrote a recursive program for the Fibonacci series, but now I want to write a program to calculate Erdös numbers. Do you know how I can do that?"

He seemed surprised that an executive idiot would know of Erdös.

"Of course," I said, "I don't need it for myself because my Erdös number is one."

After that, Iverson and I got along just fine.

◆   ◆   ◆

Computer demonstrations were a constant headache—I never got anything out of them.

Sometimes when I was feeling particularly mean I would take my frustration out on the unfortunate demonstrator. I was at one demo where I asked the guy if I could try typing in the parameters that would make the machine go through the simplex method automatically and produce the optimum solution to a linear programming problem.

I typed in the numbers, but replaced one of the zeros with the letter "o." A user-friendly system should have indicated that an illegal entry was made. But the system was user-hostile and failed. The expert couldn't figure out what happened, so he called in the programmer, who was stumped as well.

"Let me try it again," I said.

This time I entered a zero and the program worked like a charm. Later I heard that they got the message. Programmers should write user-friendly programs and not blame the users for understandable errors. They patched the program, so if you entered the letter "o" instead of a zero, the response was "Error."

It finally got to the point where I swore off attending demos altogether.

That's what I told the rep who wanted me to see a demo of IBM's new graphic computer package.

"I tell you what," he said. "We close shop at 5:00 p.m. But you name the day, and we'll let you in after five and give you a personal demo."

Knowing that it would be a feather in his cap if I attended, I let him drag me to it. As expected, the expert showed off his demo, and I had the typical mind-numbing experience. The next day, the rep called and asked how I liked it.

"I took an oath never to go to another demo. And last night God punished me for taking a false oath."

◆　　◆　　◆

In 1970 a storm was gathering over North American Aviation. We had merged with Rockwell in Cleveland, but the merger felt like a hostile takeover. Somehow, Rockwell had outmaneuvered Atwood, who was more of a patriotic country boy than a Machiavellian executive.

We disliked the Rockwells from the beginning. Mrs. Rockwell took her friends to Disneyland on corporate helicopters—something that was totally unheard of during the Atwood regime. Executives had their own barbershop and made their appointments ahead of time with Gus, the barber. Not the Rockwells, who expected service whenever the mood struck. Eventually they fired over a thousand people in the corporate offices, transferred the headquarters to Cleveland and sold the building to Hughes Aircraft.

I saw the handwriting on the wall and decided not to wait around. First, I told the organization people to take me off the organization chart so that the Rockwells would have a harder time finding me. Then I started thinking about leaving industry for a more rewarding career.

All my life I had felt compelled to teach, and during my industrial career I had given many talks, as well as authored papers and books. So I decided that I would achieve more personal fulfillment if I devoted all my efforts to research and teaching. Nowadays it's not too unusual for a person to switch horses at midstream and choose a brand new career. In fact, counselors may encourage you to do so if you're in a dead-end position. But all this would have been totally inconceivable in Hungary, the old country. It was still somewhat unusual in the U.S. in 1970 when I decided to swap a successful industrial career for a life in academia.

I had never learned anything from university professors—with a few notable exceptions—so I deliberated for a long time over whether I had the necessary stuff to become an exception myself.

In the beginning, I was under the illusion that my industrial experience qualified me to be a professor. I thought I had kept up with university life, as I had always taught in extension schools. But I had very little understanding of how academia really worked. I didn't realize how little professors knew about practical management.

I also thought professors would readily embrace what I knew about management. I totally underestimated academics' resistance to change and their love of pure theory. I found that many academics looked down on people in industry and didn't believe that people in the field could contribute to knowledge. To them, academia was the fountainhead of all knowledge.

Teaching leading-edge extension courses taught me how to deal with highly motivated students who were eager to learn, but I had no experience with reluctant students or contact with faculty life. In short, I had no idea of the troubles that lay ahead.

20

PROFESSOR AND AUTHOR

o o o o o o o o o o o o o o o o o o o o o o o o o o o o o o
He who can, does. He who cannot, teaches.

—*George Bernard Shaw (1856–1950)*

In 1970, I was still employed at North American Aviation, but was looking around for an academic position when I heard about an interesting development at the University of Southern California (USC). The USC School of Management was planning to install an IBM computer in the fall. But nobody on the faculty was qualified to install it. Not only that, no one was interested either. The dean was the only person who had the vision to see how important computers would become.

After I expressed interest in the position, the dean felt that I was qualified for the job and, moreover, with my academic credentials, would command respect from the faculty. He offered me a three-year appointment with the proviso that I spend the first year installing and running the computer. After that, I could begin teaching. Despite a big salary cut, I accepted the professorship and said adios to industry for the last time.

The USC School of Management didn't have a computer at the time, but during my first official tour I saw a punch card installation under the direction of a doctoral student. On the shelves were stacks of IBM punch cards.

"What do you use those for?" I asked the student.

"Those are the old cards, carefully stored away," he said.

"Why?"

"I don't know."

"Who does know?"

"Nobody."

"When I start work in September, I don't want to see any cards here."

I was puzzled by all this. Apparently the installation was under the sole direction of the doctoral student, without any guidance from the faculty. What was the faculty doing anyway?

Was it still clinging to archaic ways and ignoring computers? Would I have to adjust to teaching in a museum? Or, after the trial year was up, would I return to industry?

Fortunately, the cards were gone when I arrived. So far, so good. But I soon learned there were other significant differences between industry and academia. At my first faculty meeting, after the dean introduced me, I presented my ideas and invited colleagues to discuss plans for the new computer at a later date. When the time for that meeting came, however, nobody showed. My first lesson was that while industry people operate in a hierarchical structure in which one is bounded by certain loyalties and a sense of duty, academics resemble jobbers who sometimes seem linked by no more than a shared parking lot. Also, industry people are required by competitive forces to adapt to technological changes, such as computers.

The dean was very supportive and appreciated my contribution. The computer system that was installed under my direction ran smoothly and trouble-free—unlike most other academic installations. After my first year, true to his word, the dean hired a non-academic person to run the computer center, and I spent most of the next two years learning, teaching and writing about computers. I always considered computer programming a mathematically oriented task, and soon acquired a reputation as the computer guru at USC. Early on, I figured out that teaching computers could be a Trojan horse in which one could sneak math into the classroom.

My biggest problem was that I was practically clueless when it came to playing academic politics. Because I started at the top (with a salary that made me the envy of others) and didn't learn the ropes by working my way up, I was a babe when it came to presenting my ideas about developing courses, defining curricula and promoting myself. Years later I gained some insight into the politics of academia, which is captured perfectly in the following story, from J. Abner's *The Saber-Tooth Curriculum* (McGraw-Hill, 1939).

> Once upon a time there was a tribe who lived off the fish they caught by hand from a swift stream. Because the fishing was quite difficult, and the tribe depended on the fish for survival, the Petaluma State University developed an elaborate curriculum on Fish Grabbing.
>
> Everything was fine until the day an earthquake shook and rattled the ground, dumping so much mud into the stream that it became impossible for Fish Grabbers to catch fish anymore. Fortunately, some creative souls developed another method of fishing, one that relied on lines and nets.
>
> Despite this innovation, the Curriculum Committee at Petaluma State insisted that they continue to teach Fish Grabbing. Although the course no longer had any practical benefit, the committee declared that the curriculum helped to develop a logical mind and physical dexterity, and that it was historically correct and therefore "good for the soul." The committee rejected a new curriculum on Fishing With Lines and Nets because it didn't fit into a curriculum loaded with teaching Hebrew, Greek, Latin, rigorous proofs of algebra and Euclidean geometry. This classical academic attitude led to economic disaster, though theoretical research on Fish Grabbing remained a popular topic for PhD dissertations.

I began finding corollaries to Fish Grabbing early on in my academic career. For instance, I could never understand why American schools spent so much time teaching fractions. After all, students can easily use electronic calculators (fishing nets). In Hungary, of course, we had the decimal system so we wasted no time on learning fractions. It also meant that when my mother visited in 1946 and prepared to make her famous Dobos torte, a sumptuous cake with seven thin layers, she had no way of converting her grams into cups, tablespoons and teaspoons until I finally bought an affordable decimal scale during a visit to Mexico.

For that matter, I could never see the point in teaching calculus. This was one subject I could never teach successfully, although when I was a teenager I was the only one in my lycée class who could master this form of torture.

The 1987 film Stand and Deliver *presents the real-life, heroic story of Jaime Escalante, a dedicated high school teacher who inspires his East Los Angeles barrio students to pass an Advanced Placement calculus test. The movie focuses on the motivation and hard work necessary to master a most demanding and frightening subject. However, the story never shows how the students' mastery of calculus is useful, except as a brain teaser (and for shattering certain stereotypes held by testing authorities).*

The only rational explanation I ever heard for teaching calculus came from a dean at a medical school who once told me, "To keep medical fees up, we must keep the number of physicians down. Of course, the problem of keeping students out of school is a delicate one. So the best thing to do is make calculus a required course and that scares away many of the applicants."

Another explanation I could understand was given by the head of a math department: "Teaching calculus creates employment for young mathematicians."

Calculus (an abbreviation for calculus of the infinitesimal) was introduced by Newton to master the laws of motion. His discovery fueled spectacular successes in physics and afterwards became an important field of mathematics. Newton's success also created the illusion that calculus would be useful in the social sciences such as psychology and the political sciences. However, by the middle of the 1900s, when computers (finite state machines) were introduced, scholars realized that there were fields of mathematics without calculus that were also of importance. In 1956, John G. Kemeny, a mathematician and computer guru, published a critically acclaimed textbook *Introduction to Finite Mathematics* (Prentice-Hall), describing a version of math that didn't include calculus.

Years later, after realizing that calculus had limited use in decision making, I came across Kemeny's work on finite math and decided that this was the type of math we needed in our field. An editor at John Wiley Publishing agreed that there was a market for such a book in the schools of management, especially for professors and students who didn't have a solid foundation in math. We produced a beautiful book in 1977, *Finite Mathematics, Quantitative Analysis for Management*. There was only one hitch—the book didn't sell.

The John Wiley editor misjudged the market and shared my mistaken belief that faculty would be interested in teaching useful and understandable math to business school students. But what math professors really wanted to do was to continue teaching their pet subjects, and business school faculty didn't want to teach math at all. My textbook fell between a rock and a hard place because finite math wasn't accepted as a course in either the math or business curriculum.

◆   ◆   ◆

My textbook on finite math wasn't my first attempt to spread the word on teaching a more practical version of math. During my first year at USC, Roger Ross, an editor at Richard D. Irwin, asked if I'd be interested in writing a math book for junior colleges.

"It has nothing to do with decision making, management science or computers," he said. "It wouldn't be beneath your dignity, would it?"

His final words had the desired effect of getting my hackles up, so I asked for more information about the project. He explained that the book should cover such topics as fractions, percents, accounting, finance, taxes, interest, discounts—all those basic things that send students into such a tizzy. Because I wasn't working on a writing project at the time, I decided to give it a whirl and signed a contract, even though some of the topics, such as fractions, made no sense to me. In no time at all I delivered a draft containing the first three chapters.

A couple of months later, Ross appeared in my office. After much hemming and hawing, he admitted that reviewers did not take kindly to the chapters.

"You mean the manuscript is no damn good?" I asked.

"That's about the size of it," he said.

Usually I'm quite emotional about my writing, but I felt calm this time. This was more of a test of my mental prowess than anything else. And I realized that I knew enough about math to write the book, but not enough about the junior college market.

With Ross's help, I soon formed a partnership with a veteran junior college math teacher. My partner didn't write a single word, but he told me what would and wouldn't work (for which he received a third of the royalties).

After we delivered the revised draft of the manuscript to the editor, nothing happened. Finally I called Ross and he sheepishly admitted, "I'm sorry, but I forgot that we already had signed a contract with another author. As you know, we can't publish two books on the same subject at the same time." Then he made some vague promise about publishing the book the next year.

Needless to say, I was quite upset. I knew that publishing was a mismanaged business, but I thought there were limits to the craziness.

Especially when, three months later, Ross called back. "When can you finish the manuscript?" he asked.

The other book had sold only three copies, and now the publisher was desperate for our book. We finished the manuscript in six months, the book was published in 1971 and it went on to become very successful during its three editions. At one point, it was even second on the publisher's best sellers list.

◆   ◆   ◆

Over the years, I've had many publishing experiences, some good and some bad. I learned that the rules of book publishing are quite erratic and publishers don't operate in a businesslike fashion—one leading publisher even lost a manuscript of mine. Over time, however, I did learn to pay attention to my intended audience. For instance, *Problem Solving by Digital Computers with PL/I Programming*, a mathematician's view of computer programming, was published in 1970 and quickly flopped. It failed because I was interested in solving problems with math and computers, but back then people were intrigued by the computer for its own sake, not as a problem-solving tool. Moreover, at that time, professors of management despised computers. As one of the top management scientists told me, "I can't conceive of any managerial issue that would be helped by a computer."

> *In 1961, when Xerox started to market copy machines, a market researcher estimated that the market would be limited. They knew how many secretaries worked in the U.S. and were able to estimate the number of carbon copies made based on sales of carbon paper. What they failed to realize was that people would begin making copies of everything, so that the market would be many thousand times greater than predicted.*

Another textbook I co-authored in 1984 also sold poorly when it came out. This book focused on decision making under uncertainty in probabilistic environments. At the time, it took me a great deal of effort to study and research this relatively new area. I also tried a new editorial approach. Because I wanted to get rid of the boring aspects of writing, I teamed up with a partner who was supposed to critique the drafts and take care of the details. However, the partnership did not work very well, so I did most of the work myself. I suspect the reason that the book didn't sell was that over the years the academic field of decision making had completely changed. In 1958, when the material was all new, unorthodox methods of teaching were readily accepted. By the 1980s, however, the topics and approaches were well developed, cast in concrete, and novel approaches were not in demand. This failure propelled me to develop a more market-oriented approach.

The success of my first book gave me the false impression that publishing books in the future would be a breeze. The next two unpublished manuscripts sobered me up, but I never quit. I gathered a long history of dealing with publishers.

It took me years to realize that contracts were not binding at all—they were more like unenforceable gentlemen's agreements. The author commits himself to work diligently, and the publishing company agrees to not sign a contract with another author for a competing book. Beyond that, anything can happen. When the author turns in the finished manuscript, the publisher may publish it—or reject it—at their pleasure.

In the early 1980s, while learning how to use the PC, I kept detailed aid-memoirs and eventually decided to write a book on the subject. My focus was on programming in BASIC, which was very popular at the time. For several reasons, but mainly because the publisher dilly-dallied while the field exploded, the book was already obsolete when it came out in 1985. Once again I learned the lesson that publishing is an uncertain, sometimes cruel, business.

On the bright side, however, my PL/I book was successful because it eventually led to an excellent, tenured professorship.

◆   ◆   ◆

My three-year appointment at USC ended on a sour note when I was denied tenure. The business school dean was as taken aback as I was. When he began asking around, he learned that one tenure committee member had spouted forth against "that son-of-a-bitch Vazsonyi, who was running the computer—and the school—into the ground." When this grouch was reminded that it had been two years since I had maintained the computer, he said nothing. Anyway, the majority of the faculty didn't use the computer, didn't like it and just didn't give much thought to the future of computers in the business school. I still find it incredible to see how slowly this attitude has changed over the years. Even today, in my opinion, the average professor's knowledge of computers leaves much to be desired from the point of view of practical business.

The dean also mentioned that there was an undercurrent of resentment in the department. Apparently, I was the highest paid professor on the faculty. The dean considered installation of the computer the highest priority and figured (rightly!) that this was the lowest pay he could get me at. He offered to hire me on a yearly basis, and also raised the possibility of overruling the tenure committee, which he said he could do. Unfortunately for me and him, he was fired around the same time.

Besides all this, there was another problem. I was pretty good at teaching computers, but when it came to teaching statistics, the student evaluations were not so good. Like many mathematicians, I knew nothing about statistics and only many years later realized the importance of statistical thinking in decision making. So I didn't think the way I taught statistics was very practical, and it showed. I attended the classes of some of the most popular teachers, hoping I'd learn some of their successful strategies, but it never worked out. Ordinarily, the tenure committee didn't pay much attention to student evaluations. But in my case they focused on them as a rationale for not giving me tenure.

◆   ◆   ◆

I was in the process of licking my wounds and considering a return to industry when I heard from a friend at the University of Rochester's Graduate School of Business. Students at this economics and theoretically oriented school were clamoring for a computer education, but the dean didn't believe that computers were a proper academic subject. Industry people who were computer savvy weren't academically acceptable to him or the tenure committee. However, I had all the math qualifications for academia and my PL/I book guaranteed that I knew something about computers. Thanks to this unusual combination and the timing of the goddess Fortuna, I received an offer of a well-paying tenured job.

The dilemma was that after twenty-five years of living in the Los Angeles area, I had been brainwashed into believing that there was no life outside of California. Another real hitch was that Bobbi, my daughter, was living in San Francisco. Finally, after much deliberation, Laura and I decided to move—with telephones and airplanes available, we reasoned that my career was more important than geographical distance. When friends asked why I wanted to move from California to the East Coast, my stock answer was, "Because I am stupid." Interestingly enough, this answer was universally accepted.

Everything I need to learn, I learn from books. For instance, soon after moving to Rochester, I woke up one morning to see a fairyland of snow. I immediately wanted to take up skiing. Down-hill skiing scared the wits out of me, but I thought I could handle cross-country skiing. So I dashed out and bought a set of skis—and a book.

On the front lawn, I strapped on my skis, grabbed my poles and stood up with the book in one hand—and promptly fell on my face. So I retreated to the house, sipped a little red wine, then had a brainstorm. In the basement, I could prop the book on my wife's music stand, stand on skis, grip poles and follow the instructions. Laura almost died laughing when she saw me. But I had the last laugh. The first time I went out skiing, I took off down the trail and fell hard on my butt. I had to grin at how ridiculous I must have looked as I struggled to get up with my skis and poles pointing in all directions.

◆   ◆   ◆

When I settled in at the University of Rochester, I felt that I had fully arrived in academia. I had a tenured position in a top-ranking eastern university. The university had the feel of an Ivy League place—not quite like Harvard, Yale or Princeton, but close enough. According to some ratings, the Rochester Graduate School of Business was one of the top business schools in the U.S. The reason it was judged so highly was because the faculty was well known for economics. But as far as their interest in real-life business, that was another ballgame. It wasn't long before I found myself totally out of sync with the dean and any faculty members with influence.

Quite simply, they didn't know what to do with me. My industrial experience meant nothing. At USC the faculty thought that business people were idiots—at Rochester they knew it. My computer knowledge was useless. I couldn't teach about computers because that would have been beneath the school's dignity. My only saving grace, as far as they were concerned, was my math background.

Fortunately, a new, somewhat dubious, field emerged: management information systems (MIS). This popular field focused on how computers ought to be used in management. MIS proposed to replace data processing, the academic area to which the computer was typically relegated in traditional business schools. So I was assigned to teach MIS courses. The dean and the faculty didn't think much of the new curriculum, and I wasn't so hot on it myself.

When I first began teaching MIS, most of the teaching material was still steeped in data processing. So I decided to write a book on the way I was teaching, which meant I left out the highfalutin' theoretical stuff.

I was using a new MIS textbook of dubious value and students were complaining about the contents of the book. One day one the students asked me why I always refer to the book as the "Yellow Pony" book. Well, I said, this is the way it is.

A certain father was bragging about his boys to a friend. "Paul, the elder was a pessimist, Peter the younger an optimist," the father explained. The friend asked for details and the father said, "I will prove it to you. Tomorrow I am giving them a present, and you will see their reactions."

The next day at the designated hour the friend appears at the father's house. He takes the friend to the guest room where there is big heap of horse dung, a shovel and nothing else. Father tells Paul to look for his present in the guest room. Paul comes back crying, "What can I do with a heap of dung?"

Then the father tells Peter to look for his present. Soon they hear Peter singing and whistling. They open the door and see Peter busily shoveling in the dung. "Where there is so much dung, there must be a pony," Peter says.

Introduction to Electronic Data Processing was published in 1973 by Richard D. Irwin and became my best-selling book. It was eventually translated into German and Spanish, and ran through three editions. Its success had nothing to do with math, and everything to do with explaining things in simple language (something, for the life of me, I could do only in writing, not in the classroom). Although this book brought me no academic fame, it certainly helped my savings account each time I deposited a fat royalty check.

During this time, Roger Ross, my editor at Irwin, suggested that I become active in the American Institute of Decision Sciences (AIDS), founded in 1969. This group consisted of educators who made up the audience for my books. I joined the association and, afterwards, it became my principal professional affiliation. Once the name AIDS became linked in the public's mind with a newly emerging disease, the association renamed itself the Decision Sciences Institute. In the ensuing years, I was elected a Fellow of the Institute and served on their Council. In May 1989, I began writing a feature column, "The Specialist with the Universal Mind," five times a year for their regular news publication. It is now the only professional activity I faithfully keep up with. The articles provide a platform for my ideas and have established me as something of an in-house philosopher.

◆   ◆   ◆

As a confirmed Californian, I expected life to be dull in Rochester. Fortunately, I was dead wrong. When Laura and I had lived in the East before, it was during the war and we were too poor to travel. Of course, in California we were better off and we covered the West going north to Barrow, Alaska, south to Baja California and east to Colorado. Now we made up for lost time and covered the East Coast from Newfoundland to Key West several times.

But when I turned 61 years old in 1977, I could feel the threat of forced retirement hanging over my head. Congress had passed a law that tenured professors could be forced to retire at the age of 65. So being tenured meant only that I couldn't be fired in the next four years. This was hardly better than being in industry. Because there was no love between me and the dean, I was convinced that I would be cashiered at 65. So I had a few years to make some other arrangements.

I considered retiring to concentrate on book writing, but my financial position wouldn't allow me to sit back and rely on book royalties, not a particularly stable source of income. One job offer came from a business school at St. Mary's University in San Antonio, Texas. At first I didn't pursue it because the university had no graduate school and was rated quite low. However, the dean, Bob Howe, didn't let up. He invited me to visit the campus, all expenses paid, with a substantial grant. I told him I already had plans for my winter break, but he finally convinced me to fly out for one week.

When Laura and I arrived, we had quite a surprise waiting for us. St. Mary's had rolled out the red carpet—I had never met people so friendly and hospitable in my life. They gave us two rooms in the university guest house and meal tickets, loaned us a car and tossed in a generous stipend. In exchange, I was asked to conduct an open session for the faculty, so they could look me over and decide if they liked what they saw.

At the faculty session, I gave a brief description of my views on teaching management. This was followed by a free-for-all. One member of the faculty gave me a particularly hard time. She said the inventory reordering formula that I put on the blackboard was wrong. Fortunately, I remembered that one of the leading textbooks had the wrong formula in its 6th edition, but corrected it in the 7th, of which I had an advance copy.

So I took a shot in the dark and asked her if she was referring to the 6th edition of the textbook. When she replied yes, I pointed out that a new, corrected edition would soon be out.

Later I learned that this was the turning point for many people on the faculty. Their main concern was that I was over-qualified for the job and most likely a pain in the neck. But it turned out that the professor who had grilled me was the terror of the faculty, and nobody dared to stand up to her attacks. My polite, well-informed reply was music to their ears. (Five years later the holy terror was driven out when someone discovered that she had a phony doctorate.)

After clearing that hurdle, I had interviews with the president and academic vice president—both Marianist Catholic priests. Oddly enough, priests weren't on the faculty.

When the St. Mary's leaders asked me what kind of offer would tempt me to move cross-country, I gave it careful thought. The university had a pleasant group of faculty and friendly relationships with students, but the school also had limited scholarly standing. Clearly, this would be my last faculty position, so the lack of academic prominence didn't bother me too much. Besides, what I really wanted was to spend less time on teaching and more on writing textbooks.

I prepared a memo that specified a teaching load of one course per semester, with summers free. Money always interested me, and because they implied that it was no object, I specified what chaired professorships paid at first-rate universities. In all, I asked for fifty percent more than I was making at Rochester, a large grant for research expenses, summer pay and all moving expenses from Rochester.

I was all set to negotiate as I watched the St. Mary's president read my memo.

Instead, he merely looked up and said, "That's fine. When can you start?"

Later on I discovered his secret. St. Mary's had somehow forgotten to spend a large grant they had received earlier for the Emile C. Jurica Chair. Now the Jurica family wanted the university to return the money. The IRS was also threatening to confiscate the funds, so the university had to act fast. They needed somebody with the proper qualifications who could command a large salary to sit on the chair. I just happened to be the right person.

21

LIFE AT ST. MARY'S

During my last years in academia, I felt very satisfied at St. Mary's. My colleagues on the faculty were more dedicated to teaching than playing politics. Parents were committed to their children's education—most of the students were Catholics from lower income groups. Although these young men and women weren't as academically oriented as those at schools with a graduate program, they worked hard and seemed genuinely interested in my courses on computers and data processing. I felt successful as I went about my business of concealing math while teaching practical math skills with the computer.

But I can't say that all of my experiences with students were rewarding. One of my students was a most obnoxious character—his arrogance was matched only by his ignorance. When he turned in a term paper that was a senseless mess, I flunked him, something unheard of at St. Mary's.

Later, he came to my office and demanded that I change his grade. Unfortunately, I became upset and helped him out of my office with a push. As it turned out, his father was on St. Mary's board of directors and charges were filed against me, to which I readily confessed my guilt. However, the student also claimed in his charges that I gave only "A's" to good-looking girls. The president was disturbed about this sexual harassment charge and ordered an outside person to investigate.

When the news leaked out, one of my female "A" students visited me. She said that she and her friends, both "A" and "B" students, were prepared to testify that I graded fairly.

"But, I admit that I'm partial to girls," I said. "That's why, when I grade papers, I cover up the names so I don't know who I'm grading."

As for the outside investigator, he praised me for flunking the well-connected student. In his final report, he wrote: "A graduate of this caliber would have given the university a bad name."

◆   ◆   ◆

In 1984, I bought my first personal computer with the help of a university grant. At the time, no stores in San Antonio—a city with almost one million inhabitants—carried them, but I found a dealer in Austin who was willing to bring one to San Antonio and install it in my home. The computer was both primitive and wonderful.

My colleagues ridiculed my PC because this was the heyday of the Apple McIntosh. Still, the PC had 64,000 bytes of memory while the Mac had, if I remember correctly, only 4,000 bytes.

"But what do you need all that extra memory for?" my colleagues asked.

Back then, data was stored on single-sided floppies with a limit of 80,000 or so bytes. These days, of course, memory is measured in hundreds of millions of bytes and storage in many gigabytes (that is, billions of bytes) and nobody has enough.

The PC's performance was relatively poor. Authors were advised to stick with their typewriters, because if you used a PC for word processing, you would spend more time fighting the computer than writing. Fortunately, I disregarded this warning and began doing my own word processing, which meant I could stop dictating material for someone else to type.

◆   ◆   ◆

I soon discovered that Texas was a great place to live. The highway signs that said "Drive friendly" became my metaphor for living in

Texas. It wasn't fast-paced like California or the East Coast. Instead it possessed a quiet, old-fashioned southern charm. I remember once when I stopped my car at a corner to study a road map. Suddenly another motorist pulled up beside me on the left side. As I waited for his outburst of road rage, he leaned out his window and asked, "Can I help you find your way?"

With our European background, my wife and I welcomed the Spanish/Mexican heritage and unique mix of Mexican, Anglo and German cultures. We enjoyed the beautiful downtown Riverwalk and the excellent restaurants with Mexican food and chili. We had pleasant vacations on South Padre Island, and loved driving through the little Texas cowboy towns and along the Rio Grande river. We felt as if we were completing our tour of the U.S. by covering the Southwest.

Of course, we also had a few disappointments and misadventures along the way. The Alamo did not live up to the expectations created by the John Wayne movie. Laura was mugged once while walking along the river and her shoulder was broken. Winters were cold, summers were hot.

At some point I realized that almost everybody in Texas owned a handgun. This was an alien concept to me, but I thought I should try owning one myself before dismissing it completely. After purchasing a .38 caliber revolver and ammunition from my friendly neighborhood gun store, I went to a firing range and started blasting away. Firing a gun for the first time in my life knocked the wind out of me, scared me to death and gave me a life-time respect for guns. Later, while doing some research on firearms at the library, I came across an obscure local ordinance that permitted homeowners to build private shooting ranges on their own premises. In no time at all, I put the finishing touches on a range in my attached garage.

My first task was to build a safe target board. I waited for a day when Laura was out running errands, then dragged a thick board into the backyard, flopped it on the ground and fired into it. This taught me how thick to make my target board—the bullet penetrated much deeper than I expected it would.

When the day came to test out my shooting range—another day when Laura wasn't home—I set up a target on the board, donned ear and eye protectors, and commenced plinking. Needless to say, I needed practice—my shots were scattered across the target and the board—and one shot missed the board completely.

Hours later, Laura approached and asked if I knew anything about the little feathers lying on the floor of the spare room.

It seems that when I missed my target, the bullet passed through both the garage and house walls, then went through the back of the sofa in the spare room, putting a hole in a feathered pillow before dropping on an Oriental carpet in the middle of the room. With this data in front of me, I went back and revised my shooting range—my new and improved target board was so large that even I couldn't miss it.

Even though I warned the neighbors, my garage shooting range attracted some attention. One day the woman who lived next door sent her son, a war veteran, to check out the work of the mad Hungarian professor. He was so impressed that he returned later to fire off a few rounds with his own gun.

◆   ◆   ◆

After seven years, the end of my stay at St. Mary's approached, making me feel like the dinner guest who must choose the right time to leave. A new president came along who wasn't as enthusiastic about my generous salary and perks. Before long, he found better ways to spend his budget than by pampering me. With the help of inflation and no raises, he whittled down my wages and cut out my summer income. He increased my teaching load to two courses a term and began making noise about adding a third.

When I began considering retirement, I thought deeply about what this new stage in my life would mean. To me, work was both a challenging discipline and a form of creative play. Work was also my identity—my life—the source of my self expression and self esteem. I wasn't sure how retirement would fit into this until I hit on the French concept of a "rentier," someone who has financial means and doesn't need to worry about a regular paycheck. That would be me, I decided. A "senior scholar," someone who filled his days with studies and writing. After making a careful analysis of my financial situation, I found out this was possible.

To begin this next stage of life, Laura and I looked around for the best place to live. We had three important criteria:

a. A healthy, creative environment;

b. A dry, sunny climate;

c. A location close to our daughter and son-in-law, Bobbi and Sky, who lived in Santa Rosa, California.

So we made a survey of possible cities, sent out letters to chambers of commerce and visited many places in Arizona, Oregon and other states. We also considered the possibility of staying in San Antonio, where we could be near our friends and close to the resources of a research university.

Finally, we decided to move to Santa Rosa, where living costs were high, but manageable. (Little did I know that that the Dow Jones would go crazy, quadruple in ten years and ensure that our nest egg would last a good, long while.)

The only question that needed to be settled was how Bobbi would feel about us living within ten miles of her. Friends had warned us: "When you live across the country from your children, they have a good excuse not to visit you frequently. But when you live close by and they don't visit, it can lead to hurt feelings." After a long conversation with Bobbi, we realized that was one problem we wouldn't have to worry about.

The whole experience of retiring and moving brought into play all my decision-making knowledge and experience. As with many major life decisions, I'll never know if we made the right choice or not. After all, if we hadn't moved, we would never have known how the move would have worked out. And if things didn't work out, there's always the chance that things might have turned out even worse if we had chosen differently. This kind of doubt shadows most decision-making activities. We never really know; we cannot live twice.

Early in 1987 I gave notice to St. Mary's that I would be leaving. Three years later, we arrived in Santa Rosa and began a new, exciting phase in our lives. As the years have gone by, I realize that this was one of the best decisions of my life.

22

THE SENIOR SCHOLAR

o o o o o o o o o o o o o o o o o o o o o o o o o o o o o o

...studies are a spur to the young, delight to the old; an ornament in prosperity, a consoling refuge in adversity; they are pleasure for us at home, and no burden abroad; they stay with us at night, they accompany us when we travel, they are with us in our country visits.

—Cicero: Pro Archia Poeta

I was a freshly minted Ph.D. when I received my first fellowship. Though I never put the Institute of International Education's fellowship to use, it saved my life because it got me out of Hungary and started me on my long journey to the U.S. My second math fellowship came from the French government during my two-year layover in Paris. A few years later, at Harvard, I became a Gordon McKay Fellow in the field of engineering. I missed out on becoming a Junior Fellow of Harvard College, which was too bad because this was one of those no-strings-attached deals where the grantee could do whatever he wanted. Years later, the Ford Foundation provided funding for two trips to Hungary. After that, I was on my own.

That explains why in 1987, I gave myself the "MacAndrew" grant (named after the John D. and Catherine T. MacArthur Foundation's so-called genius award). I took a good, hard look at my savings, declared myself financially independent, and decided to do whatever I wanted. And what I wanted to do was become an activist who could extend math and the scientific method to all areas of ordinary life; at the same time, I wanted to fight against the nonsense of alchemists, witches, astrologers and others.

My move to Santa Rosa in December of 1989 and subsequent "retirement" marked a new phase of my life. I no longer had to support my family by teaching. Now I could dedicate my life to study, contemplation and, most importantly, writing.

Getting rid of my teaching job was certainly a blessing. I said goodbye to correcting papers, grading students, attending faculty meetings, recruiting instructors and kissing the dean's ass. I enjoyed my new leisure time, which involved gossiping with non-mathematicians in the hot tub, playing golf, going to the beach, spending time with my daughter and her husband, reading more novels, watching TV, listening to more music, drawing for pleasure and making a lot of unnecessary long-distance phone calls. Not only that, but also sending loads of e-mail, searching the Web, drinking more champagne and martinis and taking more naps.

With my "MacAndrew" grant, I no longer had to worry about my savings or bills, borrow books from the library or wonder if I could afford to pay for fixing things (especially my wayward computer).

◆   ◆   ◆

Pleasure seekers have no leisure.

—*Japanese saying.*

Idleness produces ever-changing thoughts.

—*Marcus Annaeus Lucanus.*

My Santa Rosa home, which overlooks the 4th hole of a 9-hole golf course, is nestled in a rather affluent retirement community. Most of what I learn about my fellow retirees comes from long conversations in the hot tub. (Because I've acquired a reputation as the community "genius," a neighbor suggested that I put my talents to use by writing a "hot tub gossip column" for our local paper. I graciously declined.)

What has surprised me most about my neighbors is that they always seem to be busy. They attend all sorts of meetings, spend a lot of time driving around shopping for food and goods, saving pennies and generally do what I call busy work. I plan my days without any of these evils.

My heroes never had retirement problems because they never retired. Paul Erdös could not retire from a job, because he never had one—a job would have interfered with his number one passion, math. All his life he did math, and he kept on doing it to the very end. While attending a math conference in Poland, he had a heart attack and, to use his expression, "departed". My other heroes, Theodore von Kármán and Herbert Simon, also never retired.

Most people dream about retiring and enjoying a life of leisure. But it turns out to be an illusion: people seem to be just as busy after retiring as before. They have the same "to-do" lists as before. I never had problems with over-scheduling, and nothing changed after retirement, except that I developed a more leisurely lifestyle. Today I have a ball browsing in the bookstore and talking to people wherever I can grab them. I enjoy watching the quail that run around the golf course, and the deer and rabbits who roam about eating Laura's roses. I eliminated the things I did not really have to do, or could get somebody else to do for me. I was amazed at how many things I thought I needed to do, but really could avoid.

A life of leisure means to me that I am inner-directed and my actions are not controlled by outside events. It seems to me that retirement should not be about leisure, but about taking control of your life.

Not that a life of leisure doesn't have its own set of limitations. With more time on my hands, I must make my own choices about what to do next. There are no constraints imposed from outside. For example, it is now after my lunch, after my martini, and after my nap, and I am revising notes for an article I am writing on investments, and writing a Visual Basic program about random walks.

But now a new thought surfaces: perhaps I should interrupt my writing and play golf. Since I am "retired," I can do whatever I want.

Of course, I have unorthodox ideas about the game of golf. I never make appointments to play, because I hate being pinned down. I prefer to be free as a hummingbird and flitter to my caprice, so I usually play alone. I don't keep score, and take my golf cart to whichever hole I want to play next.

Another thing that sets me apart is that I tee the ball on every shot, as do the Japanese, who use a tee to save the grass. The traffic is so heavy in Japan that they can't cope with the damage from all those clubs making divots in the grass. Occasionally, someone will point out that teeing up putts is against the rules. "What rules?" I ask. "My only rule is to have fun."

Because I usually feel better after playing six holes, my rational self tells me that I should take a break from writing. Actually, I can't concentrate one hundred percent on golf; between holes, I'm thinking about all sorts of stuff. In fact, I had a hard time learning the game at the age of 71 when I moved to Oakmont. The pro told me, "Think of batting the ball like in baseball." Well, I never played baseball so I had no idea what he was talking about. He tried several other analogies, none of which worked, and finally gave up and began to hide when he saw me coming.

◆   ◆   ◆

One day I had Dandy, my daughter's terrier of mixed heritage, on my lap and was contemplating the world, my work, my family and how lucky I was. I vaguely remember reading a story about Herbert Spencer, the British social philosopher. When he was eighty years old, sitting in his office with a stack of his books on his lap, he wondered if he would have been better off holding a grandchild on his lap, instead of being a bachelor and writer of masterpieces. Well, I don't have grandchildren, but I know about many scientists who stayed bachelors, like Paul Erdös, or had poor family relationships, like Albert Einstein. I have nothing but happiness on the family score.

In September of 1993, upon learning that I had colon cancer, I hung the sharp sword of Damocles above my place at the dinner table. The sword was there to remind me, a memento mori. As I was being wheeled into surgery with Laura and Bobbi at my side, I knew what was really important. When I woke up, I knew that my family was my first priority. I lucked out, because the cancer did not metastasize. Five years later my doctor declared me free of cancer. The incident made a profound impression on me. I understood that not only did my family come first, but that I lived on borrowed time, that I should take life day-to-day and that I may die at any time. The sword still hangs on the wall.

◆   ◆   ◆

Laura and I are inseparable. We spend very little time apart because we are interested in similar things. In the past, we traveled quite a bit, but now we travel only with Bobbi and Sky. We love our quiet life and being left alone. To my amazement, Laura edits my work without understanding a word of it. Her insightful comments always make the text better. One of my copy editors once told me that although she disagrees with Laura, she would yield to her superior judgment.

I don't have any relatives in the U.S., but Laura has a brother in Boston and sister in Portland. We keep in touch via phone, e-mail and occasional visits.

While I do my thing at home, Laura spends her time cooking, taking care of me and puttering around our house and garden. She often interrupts me with "macho" problems such as fixing the can opener, replacing light bulbs, tinkering with her cassette player, or buying a new garden hose.

We are in total agreement that our greatest treasure, blessing and success is Bobbi. She lives about fifteen minutes away. We talk on the phone every day, and meet for dinner almost every week. Often, we have sushi lunch together. She is the sun in our sunset. We also feel very good about Sky—the greatest thing about him is that he truly loves Bobbi. Also, I approve of his outlook on life.

When I left San Antonio, I was concerned that I would miss my colleagues, so I made an effort to reestablish an academic connection. I became interested in cognitive psychology and science because I felt that I didn't really understand what made people click. Sonoma State University had a large psychology department and they expressed an interest in retaining me as a visiting scholar. Unfortunately, they paid just lip service to science and were pursuing only "soft" psychology, a subject in which I had no interest. So after a wasted year I gave up and found a similar appointment at the University of San Francisco. But this didn't work out either, so I gave up completely.

Surprisingly, relationships with ordinary, non-academic human beings has more than compensated for the absence of academic connections. After I left industry, I lived in an ivory tower. But after leaving academia, my close relationships with people who did not know any math were very enlightening and changed my way of thinking. I recognized my great desire to spread the ways of mathematics to a broader group of people.

◆   ◆   ◆

In 1992 I developed a serious pain in my right leg and could hardly walk. My general practitioner sent me to a specialist who diagnosed severe arthritis, probably the aftereffect of a car accident that I had many years ago. He indicated that very likely I would need hip replacement surgery, but first he wanted to try drugs and physical therapy for a month.

As usual, I dug into the literature and found an odd paradox. Although experts strongly recommended exercise, I could find no case histories of patients who succeeded by following this recommendation. The obvious analogy was obesity. Everybody agrees that being extremely overweight is bad, but few people are successful at shedding pounds. Well, my success at dieting made me believe that regular, strenuous exercise might help my arthritis, too. Being an exercise addict for the last thirty years made it easy for me to learn the tricks from my physical therapist.

The results were spectacular! When I went to see my specialist, he was astounded. "You made my day," he said, "I've never had a patient with such a miraculous recovery."

But he added a note of caution. "Eventually, you'll need hip replacement."

During my periodic checkups, he keeps on repeating this. My reply is, "I will die 'eventually,' and I hope it comes before arthritis surgery."

This experience inspired me to start a continuing study of decision making in the healthcare industry. Lack of rational action in healthcare is matched only by strange behavior in making investments.

◆   ◆   ◆

My principal professional activity in Oakmont is writing down my thoughts. When people ask why I write, I answer with a question: Why does someone paint, write poetry, compose music, do math, live in a tree or climb a mountain? Because it is there.

I have been recording—in one form or another—my thoughts for over fifty years. I have published eight textbooks, written over seventy-five technical articles and continue to write five columns a year for the Decision Sciences Institute's news publication "Decision Line". (You can find my columns at http://www.decisionsciences.org/newsletter/archives.htm.)

Non-academics often praise me for what they call my "willpower." "How many hours do you spend working on your books?" they often ask. But a better question is: How many hours do I not spend writing? I stop writing when I have something else I want to do, such as studying, playing golf or going to the pool, or something I have to do, such as working on my income taxes or watching TV with Laura.

The trouble is in the meaning of the word "work." Ever since Adam and Eve were evicted from Paradise, people have had to earn a living by the sweat of their brows. My fellow retirees at Oakmont have fun playing golf, going to shows and doing community work, while they observe that I sit at my computer and "work." But for me writing is not "work"—it is my greatest pleasure.

I have a passion for expressing my views on the world, and make such statements to myself by writing aid-memoirs. When I learn something new, which happens all the time, I write down my own interpretation and fit it into my database network. I don't keep a diary of my life, because I don't attach that much importance to material things. My life is an intensive mental activity of thinking and feeling.

I read lots of things in books, in the daily newspaper, in The Wall Street Journal, that I want to discuss with my alter ego. I find that I don't really understand new material until I explain it to myself and write it down. I continuously overhear what I say to myself and to others.

When I came to Santa Rosa, I was halfway through my management information systems book, and spent the first few years completing it. But, that project collapsed—computers had totally changed the methods of calculating for decision making—so I was ready for a new venture.

I was going full steam ahead on Quantitative Methods for Decision Making, when suddenly the publisher pulled the rug out from under me and canceled with some meaningless excuse. Fortunately, I had no trouble getting another contract.

However, that publisher then sold some of their contracts, and mine was one of them. The new publisher, Duxbury, had some other books on decision making under contract, and did not show much enthusiasm for the manuscript. But they put it in the deep freeze, and kept stalling until there were so many competitive books that the market dried up. This looked like another death. But in 1998 they showed interest again, and wanted to use part of my book as *Operations Analysis Using Excel.*

So I lifted from the manuscript all the topics relevant and did something revolutionary. For years I've argued with my peers about math. Some have claimed that the biggest hurdle in promoting decision sciences was that high schools did not properly prepare pupils in math, and so they were turned off by our math. They considered avoiding math as proof of math ignorance, and vehemently rejected my claim that, from a practical standpoint, there is no need to teach math. But for my latest textbook, I removed all math and replaced it with computer-oriented material to take advantage of the popularity of Microsoft Excel. I used Excel as a laboratory the way engineers use wind tunnels or mathematical models. If engineers can do it, why can't managers?

Duxbury liked the material and wanted to prepare it for publication. But by that time I somewhat lost interest because I was looking for audiences beyond academia. So I managed to get two coauthors to reshape the manuscript. The book, my eighth, appeared under the name of three authors with a copyright date of 2001. This was really a non-event to me, because the fun was in the writing—publishing one more book made no difference.

But then something unexpected happened. Duxbury told me that we had the makings of a bestseller. People really liked my way of presenting decision making. Once I realized that my ideas on math had proven successful, I went on a champagne binge and began drinking two glasses every day, just to keep the doctor away.

This was a watershed in my publishing career and intellectual development. I realized that I had a potentially popular approach to spreading real-life math to a broader group of people, and I became interested in the new challenge. This meant more studying and expanding my knowledge base.

Now that there are more opportunities to publish on the Web, perhaps writers can break the stranglehold of the brick-and-mortar publishing houses. Nowadays you can publish a book yourself for as little as $100. I am convinced that this option will have a profound impact on the publishing world.

◆   ◆   ◆

I always hate it when Laura tells me to "tear myself away" from the computer. If I wrote with a pencil, she would not say, "Tear yourself away from the yellow stick that you are pushing over that piece of paper." People seem to think that I am interested in the computer as a gadget. Not so. The computer is my slave, not my master.

Actually I gave up "pushing the pencil" soon after I wrote my Ph.D. dissertation and was a student at Harvard. When I started working in industry, I would dictate into a machine and a private secretary would transcribe my work. When I was a college professor, Laura, a most superior typist and editor, prepared all my manuscripts.

I used to prepare notes, lock myself in my office and dictate. It put me under a terrible strain, but I managed. Then I edited the transcript, prepared several drafts and finally sent the manuscript to the publisher.

Word processors changed all this. I gave up dictating, started to type all my manuscripts and abandoned the concept of drafts. I now work on a piece until I feel good about it and send it out for review. After I insert the changes, I have a new copy and delete the prior version for good. But there was a heavy cost to this reengineering. I had to learn to type, manage my files and master the software (such as backing up files for safekeeping). All this was boring and frustrating.

Fortunately, one benefit was that I could stay in touch with the world through e-mail. I rediscovered the lost art of letter writing. I stopped feeling lonely. I developed an effective and practical technique for working with coauthors.

Changing my method of writing is just one revolution I've experienced. The second one was creating worlds of alternatives by computer simulation using hidden math. I have always known that simulation was a powerful tool in the exact sciences, but failed to realize that this approach holds true in the artificial sciences as well. The advent of spreadsheets (in particular, Microsoft Excel and Visual Basic) made it practical for me to gain firsthand experience and fundamentally changed my approach to decision making.

◆   ◆   ◆

During the 1990s I was greatly impressed by the importance of the visual mode of thinking. Walter Lippman said:

> What each man does is based not on direct and certain knowledge, but on pictures made by himself or given to him…[T]he way in which the world is imagined determines in any particular moment what men will do.

I started training myself to develop pictures of my ideas, and wondered if I could learn how to draw images. Unfortunately, I had to contend with my early education at the Hungarian lycée where instructors declared me hopeless as far as drawing was concerned.

So I decided to learn cartoon drawing to communicate my outlook on life in pictures. I must admit that I had a really hard time learning this. It took me about two years to develop a fairly efficient way of translating my thoughts into images. My approach combines drawing with pencil and pen, scanning pictures and using a Polaroid camera and the graphic capabilities of my computer. In 1998 I started to publish illustrations for my book on decision making. Drawing has since become an important tool for expressing myself, and I've had great fun using this communication technique.

◆   ◆   ◆

As far back as I can remember, I've felt the need—and pleasure—of discovering new ideas. Growing up in Hungary, I didn't have access to many reference books. There wasn't even a dictionary of the Hungarian language. I had only a poor, incomplete encyclopedia. When I arrived in Paris, I discovered the classic Larousse dictionary and encyclopedia and, even as poor as I was, bought a copy immediately. In the U.S., I was astounded to find the wealth of reference books that were available. The first book I bought was a good dictionary.

Lately, the advances in reference materials have been breathtaking. First there was the Encyclopedia Britannica on two CD's. Then there is the World Wide Web, which I use as a gargantuan, up-to-date encyclopedia to stay plugged in to the real world. I never feel alone because I can get in touch with almost anything at anytime. Several times a day, a question or issue arises for which I can find some relevant stuff on the Web. Book reviews are particularly important. The impact on my knowledge base is tremendous.

As I sit at my huge desk (with a roulette wheel to remind me that "chance happeneth to all"), I am wrapped in my safety blanket—my books. When I buy one, I acquire a new gateway to life that enriches my mind, spirit and personality. I have about a thousand books, approximately nine hundred of which help me think about decision making. Some have been with me for over fifty years. These are my oldest friends, full of wisdom and with whom I frequently converse. Many are recently acquired friends that I argue with. The more disagreement the better, for I have nothing to learn from those who always agree with me.

From time to time, I run out of room on my bookshelves, which means that it's time to purge. It gives me pleasure to review what I have and see what I can throw away. It is a remembrance of my past, a review of my mental journey and how I have changed and progressed. Occasionally I review a book I wrote years ago, and am amazed at how differently I would say the same thing today.

A wit once remarked that you discover you are affluent when you do not look at the right side of a menu or ask if a side dish is included. I feel affluent when I buy a book without looking at the price. Occasionally, I get a new book and have the feeling that it is no good. Then, later, I suddenly recall something I read in it, that I must go back and check. There has been much talk recently about electronic books on computers, but so far I haven't found a good use for them.

◆   ◆   ◆

Laura likes to go to a nearby lake and admire the view. One day I was sitting on the bench with her when suddenly the solution to the Steinmetz problem described in Robert and Michele Root-Bernstein's *Sparks of Genius* came to me. Apparently, in 1894, a couple of engineers approached Charles Steinmetz with a puzzle they had unsuccessfully worked on for weeks. The problem was stated as follows:

"If you take a rod two inches in diameter and cut it in half by drilling a two-inch hole through it, what is the cubic content of the volume of the plug, the metal that's removed?"

Steinmetz took a few puffs on his cigar and said, "The answer, gentlemen, is 5.33 cubic inches."

Laura noticed that something funny was going on and asked, "Are you asleep?"

"No," I said, imitating Paul Erdös, "I am zinking about mazematical zeorems."

Laura understood exactly what was going on.

It takes a lot longer to explain the solution than to find it, but here goes.

Think about the rod as a cylinder along the x axis, and the drill along the y axis. Shrink yourself to the size of a Lilliputian, to a height of half an inch, and get inside the rod along the x axis. You are inside a Quonset hut built on a very long rectangle, the width being two inches. The drill is another Quonset hut, at a 90-degree angle. I am interested in the plug that is the inside of both huts, bounded by the Steinmetz surface. It is a kind of umbrella, sitting on a 2-inch square, having four wires, that makes up the ceiling. Each horizontal slice is made up of a square formed by the wires, shrinking to nothing on the top. I inscribe a circle into each square. These circles form a sphere inside the plug. The volume of the sphere is smaller than the volume of the plug. By how much? I look at the foundation. The area of the square is 4, of the circle PI. So the ratio is 4/PI. I recall that the volume of the sphere is 4/3*PI, and so the volume of the plug is:

(4/PI)*(4/3*PI)=16/3=5 1/3.

I don't know if this is the way Steinmetz solved the problem, and why he gave only the approximate value of 5.33.

◆   ◆   ◆

My relatives and friends have urged me for years to write my memoirs, but I paid no attention to them. However, when Erdös died I found that I was one of his few friends still alive who knew him from his student days. After I decided to write my remembrances of him, several surprises awaited.

I discovered that it gave me great pleasure to write about Erdös and about the aspects of my life that interlaced with his. I also found that my writings were well-received and eventually published. This made me think that I ought to write my own memoirs, expressing my views of math, my philosophy, my human side and life in general, and explain how I earned my living as a management scientist.

After leaving academia and associating with my Santa Rosa neighbors, I discovered that things I took for granted were not obvious to others. I wondered if I could illustrate how math is used to steer the best course for solving real-life problems. I wanted to find a way to tell them about my world, the world of a scientist. To my surprise I found that this was extremely difficult.

I had to learn to write in a user-friendly style to unlock the mystery of mathematics to the non-mathematical mind. I needed examples of successful personal applications of real-life math not covered in traditional textbooks. I had to develop my story by leaning on metaphors and anecdotes and not relying so heavily on x, y, z equations or graphs. I wanted to not only explain math, but also to give the reader a glimpse into the soul of a mathematician. I wanted this to be my "declaration to the world" about decision sciences and real-life mathematics. I wanted this to be a major voyage in self-realization. My aims were daunting, but fortunately I found an unexpected ally.

I discovered, at this late date, that Bobbi, a marriage and family therapist, was a true humanist. She also understood and appreciated the role of science through her life-long contact with me. She turned out to be of immense help and inspiration. The dual perception of the scientist and the humanist, the collaboration of the father and the daughter, have created a unique blend of mental and spiritual awareness for the development of my memoirs and revised philosophy of life.

When Mischa, Laura's brother, heard that I was writing a new book, he asked, "How do you know you will live long enough to finish it?" I told him that he missed the point. I live for each day, assuming that I'll never die.

23

REMEMBERING PAUL ERDÖS

"Pusztulunk, veszünk" ("We are wasting away, perishing"), Paul Erdös would say in his phone calls, quoting the Hungarian bard Vörösmarty. By this he meant that his close friends—all mathematicians—were slowly passing away, one after another. Towards the end of his life, he kept a list of the ones who had "departed" since his last call. On September 20, 1996, with great sadness, I added his name to the list.

I find it hard to believe that never again will I receive a phone call or postcard from him beginning with the standard "Itt vagyok" ("I am here").

When we first met in 1930, I was a 14-year-old boy, and Paul Erdös, at age 17, was an old man (according to him). Until his death at the age of 83, we remained close friends.

Much has been written about this 20th century math prodigy. He worked in dozens of fields and co-authored thousands of academic papers. He was renowned for his ability to identify new problems in math and point to future directions that math should take. He was also generous to a fault, sponsoring many prizes to encourage young mathematicians to solve difficult problems that he posed.

It cheers me to recall that he spent his last day at one of his beloved math conferences. During the dinner, he was in good spirits, as always. His last joke was: "A doctor a day keeps the apples away."

His death attracted worldwide attention—articles and obituaries in the world's major newspapers. His life story captured public imagination, and two biographies of him have been published. My favorite is Bruce Schechter's *My Brain Is Open—the Mathematical Journeys of Paul Erdös*, because it stresses his broad, human side. A recent Internet search on his name resulted in 2,388 hits.

What follows are some of my memories of Erdös, snapshots of our experiences together. Some of these stories were first published in *Erdös on Graphs*, by Fan Chung and Ron Graham (A. K. Peters, Wellesley, Mass., 1998).

◆   ◆   ◆

Paul Erdös was often a guest in my home. For a variety of reasons, a visit from him was both a joyful occasion and something of an ordeal. His last stay in 1994 was no exception.

During his visits, our phone would ring constantly as his friends from around the world checked in. Because Erdös always moved from place to place—he had no permanent home—this was the only way to reach him. I remember one night, three days prior to his arrival, when the phone rang.

"Hello?"

"I am calling from Berlin," said a man with a heavy accent. "I want to talk to Erdös."

"He's not here yet," I replied.

"Where is he?"

"I don't know."

"Why don't you?"

When Erdös arrived at our home, he looked thin and worn. Of course, he had looked that way for thirty years, but this time he seemed even more tired, listless and impatient.

But his sense of humor was still the same. I overheard him on the phone saying to a friend: "Vazsonyi? He is all right—but old and deaf."

It was true that I had more trouble than usual understanding him. My hearing had grown worse, but I believe that his Hungarian accent had become thicker. Also I noticed that he reverted to Hungarian more often and occasionally garbled his sentences.

During this last visit, he had the temerity to show Laura the proof that the square root of two is irrational, something known to mathematicians as the Pythagorean "scandal." (According to legend, the disciple of Pythagoras who revealed the secret to laymen was put to death.)

They sat down at the table with a sheet of paper.

"Laura, if you don't understand a step, let me know so that I can clarify the proof," he said.

He began. "Let us assume that the square root of 2 is rational. That is, it equals a over b, where a and b are whole numbers. Okay?"

Laura nodded.

Then he went step-by-step, until he reached the contradiction.

"See, the assumption is wrong," he said triumphantly. "The square root of two cannot be rational."

Laura narrowed her eyes at him. "Why didn't you tell me at the beginning that the proof was all wrong?"

Erdös became irritated and said indignantly, "I told you to tell me when you don't understand something. Why didn't you tell me earlier?"

When he was finished with the piece of paper, I asked if he would autograph it for me. I had heard that someone had once saved a blackboard from an Einstein lecture and presented it to the Smithsonian Institution. So I told him that I intended to do the same. He signed his name, then added "PGOMLDADLDCD," an abbreviation for "Poor Great Old Man, Living Dead, Archeological Discovery, Legally Dead, Counts Dead."

Erdös began developing his own private language during the Horthy dictatorship in Hungary, when there were spies lurking everywhere. Back then, the U.S. was Uncle Sam, and the USSR became Uncle Joe, after Joseph Stalin. One day Erdös told Bobbi a nursery rhyme that began with "Sam and Joe went up the hill to fetch a pail of water."

But she quickly interrupted him. "Not so, Erdös, it was Jack and Jill."

When he turned 70, he began using "LD" for Legally Dead; five years later he referred to himself as "CD" for Count Dead. The difference between the two was known only to him.

In the international language of Erdös, as understood by many mathematicians, wives were "bosses" and husbands were "slaves"—of course, Erdös himself never became a slave. Children were epsilons, because small quantities in math are often designated by the Greek letter epsilon. He always found time to talk and play with children. He never failed to stop a mother with a youngster and ask (usually to her great bewilderment): "How old is the epsilon?"

Communists were on the "long wave length" because that is the wave length of the color red. An alcoholic drink was "poison." "Give me an epsilon of poison" was a request for a small drink. Classical music was "noise." He could not live without it. The baroque music of Bach, Vivaldi and Boccherini was his favorite.

One particular phrase that caught on in the international mathematics community was "OM," which referred to someone's bad performance. In mathematics, when you make a general estimate of a quantity, you use the word "ordo." The mathematician Mahler was one of Erdös's friends, and also one of the worst bridge players in Manchester. Hence, when somebody acted poorly, Erdös would say he performed "ordo Mahler," or "OM."

His special language was so contagious that even Mahler used "OM" without knowing where the expression came from. When he was finally told, however, he had a good laugh.

God was the "SF" (Supreme Fascist). The SF kept the "Big Book," where beautiful proofs of math theorems are listed. (To this I would add that Lucifer keeps a Little Black Book that contains all the beautiful theorems for which the SF has no proofs.)

Lecturing on math was known simply as "preaching."

According to Erdös, a mathematician who stopped doing math was "dead." When I switched my allegiance to engineering and business, Erdös pardoned my ignominious death by saying that I was a victim of WWII.

In 1960, when I resurrected myself by proving a rather difficult theorem in geometry, Erdös told Laura, "It's strange. Vazsonyi is dead, but he never lost the touch. Yesterday he found a proof straight from the Big Book."

Erdös would also play around with the English language by pronouncing words using Hungarian phonetics. The sounds for a, e, i, o and u are roughly equivalent to the vowel sounds in father, bet, tip, coin and rule. In 1965 I was once astounded to visit Erdös at the University of California in Los Angeles and find all the mathematicians in his company—Americans, English, Japanese—speaking this strange dialect.

As for his handwriting, it was abominable—readable, but childlike. This might explain why Erdös had so many co-authors—I don't believe he was physically capable of writing a paper by himself.

◆   ◆   ◆

Years before Erdös gained worldwide recognition as a math genius, I received an emotional letter from his mother saying, in effect, "What will become of my son?"

After all, he didn't have a job, home or savings. He traveled continuously; all his possessions fit into two suitcases. He had friends everywhere, but never had a deep relationship with any woman besides his mother.

Erdös's mother was a dominating figure in his life. After her two daughters died of scarlet fever, she took extreme measures to shelter her son. Her efforts to protect him from dangers (especially other women) were legendary.

I remember once meeting Erdös in the City Park of Budapest with my girlfriend Aranka. We walked back to Erdös' apartment house. As we entered the courtyard, we heard an angry shout from an overhead balcony: "Who is that woman?!"

"Just Vazsonyi's girlfriend Aranka," Erdös replied meekly. Even though he was 23 years old, a girlfriend for him was totally out of the question.

Erdös never attended public schools; instead he stayed home where his parents, both math teachers, gave full attention to his education.

In our time, he was the youngest Hungarian Ph.D. in math. (I was the second youngest.) After earning his Ph.D., he received a grant of 50 pounds from a British math professor and left Hungary for the first time to begin a four-year period of math research in Manchester, England.

Erdös had been so sheltered that, when he arrived in Manchester, he still needed someone to make his toast and butter it, as well as cut his meat. Gradually, he learned to do a few things for himself, but he mostly relied on friends to do everything else. For example, one day we were having breakfast together and he couldn't open the little cream container. So I opened it for him. The next day at breakfast he simply handed the cream container to me without a word.

I reassured his mother that Erdös had nothing to worry about. The ordinary rules of life don't apply to a genius. He didn't need a regular paycheck because he had unlimited credit with his friends—thousands of friends all over the world. We loved him, would gladly do anything for him and took turns caring for him.

Of course, from the moment Erdös arrived at your house, you ceased to have a life of your own. Among other things, you became his private switchboard operator and chauffeur.

One time he asked me to drive him to the San Francisco Airport. I balked at driving him sixty miles and instead dropped him off at the local bus terminal.

To allay his worries, I carefully explained what would happen when he stepped off the bus at the airport. I told him that he would find an outdoor baggage check, and that the airline attendant would take his suitcase and check him in. He looked doubtful, but said he would try his best.

A few days later he called. "You were right," he said in amazement. "I had no problem at all."

Laura, as all wives did, became his domestic servant during his stay. She was responsible for cooking, sewing, mending, laundering his silk underwear and shirts (he had sensitive skin), ironing, etc.

Even though he was an early riser and knew where to find breakfast foods, he always waited for Laura to fix his toast with jam, cereal (with brown sugar, raisins, nuts) and an egg.

He considered everything relating to his appearance to be trivial. In math, "trivial" refers to obvious theorems—Erdös extended its meaning to all useless actions, thoughts or things. For instance, Laura might ask Erdös about a bundle in the corner of the room, and he would reply that "it was trivial," meaning his other pair of pants.

◆   ◆   ◆

Erdös worked all the time, but he never had much need for a desk or office. In the early 1940s, when he had a grant at the Institute for Advanced Study in Princeton, he was criticized for spending all his time either talking to other mathematicians or playing Go, his favorite board game. Yet, at the same time, he jointly published more papers than the rest of the grantees combined.

In August 1941, while at the Institute, Erdös also made news in a New York City tabloid under the headline "The three most intelligent spies ever arrested by the FBI." It seems that Erdös was strolling along a New Jersey beach with two colleagues, one of whom was Japanese, and neighbors reported the suspicious-looking characters to the FBI. In those days, many folks were hysterical about a possible Japanese invasion and the seashore was off limits. When the G-men arrived, they asked Erdös why he didn't obey the off-limits signs.

"You zee," he replied, "I could not read any of the zigns because I was zinking about mazematical zeorems."

After the FBI hauled these three into town, they checked with the Institute and subsequently released the mathematicians with apologies.

No matter where Erdös was, you always had the feeling that he was focused on math. You might be eating lunch with him, when suddenly he would jump up and run toward the wall. If you didn't know better, you would catch your breath and wait for him to crash. But, no! He would miraculously stop and turn around. Of course, there was a phase when he developed some trouble with body control and on several occasions did smack into the wall.

Occasionally, there were outward signs of his mind at work. I'll always remember the image of Erdös perched on a Laguna Beach rock, shading himself with a black umbrella in one hand as he poured over a math journal in the other hand. Any place other than California and he might have drawn attention.

Erdös didn't believe in vacations, saying, "There will be plenty chance for that when I leave." Nor would he take off time for his health. Even when his cataracts became so bad that he could no longer return Ping-Pong lobs (his favorite game), he still refused to have them removed.

Incidentally, his Ping-Pong style was terrible compared to that of his graceful, life-time math collaborator, Paul Turan. But Erdös' reflexes were so fast that he could return every shot. When he played Turan, he would eventually wear down his friend until he made a mistake. With children, Erdös would show off his fast reflexes by dropping a quarter, then snatching it out of the air. "Can you do that?" he'd ask.

His devotion to math included total devotion to his mathematician friends. Once Erdös was visiting me in my London hotel room when he announced, "We must go and see Rami Zhu."

We took a cab to the other end of London. Upon arriving at his apartment, Erdös opened with his standard gambit, "What are you doing?", meaning, what math problem are you working on? After his friend informed him, we dallied for another five minutes before Erdös said, "We must go."

One day while Erdös was staying at my house a package arrived. It was filled with amphetamines. He was taking them for years, mostly to pep himself up. Somehow he managed to get them through his friends.

I expressed some concern. "Can't you live without them?"

"I bet Graham $500 that I could give them up for a month," he replied. "I did and won the bet, but I also discovered no theorems. Graham held up the progress of math for a month."

Ron Graham, who led mathematical research at AT&T and Bell, as well as found time to master the trampoline, coauthored 26 papers with Erdös, and took care of all his administrative matters from the Erdös Room of his house.

◆   ◆   ◆

Erdös's visits were not necessarily pre-announced. Once I was sleeping early one Sunday morning in Jeanette, Pennsylvania, when I heard a terrible racket downstairs.

"Damn," I thought, "the paper boy is giving me trouble again with the Sunday paper."

So I leaned out the window to raise hell, and behold, there was Erdös banging on the door.

"Why didn't you call me on the phone?" I asked.

"Why would I do that?" he said.

Another evening he appeared in our Cambridge, Massachusetts, apartment. Sweat was rolling down his nose.

"It's impossible to sleep in my attic room in this vicious heat," he said.

We had no extra bedroom so Laura made up the sofa in the living room. Later he spilled his cologne, which he had a great fondness for, all over our coffee table.

Sometimes his departures weren't planned either.

Once Professor Szegö of Stanford fame was about to give a party. His wife came to me practically in tears.

"Erdös dropped in three weeks ago and he is still staying with us," she said. "I am at my wits end."

"No problem," I said, "tell him to get out."

"I can't do that. We love him and don't want to insult him."

"Do what I say. He won't be insulted at all."

An hour later, Erdös called me and asked if I would drive him to a motel. I played dumb and asked what happened.

"Oh, Mrs. Szegö asked me to move out because I stayed long enough," he said nonchalantly.

◆　　◆　　◆

Compassion for others, a trait not commonly found in most scientists, played a large role in Erdös's life. He never passed a beggar without giving him money. He was particularly generous to mathematicians, establishing grants for those in need. When he preached, he frequently announced conjectures and offered prizes, sometimes as high as $10,000, to the first person who could prove or disprove them. There is a story that he once gave a lecture in Tel Aviv. The next morning, mathematicians formed a line outside his door to claim their winnings.

The sum total of his promised grants ran into many thousands of dollars. He was once asked by a journalist what would happen if all his conjectures were solved at the same time.

"This is like a bank," he replied. "It's unlikely that all the depositors would arrive on the same day to claim their money."

It was well known that Erdös collected donations for good causes. One day a few so-called friends made him an offer. Knowing of Erdös's bizarre attitude towards women, they offered him a $100 donation if he would accompany them to a burlesque show. To everyone's amazement, Erdös accepted the offer. After leaving the theater, they paid him and asked him how he liked the show.

Erdös smiled. "You trivial things, I tricked you. After I took off my glasses, I didn't see a thing."

◆ ◆ ◆

Erdös had a lifelong passion for politics. During the China civil war, he collected donations for needy communists. As for his personal beliefs, he was once asked by American immigration officials if he was a communist himself. He answered that it depended on what they meant by the term communist. Because of this, his reentry permit for the U.S. was denied. When he left the country to visit Europe, he stayed away for many years.

◆ ◆ ◆

One day in the early 1960s, while I was still at North American Aviation, my secretary buzzed me and said that I had an urgent phone call. It was Paul Erdös.

"I am here ("Itt vagyok") at UCLA, in Boelter Hall," he said. "Szervusz, Vazsonyi, how is Beatrice, your boss child? I must see you right away."

I hopped in my car, drove to UCLA and found Erdös playing Go with Dr. Po.

Erdös introduced me by saying, "This is Vazsonyi. He is an executive at North American Aviation. His Erdös number is one. But now he is dead."

Dr. Po nodded at me. "My Vazsonyi number is two."

As I waited for Erdös to finish his game, I overheard two young mathematicians having an animated discussion about a diagram on the blackboard.

"What's that about?" I asked.

"Quiet," said Erdös, "you are supposed to be dead."

The young mathematicians were more tolerant, however, and explained they were talking about a theorem for which there was no geometric proof.

I call it the Theorem of Penta-Chords. Consider a circle and the arbitrary A1-A2 chord M is the midpoint on the chord. Draw two other arbitrary chords, B1-B2, C1-C2 through M. Draw the two chords B1-C2 and B2-C1. Find the points D1 and D2, the intersections of chords A1-A2 and chords B1-C2 and C1-B2. The theorem says that M is the midpoint between D1 and D2.

I recalled Reverend Sutak presenting a lecture on projective geometry when I was a student at Budapest's Pázmány Péter University in 1936. The highlight was when Sutak, in front of a standing-room-only audience, showed the interval AB, and the midpoint M. Sutak explained that M was looking for his harmonic associate but couldn't find it. At this point, His Excellency (Meltosagos Ur, the official title of a professor) galloped around the class in his gown and looked for the associate. When Sutak arrived back at the blackboard, he banged it with all his might and announced that M got to infinity, with M crying out: "You are my harmonic associate!" ("Te vagy az én haromonikus társam!")

Back to the blackboard at UCLA.

"Doesn't look too hard," I said.

"Maybe not for an industrial tycoon," they joked.

Afterwards, my drive home on the San Diego Freeway was horrible. I had nothing else to do but think about Erdös's odd behavior and the geometry puzzle. I chose to concentrate on the latter. And by the time I parked my car in my driveway, I had the heuristics for the new proof.

Excited, I called Erdös and stuttered as I tried to put my proof into words, without paper. (I have never used paper for math, not even for my dissertation.) Erdös mumbled back that the proof was no good. But finally he became convinced.

"Supreme Fascist!" he declared. "Straight from the Big Book. Dead men do prove theorems. You must publish this."

I felt elated—I had removed the theorem from Lucifer's Little Black Book.

Later he told Laura, "Strange thing, Vazsonyi has been dead for a long time, but he never lost the touch."

◆   ◆   ◆

Towards the end of that visit with Erdös at UCLA, he turned to me and said, "I will come to see you Sunday—you can cook me shish kebab. But you don't have to drive me around anymore."

He raised his right thumb and gestured behind him.

"What do you mean?" I asked.

Without turning around he said, "She drives me around."

I looked in the corner of the room, where I saw a woman sitting. I'll refer to her as OW (the Other Woman).

I had no idea about the extent or length of the relationship between Erdös and OW. I do know that it was certainly Platonic. One weekend we all went to Laguna Beach. When we arrived at our lodging, a crisis developed. There was one room for my family and another room for the Erdös party. But where would OW sleep? When the manager suggested that she and Erdös sleep in the only available room, he became visibly disturbed and yelled: "Impossible!" The impending catastrophe was somehow resolved.

During that same trip, we stopped to visit a Catholic mission, but OW refused to pay the admission fee and waited outside. She was an adamant Protestant and didn't like the idea of giving money to the

Catholics. Erdös had no such hang-ups, so he entered and happily fed the pigeons with Bobbi.

One day OW told Laura that she was finished with Erdös. She was tired of being his chauffeur. And that was it. Some time later I heard that she departed. The relationship would have ended anyway because Erdös' mother appeared on the scene in 1964 and resumed her attitude of protection.

I remember a visit from Erdös and his mother when we lived in Manhattan Beach. We were hundreds of feet above the waves, yet she was concerned that he would be washed away when he went for a walk. While visiting the University of California in Los Angeles, we rented a fine suite for them in Westwood but his mother was totally dissatisfied with the place. "It is too dusty," she said. Erdös asked the desk to put a cot for him in the bedroom, and her objections evaporated.

They were inseparable until she died during one of his lecture tours in Calgary, Canada, at the age of 93.

"They misdiagnosed her," Erdös said later. "She should have lived longer." No mother has been loved more by a son than Erdös' mother.

"Strange," Erdös once told me, "I was always concerned when flying on a plane. But after my mother died, I lost my fear."

"You look depressed," a friend once told him.

"Well, you know my mother died," said Erdös.

"But that was five years ago," the friend observed.

"I still miss her," Erdös responded.

Epilogue

I have come to the end of my memoirs but not to the end of my life. At the age of eighty-five, my mind tells me I don't have much time left, but in my heart I act as if I will live forever.

When I look back on my life I see the magical role that math has played. From the days of my first meeting with Paul Erdös, discovery of the Weiszfeld algorithm, the Középiskolai Matematikai Lapok, winning the math competitions, I still identify with the name my Parisian friends gave me, the Hungarian "bossu." This reminds me of J. K. Rowling's recent best-selling series on Harry Potter. I may not be wearing strange robes, but my invisible hump still gives me the magical power to spread math to the Muggles, those ordinary folks without the interest or inclination for enchantment. I have learned enough of their language and ways to know they use the magic without being aware of it. They boot up the computer, hit the keys, and "presto!" Like the checker at Safeway, who operates the scanner but doesn't see the web of magic behind the numerical codes she pops in by the bushels.

I am happiest when I am soaring around in all directions searching for spots where I can use the magic wand of real-life math. At present I am fascinated by healthcare, the new American jungle. This is not surprising since I am navigating it like any other Muggle.

I told my doctor I finally joined the human race by struggling with the boring health problems of old age. As my hero Feynman said when he was dying, "Dying is boring." Old age is not for sissies. My legs "refuse to do their office," my eyes need drops thrice a day, and I have to use closed captions on the TV. I keep a pair of hearing aids in my desk drawer, the best money can buy. They don't seem to help. Parts of my machine are wearing out and I cannot find spare parts. I can walk around the house but I cannot walk the golf course as I once did.

Old age has caught up with me in other ways, too. Paul Turan died. Paul Erdös died. Herbert Simon died. Dick Chaney, my best friend, is dying of cancer. Laura, at ninety, broke her hip and has not been the same.

But as always, I am happiest when I'm working on math. Every day I get up, wrap myself in heating pads for my arthritis, take my Dextrostat pill to wake up, read my email and the paper. Since the collapse of Health Plan of the Redwoods, our local HMO that serves 78,000 people, a day does not go by without an article lamenting the problems of its participants.

I am curious. I study dozens of web sites and have an overwhelming feeling of déjà vu. Wind back the clock fifty years. Observe the level of confusion in factories. I am told that production could never be improved by using the computer and/or mathematical models. The problems are just too complex, the experts said, and production or marketing could not be improved because of "the human element." These same nay sayers insist that computers would never replace typewriters, and no one imagined the computer would provide a resource better than an infinite encyclopedia, the World Wide Web.

Today no industry would attempt to compete without information systems and management theory. The health care system is no exception, but like an errant dinosaur it continues to lumber along. I believe that the healthcare industry and its hoards of members would greatly benefit by using the bread-and-butter techniques of decision theory.

Some of these principles are already applied to health care by maverick wizards and more will be used in the future. But the great majority is ignorant, skeptical, or just doesn't pay attention. The math wizards speak a different language from the Muggles. Sir Snow Charles explained this gulf in "Two Cultures and the Scientific Revolution." But as the great Austrian physicist and philosopher Ernst Mach once pointed out, the ordinary person can reap the benefits of science without understanding it. It takes the creative genius of a mathematician like von Neumann to invent the computer, but little children and grandmothers have no problem using it.

Fortunately, I am not alone in believing such an extension of science is possible for healthcare. Billions of dollars are presently being spent digitizing the healthcare system. Many large consulting firms are busy improving quality and reducing costs. Of course, there are frustrations and disappointments. Many projects cost more and produce less than advocates had hoped. The best practices in health care are in their infancy.

As you can see, I am still curious in a wide variety of things and receive great joy in finding out what makes the world tick. Just last week I projected myself fifty years into the future and wrote an article on the state of health care in 2052. I sent it to several doctors and it was met with both interest and resistance. I've always been ahead of my time and this gets me into trouble with the Muggles. I have a deep-seated conviction, in the bottom of my heart, that math can help human beings improve the quality of their lives, even if they don't know it yet. This has been my guiding force and the legacy I want to pass on to generations to come.

Index

0-595-26062-4